WITHDRAWN

Eyewitness Accounts of the American Revolution

The Adventures
of
Christopher Hawkins

The New York Times & Arno Press

Copyright © 1968 by Arno Press, Inc.
All Rights Reserved

✲

Library of Congress Catalog Card No. 67-29042

✲

Manufactured in the U.S.A.

THE

ADVENTURES

OF

CHRISTOPHER HAWKINS

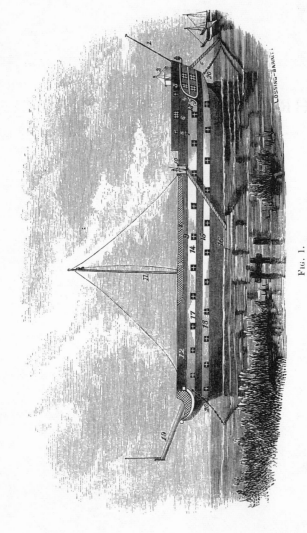

FIG. 1.

THE "JERSEY" PRISON-SHIP;

As moored at the Wallabout, near Long Island, N. Y.

THE

ADVENTURES

OF

CHRISTOPHER HAWKINS,

CONTAINING

Details of his Captivity,
a first and second time on the High Seas, in the Revolutionary War, by the British, and his consequent sufferings, and escape from
the JERSEY PRISON SHIP, then lying in the harbour of
New York, by swimming.

Now first Printed from the original Manuscript.

WRITTEN BY HIMSELF.

WITH AN

INTRODUCTION AND NOTES

BY

CHARLES I. BUSHNELL.

NEW YORK:

PRIVATELY PRINTED.

1864

CALVIN T. RYAN LIBRARY
KEARNEY STATE COLLEGE
KEARNEY, NEBRASKA

CHRISTOPHER HAWKINS.

(*The Son of the Author.*)

TO

MY FRIEND

CHRISTOPHER HAWKINS, ESQ.,

OF NEWPORT, N. Y.,

THE

WORTHY SON OF A PATRIOT SIRE,

THIS VOLUME

IS

RESPECTFULLY DEDICATED

BY

THE EDITOR.

Entered, according to Act of Congress, in the year 1864, by
CHARLES I. BUSHNELL,
In the Clerk's Office of the District Court of the United States for the
Southern District of New York.

LIST

OF

ILLUSTRATIONS.

INTRODUCTION.

HRISTOPHER HAWKINS, the author of the following narrative, was the son of Hesabiah Hawkins, and was born in North Providence, R. I., on the 8th day of June, 1764. On arriving at sufficient age, he became engaged in the duties of a farm, in which occupation he continued until he had reached the twelfth year of his age, when he was bound to Aaron Mason, of Provi-

dence, as an apprentice to learn the tanner's trade. In this employment he remained for about twelve months, when he ran away and enlisted as a privateer. His adventures subsequently, and to the time of his return from his second captivity with the enemy, are the subject of his narrative, and it is, therefore, unnecessary to repeat them here.

After his return home the second time, he worked for a while with Obadiah Olney, of Smithfield, R. I., and subsequently with William Whipple, of Fairfield, Herkimer Co., N. Y. When about twenty years of age, Mr. Hawkins was married to Dorcas, daughter of Thomas Whipple, of Smithfield, a farmer by occupation. About the year 1786, Hawkins emigrated from Rhode Island to Norway, in Herkimer Co., thence moved to Fairfield, and in the fall of the year 1791 moved into Newport in the same county, thereby becoming the first permanent settler of the town. He employed himself chiefly as a farmer, although he occasionally did some work as a carpenter, having while in Providence been engaged for a short time in a ship-yard, where he acquired some knowledge of the trade.

In his early life, Mr. Hawkins had but limited opportunities for education, but this deficiency he subsequently filled, in a great degree, after he had attained his majority. He was a man of energy, of strong common sense, and of excellent judgment. In consequence of these qualities, as well as for his practical business turn, he was frequently appointed by the local and state authorities to lay out wards, partition fences, and settle contested claims. He was at one time a Commissioner of Roads, and was the first Supervisor of Newport, having been chosen such in 1807 at the first meeting of the town after its erection. He held the office for fourteen years, when, after a short interregnum, he was again elected to the same situation, and served for six years longer.

It may be interesting to the reader to learn something of the personal appearance and character of our hero, and we will therefore gratify the desire. He was about five feet ten inches in stature, and rather slim, with high forehead, rather large mouth, and when young, his hair was black. He had a fair complexion, with blue eyes, and heavy eyebrows, and his expression was that of firmness and determination. Though rather sarcastic in his manner, yet he was kind-hearted and charitable, quick to discern merit, and liberal to the poor and distressed. Industrious himself, he loved to see others so. He detested pride and presumption, and gave no encouragement to meanness or extravagance. In his religious feelings, he was inclined to Methodism; in his political views, he was a Federalist, and continued so to his death. He was an affectionate husband and a kind parent, a citizen of the purest and most lofty patriotism, a gentleman of scrupulous honor and of unblemished integrity.

Mr. Hawkins had by his wife seven children, of whom there were six daughters, who all survived him but one. The son, who bears his father's name, is still living. Mr. Hawkins died in Newport, Herkimer County, N. Y., on the 25th day of

February, 1837, in the seventy-third year of his age, and was interred in a burial ground at that place. For several years previous to his death, he was afflicted with asthma, and was consequently unable to labor. The disease of which he died, however, was dropsical consumption, and his death, though expected, was sudden. He was sitting in his chair: his attendants left him for a few moments, and when they returned, his spirit had fled. He had died apparently without a struggle.

It is proper to state that the narrative is now given to the public for the first time, having been placed by the family of Mr. Hawkins in our hands for publication. The work, though somewhat faulty in orthography and the use of capitals, is nevertheless a meritorious one. It is truthful and candid, and upon the whole, a well written production. It is, moreover, full of incident and adventure, very minute in its details, and of intense interest. It will, we think, be considered as a valuable contribution to the Revolutionary history of our country.

To enhance its value, and add to its interest, the Editor has appended some explanatory and illustrative notes, which he hopes will be found worthy of attention. With these few prefatory remarks, we will now introduce to the reader, the hero himself, and leave him to tell his own story.

PREFACE.

HE sufferings of my youth is still fresh in my memory, and ev'ry incident or event set forth in the following work I have no doubt is correct, and indeed so far as I was personally concerned I know it is so. No literary ambition has prompted its publication. I am an unlettered man, and cannot possibly have a desire to be ranked among the *literati* of my own or any other conntry. The literary critics of course will not notice my work, for in it, there can be no food wherewith to feast their refined and delicate appetites. To refined and classical writing I offer no claim. It is my desire to leave behind me a faithful and unvarnished narrative of my early sufferings, in which I was not alone. My intention in publishing this narative is confined to the attention of my children, grandchildren, and their descendants, with the hope that they will duly appreciate not only my own sufferings, but those of my contemporaries in the arduous struggle of my country for independence, in which, success crowned the efforts of those who embarked in the American cause. To my descendants and those of my fellows I dedicate this limited narative, at the same time in the hope that their generosity will pardon anything which can be construed as arrogant in this production. I am well aware that a correct and minute history of the American revolution has been published. In the meantime I cannot conceive that such an work shall supercede personal narative which has connection to that event. My principal design is to amuse and inform my friends and descendants with the sufferings of my youth. If any one shall be so incredulous as to disbelieve this narative, I hope that some of my early cotemporaries are still alive, and if they are, I refer to them the truth or falshood of this narative, and feel confident that they will sustain me in ev'ry particular, claiming importance.

NEWPORT, N. YORK, *April 3d*, 1834.

Christopher Hawkins

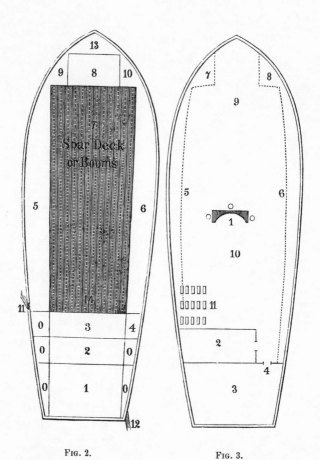

FIG. 2.

THE GUN DECK,

with its Apartments.

FIG. 3.

THE MIDDLE DECK.

(The arrangement of the Lower Deck was similar; but without Bunks.)

REFERENCES TO THE PLATES.

FIGURE 1.

Exterior View of the Ship.

1. The Flag Staff, which was seldom used, and only for signals.

2. A Canvas Awning or Tent, used by the guards in warm weather.

3. The Quarter Deck, with its barricado about ten feet high, with a door and loop holes on each side.

4. The Ship's Officers' Cabin, under the quarter deck.

5. Accommodation Ladder, on the starboard side, for the use of the ship's officers.

6. The Steerage, occupied by the sailors belonging to the ship.

7. The Cook Room, for the ship's crew and guards.

8. The Sutler's Room, where articles were sold to the prisoners, and delivered to them through on opening in the bulk head.

9. The Upper Deck and Spar Deck, where the prisoners were occasionally allowed to walk.

10. The Gangway Ladder, on the larboard side, for the prisoners.

11. The Derrick, on the starboard side, for taking in water, etc., etc.

12. The Galley, or Great Copper, under the forecastle, where the provisions were cooked for the prisoners.

13. The Gun Room, occupied by those prisoners who were officers.

14–15. Hatchways leading below, where the prisoners were confined.

16. Foot of the gang plank.

17–18. Between decks. where the prisoners were confined by night.

19. The Bowsprit.

20. Chain Cables, by which the ship was moored.

FIGURE 2.

The Gun Deck, with its Apartments.

1. Cabin.	9, 10. The Cook's Quarters.
2. Steerage.	11. The Gangway Ladder.
3. Cook Room.	12. The Officers' Ladder.
4. Sutler's Room.	13. Working Party.
5, 6. Gangways.	14. The Barricado.
7. The Booms.	000. Store Rooms.
8. The Galley.	

Figure 3.

The Upper Deck, between Decks.

1. The Hatchway Ladder, leading to the lower deck, railed round on three sides.

2. The Steward's Room, from which the prisoners received their daily allowances, through an opening in the partition.

3. The Gun Room, occupied by those prisoners who were officers.

4. Door of the Gun Room.

5, 6, 7, 8. The arrangement of the prisoners' chests and boxes, which were ranged along, about ten feet from the sides of the ship, leaving a vacant space, where the messes assembled.

9, 10. The middle of the deck, where many of the prisoners' hammocks were hung at night, but always taken down in the morning to afford room for walking.

11. Bunks, on the larboard side of the deck, for the reception of the sick.

NARRATIVE.

 N the month of May 1777 I left Mr.
Aaron Mason (1) of Providence, R. I.,
to whom I was an indented apprentice, went to New Bedford, Ms.
and entered on board a privateer
Schooner, mounting twelve small carriage guns, by
the name of the Eagle, Mowry Potter, (2) Master.
This vessel was bound on a cruise in quest of the
british vessels, or rather such as we could make
prizes of. This was the first time I had been
engaged in any sea service, and being only in the
thirteenth year of my age, of course I knew nothing

of a seafaring life, for after the vessel had sailed from the sight of land, she seemed to me as steering in the same direction as when she left the Harbour, and the illusion was not dispelled even when the sun rose above the horizon in a clear day, for some days. Nothing occurred worthy of any notice after leaving port, except occasionally taking fish on the Newfoundland coast, until we came in sight of the English coast, and nothing then of any importance to us but disappointment, for both officers and crew had been promising themselves as many British prizes as could be manned from our crew, as they pretended to cruise in the track between New York and England. After remaining on the English coast a short time, we tacked about for America without speaking a single sail on our outward cruise. After we had been several days on our return, we espied one morning a "sail." We made for her and hailed. The vessel proved to be a schooner unarmed. She answered our hail by stating that she was a french vessel from the West Indies, and bound to Halifax. After being hailed and threat'ned from our Capt. she short'ned sail, and was boarded by our first Lieut. (John Paine).

After boarding and examining her papers the Lieut. returned and confirmed the answer before mentioned, and stated his conviction that she was a french vessel and laden with flour. John Ward our boatswain and a large majority of our crew, were much dissatisfied with this report. Ward was loud in his denunciations of the conduct of the Capt. and First Lieutenant towards this vessel. Ward and all the best informed of our crew had no hesitation in pronouncing her a British vessel, with false papers prepared for the occasion, and also that the pretended french vessel's crew were dressed in disguise, the crew had the french turban on their heads. Our dissatisfied crew were now for making the port of New Bedford (²) from whence we had sailed. On the second or third day after speaking the pretended french vessel, early in the morning we espied a sail on our weather beam—the officers concluded to make sail for her: many of the crew yet in surly mood about the other vessel exclaimed, "if she prove lawful prize our officers will not take her." After giving chase some time we gained but slowly upon her. She was a fast sailor—the officers concluded to give

our schooner more canvass, and get to windward
of our chase as our vessel sailed best before the
wind. This done we came so close late in the day
to discover that our chase was a large Brig, copper
bottomed, and british built, but nothing appeared
to shew that she was armed. It was by this time
near sun-setting. We then run up our colours, and
gave her a bow gun, without effect. Another gun
or two was ordered, and directed to her sails or
other rigging—these were given but disregarded.
This had brot. us to early twilight. Our second
Lieut. observed that this cleaned our way. the Brig
had evry sail set and the second Lieut. advised to
trim our schooner in the best manner and cease
firing—all things were executed agreeably to his
suggestion. The 2. Lieut. took the helm and seemed
in command—ordered the boatswain after trimming
the sails and the greater part of the crew to be
seated aft and attend to the singing of some of the
crew, (Capt. of Marines). We now *neared* the Brig
very fast. Weather hazy, but a handsome breeze.
We had before it became entirely dark got so near
the brig that the 2d Lieut. asked permission to
haul our wind and give her a broadside—this

was granted by the Capt. with a proviso, that he
(the Capt.) as the schooner luft would hail the Brig.
this he did a first and second time—the first without an answer—to the second hail the answer was,
that said Brig was from Liverpool and bound to
New York. This answer put our crew in ecstacies.
But our Capt. soon dispelled these joyful and
agreeable sensations. The Capt. of the Brigg interrogated our Capt. Potter as follows, "For God's
sake what do you want of me?" "Back your
main top sail and shorten your other sails, lower
your boat and come on board me," was the answer
of Potter—this was disregarded. The Brig kept
her course with all sails set. The second Lieut.
again asked permission to give her a broadside—
we were within short shot of her—this our cowardly
Capt. did not please to give, but evaded the question by ordering the guns loaded, matches well
lighted &c. The second Lieut. yet at the helm.
At this time my situation did not appear so pleasant to me. The idea of broadsides, blood, death
&c. rather disturbed my mind, for the time being.
This had been created by our cowardly Capt. who
had been saying, that said brig had guns on board,

and would blow our little Schooner to atoms in short time. In the meantime our two vessels kept near each other, and the brig not appearing to regard us. It was now resolved to give the brig a broadside which was immediately done. this salutation brought the commander of the brig to take some notice of us—again he interrogated, "What in God's name do you want or wish of us?" Our Capt. answered, "shorten your sail and come under our lee, and hoist out your boat and come on board me"—to me this seemed quite paradoxcal—the idea that a vessel four times larger than ours could come under our lee. This resulted from youth and inexperience in seamanship. The Commander of the brig now commenced a sort of seeming sympathetic appeal to our Capt. Potter by stating to him, (Potter,) that he (the Comr. of the brig) wished for permission to lie by us until morning, for said he, my boat is lashed fast under my booms, and I cannot get her out—In the morning if you will lie by me to-night I will come on board you. Our Capt. Potter responded, Aye! Aye! This answer produced a general murmur through far the greater portion of our crew. The boatswain was a bold,

hardy and excellent seaman, jumped about and
swore like a madman. Ward [boatswain] exclaimed
in the presence and hearing of Capt. Potter, that
the brig would get away from us before morning,
and indeed so did the remainder of the crew, the
first Lieut. and some few excepted. What would
you do inquired Capt. Potter. The 2d Lieut. with
others answered, "Why! board the brig and take
possession of her ourselves." Capt. Potter inquires
who will go with you, to the 2d Lieut. who had
offered to command the boat. "I will" answered
a great number of voices at the same instant.
"Well," says Potter, "it is now dark, and she is
armed—things must now remain as they are—she
will sink you and we have no other boat, and further I have given my word to lye by her until
morning, and that is enough—now keep a good
look out for her until morning. I command this
vessel and will be obeyed." "The devil keep a
good look out," said our boatswain, for it is now
very thick and hazy and we are soon to have a
storm. Potter and Paine, (the first Lieutenant,)
went below. As soon as the Capt. & 1st Lieut. had
gone below, the remainder of the crew proposed to

the 2d Lieut. to confine the Capt. & 1st Lieut. to
their cabin, and immediately take possession of
said brig—this was opposed by the 2d Lieut. for the
reason that the act would be piratical, and perhaps
might amount to a hanging matter. This enterprize was then abandoned. A man was sent to
mast head to keep a look out but he lost sight of
the brig before morning, and she had completely
made her escape from us. Capt. Potter came on
deck in the morning about one o'clock. He
enquired " have you lost sight of the brig." Yes
sir, was the answer. Potter continues, " It is
damned strange you could not keep sight of her."
It is damned strange if we could, (observed the
boatswain,) in such a night as this, when she was
using all means to get clear of us. I was well
assured of this. Dont be troublesome Ward, said
Capt. Potter, to the boatswain. No sir, (answered)
the boatswain) only for your good and mine. After
a few sulky moments it was determined to stand on
for Sandy-hook, thinking at day light she might
possibly be in sight—this hope proved futile. In
the morning at day light the atmosphere was dismal and the wind rising to a gale from the North

East. through the day all hands were obliged to keep on deck. The hatches and companion way were lashed down and tarpaulins nailed over them to keep the water out, for by this time the sea made a breach over the deck from stem to stern by every successive wave. The 2d Lieut. yet kept at the helm. Our safety demanded the utmost activity and caution and none but the 2d Lieut. in such a perilous time could be entrusted with steering the schooner. The gale did not abate much during that day and the following night we found it necessary to throw six of our heaviest guns over board to lighten our vessel—this hard fare evidently had a great impression upon the crew, for their spirits were much depressed and I wished myself on land— we had nothing to eat or drink above deck except some bad water—we had now fasted the whole day and night coming on. some one inquired of the Capt. if there was nothing eatable in the cabin. He answered that I knew best (being cabin boy). Can you go down if the top of the companion way is raised up and get something to eat for us. I answered, I would try. I was let down into the cabin and gathered all I could find to eat or drink

and hauled up again, not being able to get provision from the hold, the bulk head being strong—
this was a very small meal for each of the crew
when divided and nothing else could be obtained
through the dismal and painful night ensuing—the
gale was hard so that ev'ry one was either lashed
to some part of the vessel, or clung to some of her
rigging—no one slept on board our vessel the succeeding night—the white heads often broke over
our Taffil and kept us awake. On the morning of
the third day of the gale the wind abated in its
violence in a small degree and hauled a little to the
Northwest; as the wind abated the swells arose, the
water did not break over us so much as in the
violence of the gale. In the fore part of the day
hunger and fatigue had much dispirited the crew.
Nevertheless it was determined to enter the hold of
the vessel if possible and obtain something to eat—
this with some difficulty was effected, and served to
the crew on deck—my share was a hard biscuit and
small piece of raw pork—this to me although a boy
was a delicious meal. I seated myself to eat my
meal under the lee of the vessel's boat on deck.
Among my reflections while devouring my food,

the thoughts of home rushed into my mind. I was
in rather a melancholy mood and cast my eyes
about hoping to discover land—in this endeavour to
see land looking to the leward, I discovered something in appearance resembling a very small bush
without leaves. I mentioned this to the crew,
many of them tried to discover it without success.
The 2d Lieut. who was yet at the helm called a
skilful sailor to take it, and said he would undertake
the discovery himself. He came to me, and I gave
him the course, and at the top of the next swell he
succeeded and confirmed me in my assertion, and
remarked that it was "a sail" and square rigged
under bare poles. The crew in some degree had
regained their wonted spirits, and many of them
concluded the sail was the brig we had suffered to
run away from us, and cheered themselves with
strong hopes of again coming up with her. One of
the crew, a small but active hand, observed that we
will tell her we have come again tomorrow, alluding
to the compromise our Capt. had made with her
when she was fully in our power. We made for
the sail as much as wind and weather would admit,
and as we *neared her* we set more sail, and partly

obtained the windward of her—she now discovered
us, and in turn made sail for us. We had our close
reefed top sails set. We now plainly discovered
that " the sail " was a ship—by this time our spirits
had become damped, and our course immediately
shifted from a *chase* to a *run away*. We aimed to
get before the wind as our vessel sailed best in that
situation, but our exertions were fruitless—she came
up with us in a very short time and it was our ill
fate to learn that she was an English sloop of war—
the Sphynx of twenty guns.(4) In half an hour she
spoke us, and by her sailing seemed to disregard
wind or weather. When our answer had been
given and our character known we were ordered
under her lee. The crew then exclaimed " we are
taken."(5) With respect to myself I reflected. If I
can get a better ship for my money I am glad of
it. these conclusions were induced from the superior
appearance and sailing of the captor when compared to the captive, and from youth and inexperience. As soon as we were ordered under the
lee of the captor, confusion ensued among our crew,
each selecting his own effects. We had taken in
none of our spread canvass—a small black cloud

was rising up and a squall succeeding struck our vessel and laid the vessel on her beams end, and remained in that situation a sufficient time to allow our surgeon to go out upon the side of the vessel supporting himself by holding upon the main chains turning his feet towards the keel. In the meantime great exertions were made on board the captor to send their boats to our vessel to save us from perishing, apprehending from the situation of our vessel that she would immediately sink, but contrary to expectation our vessel "righted," and the boats of the Sphynx were soon along side to convey us on board her. I was the first to board one of their boats which proved to be the Capt's Barge. She was soon loaded with part of our crew and their baggage. I placed myself on the stern of the boat, arriving under the quarter railing of the Sphynx. Many ropes were thrown to us from on board. I fast'ned the end of one around my breast, and called to those on deck to "haul away"—some one cried out on the quarter deck, "Put it round your damned neck you damned yankee, and we'll soon haul you up," but an officer on board said "haul him up"—the barge was then under the lee-

quarter. I was soon on the quarter deck. The
buttons on my clothes soon attracted the attention
of the british seamen, being pewter, and the motto
on them not suiting their taste quite so well—the
motto being Liberty and property—a knife was
called for to sever them from my clothes—an officer
on board ordered them to let me alone, but I kept
them for the crew to look at and make their rough
and loyal observations about. The swells were yet
running very high and considerable time taken up
in removing the prisoners from our schooner to the
ship—which was finally effected without disaster.
As soon as the prisoners were taken from the captured vessel a boat was sent to her with orders
to the crew to set her on fire if she would burn, if
not to scuttle and sink her—the latter alternative
was adopted without taking a single article from
her, either furniture, rigging, tackle or provisions.
This done our crew were all put into the cable-tier.
The Capt. (Potter) and two boys excepted, and of
the two boys I was one. We were allowed to run
about deck and between decks among the common sailors, who fed us with as much food as we
wanted. The evening after our capture, the Capt. (e)

of the Sphynx ordered us (the two boys) into his Cabin by his waiter. As soon as we entered the Cabin he sent for the boatswain's mate, who soon shewed himself. The Capt. then ordered him to tie us (the two boys) each to a cabin gun carriage, and as far asunder as possible for the purpose of keeping us from the hearing of each other. The boatswain's mate was not so delicate as to conceal from our view his whipping instrument, which by sailors was called a *cat*—by others a cat with nine tails (7)— the appearance of which did not please us much. He first devoted his attention to the other boy whose name was Paul Howe or Paul Wright. The *cat* was laid on the gun in sight of Paul. he soon commenced tieing him (Paul) to the gun, the sight of the *cat* and the process of tieing moved Paul's feelings so much that he bawled out with terrour— he made a noise as loud as a mad bull. The boatswain's mate as soon as he had fast'ned Paul, left him and came to me and began his operation of tieing me to the other gun. He soon began to console me however by observing that he hoped I would not make such a damn'd crying as that fellow does—he further said I guess you will not get it very hard. I answered, "If I do it will be damn'd hard," for I had begun to be learned in sailors' phrases. He (the mate) replied. I see you will not bawl before you are hurt. Having tied me, I was left in that situation and he returned to Paul. By this time I learned that we had been thus put in "durance vile" for the purpose of putting us under examination in relation to our vessel, her cruise, captures &c. Paul's examination was soon commenced, but I could not hear much of either questions or answers, as the Capt. questioned him in an under tone of voice, the bawling of Paul prevented me from hearing much if any of their dialogue. He was soon again left and their attention was directed to me a second time, which was for examination. Before commencing the Capt. remarked to me in the following words, Now I want the exact truth from you concerning your cruise. I answered, I shall tell you the truth as far as I know it. He rejoined, "It is what I want of you." The Capt. put a long series of questions to me on the subject, and I answered them severally as he propounded them—before getting through he ordered me to be released from my uncomfortable

situation at the gun which was done and the examination resumed and continued to a close. As
soon as I was untied however he offered me Porter
or wine which I declined—a seat was offered me
and also declined. My answers and the details
annexed seemed to give satisfaction, sometimes provoking a smile and even a laugh from the Capt.
and those around him—some of my answers however were not so pleasant. That portion which
related to falling in with the brig seemed the most
pleasant to them, particularly the conduct of our
Capt. Potter in suffering the brig to run away from
us after we had captured her. Our captor kept on
her course for New York and in three or four days
after our capture we made the highlands of Never
Sink (s) as they were called. While steering for the
port of New York off Sandy Hook as I was running
about deck I saw a large number of vessels aft
coming into port, or apparently so, and among them
a large Brig several miles from our ship (say 4 or 5).
I mentioned to some of the common sailors that
that brig (pointing her out to them) is the one that
escaped from us in the night before you captured
us. This assertion caused a laugh amongst the

under officers and seamen who heard me. My pretended discovery soon got to the ears of the officers on the quarter deck—the Capt. sent for me, it being in the day time and inquired whether or not I had ever seen that Brig before (pointing her out) I answered him in the affirmative, the substance of which was much the same as my story told a few minutes before to the under officers and common sailors. Are you sure of it said the Capt. I think I am. This conversation with the Capt. caused a hearty laugh among the officers on the quarter deck at my expence. But the Capt. ordered the main top sail to be backed, and said, we will wait for her to come up—she now came up very fast. I still remained on the quarter deck—as she neared us I called the attention of those around me to the appearance of the Brig and observed—there don't you see her copper bottom? Some one inquired, had she a copper bottom? did you see it in the night? As she escaped from us in the night the inquirer supposed I had only seen her *in the night.* I answered that I saw her in day light as well as in the night and added "I know it is the same Brig. I know her also by the trim of her sails." An old

grum looking officer standing near, (the boatswain
or quarter master) in a surly manner said, What a
damned rebel fool you are. The Capt. rebuked his
insolence and said, we will wait for her to come up
for our own curiosity. She was soon near enough
to be hailed which was done by the question,
Where from? From Liverpool. Where bound? to
New York. had you a good passage? Yes, all but
a late gale. Have you fell in with any vessels at
sea? But one, a small privateer Schooner, and that
I ran away from in the night. What is your cargo?
Dry goods mainly, and ballanced with salt. What
is the amount of your invoice? The amount was
great but I cannot now recollect it. The Capt. of
the Sphynx now observed to the Capt. of the brig,
The Capt. and crew of the schooner you got away
from I have now on board and she has gone to the
bottom. The crew of the Brig then gave three
hearty cheers, keeping under weigh into the port of
New York. The cheering and glee amongst the
crew of the Brig gave me very unpleasant sensations, but I was compelled to submit to it without
any audible disapprobation. After arriving in the
port of New-York (∘) we were immediately put on

board a prison ship, I think "the Asia"(₁₀)—She was an old transport ship lying near the mouth of the east river and not far from the place where the old Jersey prison ship afterwards lay. In a day or two after this, newspapers from the city of N. Y. were brought on board our prison ship, detailing our affair with the brig at sea and reprehending the conduct of our Capt. Potter in no measured terms and stating the value of the Brig and cargo. It appeared that her cargo consisted of fine broad cloth for the officers of the army and navy, silks &c. and salt worth three dollars per bushel in the states. Our Capt. Potter was compelled to hear these details all read, not being able to get out of the hearing and also the severe denunciations of both American and British seamen with respect to his conduct before alluded to. Although I considered myself extremely the sufferer by his conduct, I could not help sympathizing with him in his then very unpleasant situation. His countenance denoted a mind full of dejection, apparently bordering on a state of inanity—four hundred men were gazing at him nearly at the same time and among them fourteen American sea captains. Many would inquire on seeing him near them, Is that the Capt. Potter who captured the Brig and suffered her to run away. I sware if I were one of his crew I would murder him. This and similar expressions were often uttered in his hearing among British as well as Americans. (11)—After having been on board the Prison Ship about three weeks, an under British naval officer came on board in quest of waiters, intending if any boys were on board to take them away, mentioning that he had leave to do so from the post Admiral—he soon selected Paul, before mentioned, and myself, having leave as he said, to take two boys. Paul's father was also a fellow prisoner and captured with us. The father and son both set up such an uproar and lamentations that the officer was induced to leave him. The officer selected another prisoner by the name of Jacob Good in Paul's stead—then taking our names left the prison ship reminding us that he should call and take us away in two or three days, that we were destined to go on board the British frigate Maid-stone (12) of twenty eight guns to which vessel said officer had been transferred by recent arrangement, and was at that time removing his effects on board

her. When the officer left the ship he handed each
of us a quarter of a dollar—I refused to receive the
money offered me saying I had heard of silver
Copeing (₁₃) before. The officer replied, Why you
damn'd Yankee I dont mean to buy you with this
money—I have you safe enough—I gave it to you
for use as you pleased until I call for you. I kept it
and no more was said, the officer went away laugh-
ing. This officer came on board the day appointed
and called for us. Good & myself presented ourselves—he directed me to get in readiness to go
with him but told Good he should not take him,
much to Good's apparent disappointment—he was
mortified at the neglect of the officer for he was
anxious to leave the prison ship. Good remained
behind but he soon swam away from the prison ship
reached the Long Island shore and finally escaped,
and again reached Providence where he had then
lately resided with a Mrs. Crawford, (₁₄) and in
whose service he again entered. All this, (running
away from the prison ship) he performed at noon
day, in spite of the vigilance of the British officers
and guards. He was fired on by the guard on
board ship without injury many times. Jacob took

ALAN GARDNER,

(*Captain of the Maidstone.*)

advantage of the absence of the ship's boat, for his escape. After the guard had ceased firing upon him a hallo was set up by the british on board the ship to the people on shore to stop a run-a-way rebel—the people on shore could not see him and he passed them some distance to effect a landing. After landing he took to his heels and a number of large dogs were set to him but when the dogs came near him, Jacob turned pursuer, clapped his hands and sent the dogs forward of him at full chase after other game—whether they came up with it or not Jacob did not stop to inquire. This adventure of Jacobs I afterwards had from himself and others. I knew nothing of it personally. I have no doubt that what is here stated with respect to him is substantially correct. I was immediately taken on board the frigate by the officer as his waiter. This frigate was then commanded by Capt. Lewis Gardiner,* (15) James Vashan (16) 1st Lieut. I have since observed that both these officers have been Admirals in the British Navy. The Maidstone was preparing for sea when I was first put on board and bound on a cruise. She was an old ship but an

---

* A mistake in the name. Should be Alan Gardner.

excellent sailor. The officer who had removed me on board the frigate as his servant, soon wished me to sign the books, having learned that I could write my name, for the purpose as he said of drawing my wages. This I refused to do and said I had rather go and see my mother, (17) rather than sign away my liberty. Then, said he, I will do it for you, which he did, and further said, there you damned Yankee it will make no odds with you. I have you fast enough. The name of this officer was Richard Richards. (18) He had a right to two servants, and he soon secured it by obtaining one Stephen Stone, an English boy from Yorkshire. He was three or four years my senior in age, but failed in a degree in activity and too often indulged the inebriating draught. His habits prevented our Mr. Richards entrusting him with anything requiring care or fidelity. Fortunately for me I did not indulge intoxication from ardent spirits or any other beverage. I was soon entrusted with Mr. Richard's domestic affairs, so far as related to his Cabin operations, so that my Yorkshire lad had to follow my directions with respect to cooking, cleansing the Cabin &c. Although fellow servants we did not always keep in the best of humour towards each other. He did not always obey my commands so readily as I desired and was too much a defaulter to keep me in peace with his ill behavior. Sometimes it promoted a broil between us which would end in a trial of muscular activity and generally I came off conqueror, although he possessed as much and perhaps more strength than myself. Boxing was not allowed on board the frigate yet the boys would sometimes play the pugilist, and no notice would be taken of it by the officers. On one occasion my Stephen did not clean the knives and forks in a proper manner for which I called him to an account in a manner that so much displeased him he called me a "damn'd Yankee" and at the same instant stabbed me with a table fork which he held in his hand—by this stab he wounded me in the breast—the blood soon made its appearance running down my clothes freely. This took place in the cooks room near the Coppers—in presence of many of the sailors who were much exasperated with Stephen for his barbarity and immediately removed us both to the quarter deck—he to be punished for the assault and myself to enter com-

plaint against him. He was immediately sentenced
to receive two dozen lashes from the boatswain's
mate for this outrage, and tied to a gun. He now
began to beg my forgiveness. I interposed in his
behalf with great anxiety, but to no purpose except
saving one of the dozen. The dozen that he
received was most horribly inflicted—the blood ran
down to his heels. The boatswain's mate who
administered his punishment was a hard hearted
wretch and appeared destitute of human feelings.—
his name James Richardson. The witnessing of
this punishment and the shrieks of the sufferer
made me sick at the stomach. The other boatswain's mate was John Henly, a humane man and
beloved. Richardson was a Scotchman. After
this Stephen and myself had very little dispute
while I remained on board the frigate, which was
quite a year after this event. This frigate (19) while
I was on board her cruised on the coast of the
United States, for some time on the coast of
Virginia, where she captured a number of red
cedar pilot boats laden with tobacco which was
valuable and generally outward bound—the boys
on board always sharing equal with the common

sailors—the prize money ([20]) was soon expended, for the sailors' creed then was, "What I had I got, what I spent I saved, and what I kept I lost." The vessels which were captured during the time I was on board the frigate were small—the crews taken out and the craft sunk or burnt—all the young men and boys would be retained in the service of the frigate and against their desire or choice. The frigate seldom lay at a wharf or came to anchor except at some distance from land. I was not on shore save once during the whole of my stay on board the frigate, which was fifteen months. This was on a small Island in Naragansett bay, between Connecticut and Rhode Island—the company consisted of thirteen boys and others in the ship's yawl for the purpose of gathering twigs from the birches to make scrub brooms. Mr. Richards directed those who had charge of the boat to "keep a damn'd sharp look out for Kit." I must here be permitted to mention an incident although not immediately concerning my narative—late in the fall of 1777 while at sea we spoke a brig, then directly from the port of New York—our Capt. inquired "what news from New York"—he received for

answer that it was reported in N. Y. when the brig
sailed that Burgoyne had capitulated with his whole
army. I was on the quarter deck and heard this,
which pleased me exceedingly, and in my transports
of joy run fore and aft on the gun deck crying the
news. A midshipman observing me, said, away
with you, you damn'd yankee, with your damn'd
lies—there is not yankees enough by G—d on the
whole continent to take him, for he had with him
ten thousand of the best troops of Lord Howe's
army. I know it is a damn'd lie, but the next day
we fell in with a ship and hailed her—she also
proved to be from New-York—had sailed since the
brig we had spoken the day before. Our Capt.
inquired " what news," he was answered, " unpleasant news. Burgoyne has capitulated with his
whole army." Back your topsails and I will send
my boat on board of you. The boat was sent on
board. When it was returning I got to the quarter
deck where my duty often led me and was not
noticed. As soon as the boat returned the news of
Burgoyne's capitulation was confirmed. (21) I went
immediately to the main deck, with joy beaming in
my countenance, exclaiming, what do you think

now of your great Burgoyne? Damn you be off you damn'd saucy bo-g-r cried a number of voices at the same time. What, said I, looking at them earnestly—this short question put them in silence for I had seen many of them take a dozen for useing these words, "damn'd saucy bo-g-r," when all other profanity would be winked at. The Maidstone was lying at anchor one evening at Newport in Course Harbour,* in the course of the night orders were given to get under weigh for what purpose the officers only knew—we stood out, and in the morning at daylight we saw a ship off Point Judith point (22)—standing out—we made sail for her and soon came near her—she proved to be the ship Columbus (23) privateer and American—then out of Providence. The crew of the Columbus did not seem to like our appearance much for they soon run her a shore at Point Judith, got out one carriage gun, a 4 or 6 pounder, and drew it up a hill a short distance from the Columbus, and halted—in the meantime the Maidstone approached as near the Columbus as prudence would permit for fear of grounding, dropt her hedge anchor and came to a

* Coaster's Harbor.

stand. The crew of the Columbus had taken mus-
kets and ammunition from her after running her on
shore. This we soon learned by their opening a fire
upon us with musketry and the carriage gun before
mentioned—a shot from the cannon hull'd us once
under our quarter at the edge of the copper and
which sprung a leak into the bread room which
afterwards moulded our bread and we were obliged
to eat, and the british sailors often damned the
yankees for their insolence. I noticed that some of
our officers were a little cautious of the balls from
the cannon on shore—the balls whistled over our
heads and some of our quarter deck gentry *dodged*
or *bowed* a little. But we brought some of our guns
to bear upon those on shore which after some time
dispersed them. Our yawl was manned and com-
bustibles put on board to assist in burning the
Columbus—the crew of the yawl boarded and set
fire to her, but some of them paid severely for their
temerity—five of them were dreadfully wounded
after they had gained the yawl to return after setting the Columbus on fire, by the crew of the
Columbus, who ran down the hill and fired upon
them. (24) When the yawl returned to the frigate

the five wounded men lay in the bottom of the boat, apparently dead—wallowing in their gore. Capt. Gardner saw them and shed tears—not one of them however died of their wounds. The inhuman wretch Richardson and boatswain's mate before spoken of, was among the wounded. It was sometime before he recovered from his wound—when Americans were near enough for him to notice them, such was his malignity he would grate or gnash his teeth from rage, but the poor devil could not help himself. This same Richardson had good reason to remember the yankees as he was pleased to call them, although from his own misconduct and inhumanity. I will relate one case. In one of our cruises a short time before burning the Columbus, an American vessel was taken, on board of which among other sailors was one by the name of Barney Clark, a small but very athletic man and young—he was retained as a seaman on board the frigate against his will. After Clark had been on board about three weeks, orders were given to about ship—when such an order was given all hands were called and at the time before mentioned Clark was below shifting his linen—he was however soon on deck

through the fore hatch. Richardson being boatswain's mate stood near the hatchway, and as Clark
was passing him gave him (Clark) a blow with his
rattan—this insult Clark had the boldness to resent
and which ended in a boxing match between Clark
and Richardson, and resulted in Clark's favour most
triumphantly, for Richardson was horribly whipt,
and so badly off was he that he was confined to his
hammock for some weeks, and for some days after
the combat was completely blind. For this fight
Richardson was cashiered by a Court Martial. I
witnessed the battle—I felt very uneasy when it
was about commencing from the fear that Clark
would be vanquished, from the circumstance that
Richardson was much the heaviest and apparently
the strongest man, but he was compelled to yield to
the hardy American. In the contest Clark rec'd
but very little injury, having escaped with a mere
scratch in the face. Richardson was bruised to
black and blue from the lower part of his breast to
the top of his head. I saw him the next day after
the affair in his hammock, and a more horrid spectacle I never beheld in the carcase of one man.
The sight of a yankee troubled his vision ever after,

as long as I knew him. The pilot on board the
Maidstone was an American. He was a Virginian
and I think born in that state. His name was
Philips if my memory be correct—he had a small
family on the western shore of the Chesapeake bay,
not a great distance from the Capes Charles &
Henry, which he visited once or twice in the night
while yet I was on board the frigate. He went on
shore in a boat belonging to the frigate which
awaited the termination of his visit to his family—
he messed in the same Cabin with us, was a jovial
money getting sort of man and beloved by the
whole crew. Mr. Richards took him into our mess,
to accommodate him, and with my assent or permission. He was very affable and so far as I can
judge from what I then knew of him was a man of
good information and judgment. He was well
acquainted with the coast from New York to New
Orleans, and was very successful in directing the
frigate to points or places to take prizes. The commerce of his countrymen was much annoyed by his
skill, for he caused many prizes to be taken on the
coast. Although then a boy under fourteen years
of age I could not avoid noticing his unpatriotic

conduct towards his country and fellow citizens, and when alone with him in a good natured manner took the liberty to remind him of it. He would always turn the conversation to some other subject, not wishing to make any remarks on his national feelings. He had a large amount of money on board all in gold. He gave his money into my custody when he came to mess with us at the instance of Mr. Richards—after some time he set the ship's carpenter to make him a box to pack his gold in. The box was made and delivered to him, which done he called on me to assist him in packing it into his box which I readily obeyed—when we had finished he gave me a guinea which I willingly took. On one occasion in reply to some observations I made to him in relation to his avocations, he said that he meant to keep in the business he was then in until he should fill his box with gold, if the war continued long enough, and then return to his family and country and remain there if his countrymen would permit him, if not, he should remove his family to some country where he could live in peace. All this was on our first cruise, but he was with us two more cruises while I was on board.

The last cruise I went in the Maidstone our success was so great in taking prizes that it came to the turn of Mr Richards, my master, to be put on board a prize we had taken as prize master and to take the prize into the port of New-York for adjudication—the prize was a french Schooner—Mr Richards had several times in our light conversation asked me whether or not I would run away from him if I had a good opportunity—I had invariably answered him that I would. He would then observe that I was very much out of the way in such a conclusion and would make me great promises as an inducement to stay with him on board, not forgetting to mention that he could or would retake me 99 times in a 100 escapes by me, if I could effect so many. When we were about to leave the frigate to go on board the french prize schooner he inquired of me about leaving him if an opportunity offered. I answered evasively lest he would be careful to prevent me. The crew which was put on board the prize Schooner was a very indifferent one and composed mostly of invalids, with one exception, and he was soon after taken sick. The frigate which was bound in took the prize in tow but things did

not go well in this way, sometimes the tow line
would slake—and then bring up—at last the tow
line parted and sent the prize adrift. The Capt. of
the frigate hailed and told Mr Richards he must
take care of himself without the aid of the frigate.
We were left in this situation by the frigate with
our flimsy crew—the weather was rough when the
frigate parted from us. A sail was in sight at the
time we went on board the prize which gave us
chase. When the frigate parted from us she in
turn gave chase to said vessel but without success.
The officers of the frigate concluded it to be a sloop
which we had chased several times before without
coming up with her. They supposed the sloop to
be commanded by Capt. John Hopkins, (25) and that
there was no use in giving further chase. The
frigate then left her chase—this chase I did not see
much of but was informed of it by others. After
several days we arrived with our prize in the port
of New York. Here I was permitted to go ashore
almost as often as I pleased. The crew or the
greater portion of it remained on board until the
prize was libelled and condemned. During all this
time I made no attempts to leave the british service

concluding that my motions were strictly watched
by the officer Richards and perhaps others. The
Maidstone arrived at New-York on or about the
time that the prize got into port. As soon as the
prize had passed a final adjudication the crew were
ordered on board the frigate whither they immediately went—having been on board the frigate
a few days she yet lying in the east river nearly
opposite Governors Island, (₂₀) and again about sailing on a cruise, Mr. Richards ordered me one day
about one o'clock P. M. to take such of his wearing
apparel as required washing, carry it on shore to a
wash woman in the city whom he named and
directed me to, and have the clothes washed with
orders to return to the frigate at 5 o'clock P. M. I
determined to avail myself of this opportunity to
effect my escape. A servant to the boatswain by
the name of William Rock, an english boy born in
London accompanied me on a similar errand for his
master—after arriving in the city, we left the
clothes as we had been directed. When we had
disposed of our charge we walked about the city
some time—I soon intimated to Rock my intention
of escape. He then said he would escape with me.

I undertook to dissuade *him* from attempting it, and as a reason that he was an englishman and had no family connections in America—thus being situated if he should not succeed *he* would be severely punished. That my case was very different from his—that I had parents and a large circle of family connections who were interested in my fate, and all of them engaged in support of the cause of American independence—that I considered the attempt on my part hazardous in the extreme, but I considered it my duty however perilous the effort might be, to undertake the enterprize, and more especially as I was compelled on board the frigate to perform service against my country. This reasoning had no impression upon the mind of Rock. He would go with me. I then told him he must act under my directions wholly. This he promised me faithfully to observe. This William Rock was several years my senior in age—was industrious and rigidly honest. His information with respect to the colonies was limited to a degree bordering upon incredulity. When walking with me in the city of New York, and after I had mentioned to him my determination to escape, he enquired where I was going, for he had understood I was an American and had parents living there. How can you get there, and when you do get there the wild beasts will tear you in pieces. From these observations I was convinced of his total ignorance of the colonies, their inhabitants, inteligence, manners, customs &c. and put the following question to him, "Where do you think you now are?" He answered, "Why, we are in a british port." I replied, "No, we are in an American port. It is true the british now controul it by force—you will find in America the arts and sciences diffused throughout the civilized portion of her inhabitants." He was fully aware that the wild beasts and savages were the terrour of all the American people, for he said "Hawkins, if we should have the luck to get there (meaning America) would not the wild beasts and savages devour us immediately." (27) At this I laughed heartily in his presence and observed to him that no more danger would attend us in my intended rout to Rhode Island than in the place where we were then walking from the wild beasts and savages—that the greater portion of New England was wholly exempted from the incursions of

wild beasts and savages, and certainly in a great
degree at least I entertained no apprehensions from
them especially in my colony of R. Island. These
assurances quieted his feelings. He immediately
and very earnestly observed, " then I *will* go with
you if it be to the end of the world, if *this be the
case.*" It was at this time that I much desired a
new suit of fine broad cloth clothes that had been
made for me after we had arrived in New York at
the expence of Mr Richards and the pilot before
mentioned. These had been purchased for me by
them for my good conduct in getting the prize into
port, for after the able seamen before mentioned
had become sick no one on board could go aloft to
do anything but myself—or at least it was so pretended. For my attention in this case, and other
services these clothes were given me. I could not
bring them away with me when I left the frigate
without detection of my intention. I left some
money on board in the custody of Richards. It
was prize money and amounted to at least fifteen
guineas. Richards kept this from me to keep me
from leaving. The guinea that the pilot had given
me Richards knew nothing about—so that when I

got into the city I had this guinea and a silver dollar besides. Rock had only a dollar. I will here mention an incident which occurred on board of our french prize schooner, the next day after we took possession of her—I do it for the purpose of exposing the silly superstition of the sailors, as well as others of those times. An old english sailor came tumbling towards several of us who were on the quarter deck exclaiming with much trepidation and apparent alarm "that this damned french vessel is haunted," for said he "I heard a damned scratching somewhere, saying 'quit,' and you were all aft." I went quickly forward and struck a small cable that was coiled on deck and covered with an old tarpaulin— quit was again repeated, the voice that uttered it seemed to be under the Tarpaulin—I removed the tarpaulin and a large cock Turkey appeared. I loudly observed that I had found the spirit. It was soon viewed by nearly all on board to the no small meriment of the whole crew not excepting the old sailor who had been so much alarmed at his discovery. But to return to our escape. The evening after leaving the frigate, we (Rock & myself) slept on board an old dismantled vessel lying not far from the Fly Market (28)—we slept in the shot lockers, myself in the starboard one and Rock in the larboard one. We left the vessel as soon as the day dawned. We immediately went to the ferry stairs near the market where we found a boat with milk, sauce &c. which was unlading and destined for the Market. I proposed to be taken with Rock across in the boat to Brooklyn after the boat should be discharged of her Market freight. We soon made a bargain and about the time we were stepping on board the boat I cast my eyes towards the market. I saw a boy by the name of John Sawyer walking slowly towards us. He was an American boy, belonging towards the easterly end of Long Island, at or near Sag Harbour—had been taken prisoner at sea, kept as a servant to the Capt's Clerk, on board the same frigate with me—I hailed him instantly. He had left the frigate that morning in the first boat under the directions of his master to visit the market to purchase milk. When I hailed him I said, come John, the boat is ready. Ay, Ay, answered John. He soon joined us and we crossed the east river to Brooklyn. It pleased me much to get a sight at Sawyer. It was unexpected to me.

As soon as I had hailed him, " Come John the boat is ready," he understood me at once, and on seeing and hearing me he at the instant cast the bottle from his hands under a flight of steps near the market, and walked directly to the boat. He was not at a loss to understand our meaning. He well knew that a run away manoeuvre was being entered into. During our stay with the boatman nothing was said between us about our leaving the frigate, nor of our operations or intentions. As soon as we got clear of the boat we travelled several miles at a rapid pace. After we had progressed several miles we began to converse about our adventures. John Sawyer informed me that I was missed the evening before by Richards, about dusk, and that he called me several times, and made strict inquiry of Stephen Stone, his other servant for me. Stephen of course had not seen me since I left the frigate the afternoon before. One sailor said " Kit had paddled the hoff"—another, in a taunting manner, " He has gone to see his mother !" These observations provoked master Richards to anger to such a degree that he treated them rather irreverently. The next morning Richards came on shore in the same boat

with Sawyer, but it was yet so dark that Sawyer did
not discover him until leaving the boat after it had
arrived at the wharf in the city. Then it was that
Richards disclosed to Sawyer his object in coming
a shore so early in the morning—and that he was in
quest of me. He supposed that I had either got
lost in the city, had mistaken the wharf where the
ship's boats arrived and departed, or had taken
lodgings with some acquaintances which he had
made when on board our prize and while we had
been in New York—while walking the street with
Sawyer he thought he should find me at or near the
market, but when they had arrived within a short
distance of the market Richards concluded to visit a
barber's shop then opposite to them in the same
street they were then in. He directed Sawyer if he
should see me, to order my stay at the market
whither Sawyer was going, until he (Richards)
should be there which would not exceed twenty
minutes from the time Sawyer left him. It seems
then that at the time we entered the market Mr
Richards was very near me, and but for his attention at the barber's shop would probably have
taken me. After we had travelled some distance,

Rock began to complain of hunger and fatigue. It was suggested to call at some small house out of the road and obtain something to eat. This I strongly opposed as that course would induce a suspicion of our true situation, and proposed calling for our breakfast at a tavern then in sight, in a bold but careless manner. It was at the same time proposed to fix a plausible story between us to use provided we should be taken up which was more than probable for we well knew that nearly if not all the country embraced within the limits of Long Island was governed by the british and their tory adherents, and that we should be examined not only in the hearing of each other but separately. I was appointed to invent our brief but fabulous history. I accepted the appointment—And suggested as follows, "We must say that we have been privateering to catch yankees, out of New-York, have recently returned from sea and are now going home to Sag-Harbour to visit our relatives, friends and neighbors." This was adopted, and Sawyer observed that nothing could do better as he had an uncle residing at Sag-Harbour by the name of Daniel Havens, (29) and that his father had lived there, but now resided

on Shelter Island (30) not far distant, and he had a
sister married and then living at or near Sag Harbour. Our contingent history having been agreed
upon we went forward to the tavern before mentioned, called for our breakfasts which was furnished
us, and for which we paid a shilling each, N. York
currency—we learned at this tavern (31) on inquiry
that we were nine miles from New York, and that
three miles further travel would take us to Jamaica.
We immediately went forward, having determined
to keep the main road to Sag Harbour, we went
boldly on our journey—were stopped in our course
once that day on suspicion as run a ways from his
majesty's navy—our story was told, and we were
suffered to proceed with very little delay. The
next day were again stopped by two or three
men travelling in the direction for New York—we
were again examined but separately, and supported
each other in our several examinations. Notwithstanding there was no descripencies in our stories,
the examinants had considerable hesitation with
respect to suffering us to proceed. They accused us
of having run away from a british man of war—
said they could get forty dollars a head for us which

sum would pay one half the price for a fine horse &c. These men had eight or ten horses with them destined for the New York market. After I had spoken in an under tone to Sawyer & Rock, that we should get a good ride by going back and that on our arrival at New-York we should be instantly released through the interest we could make with our late officers and these men would be obliged to bring us back at their own expence &c which was heard by our examinants as I intended it to be, I walked up to the best horse I could select and said, "I will take this horse." "Stop," said one of the examinants, who seemed to be the leader of the party, "I do not know what to make of you. That fellow," (pointing to Rock) "I could swear is an english boy, but you two (meaning myself and Sawyer) seem to know men at Sag-Harbour—one of you say that Capt. Havens is your uncle—I know him, and I must let you go on." We then went on full of glee and laughed heartily at our success, and arrived at the house of Capt. Havens in Sag Harbour without any further molestation from the tories or british. Capt. Havens received us with cordiality and even politeness welcomed us

to his house, entertained us with the best victuals
and drink his house could afford—he invited us to
tarry with him until an opportunity offered for us
to cross the sound in safety to the Connecticut shore.
He advised us to keep very still and out of sight as
much as possible or convenient. He promised to
arrange matters so that we could cross the sound
which he said would be in a day or two—all which
he performed in the time he mentioned. Sawyer
proposed visiting his sister that evening who resided
about two miles from the house of Capt. Havens—
Rock and myself proposed going with him but we
were reminded by Capt. Havens that our movements must be conducted with the utmost caution
or we should not only get into difficulty ourselves,
but himself also. He said, boys there are british
officers walking our streets in disguise—you would
not mistrust them. You may go in the evening in
a still manner to the house of John Sawyer's sister.
We went according to his directions, and spent the
night with his sister and her husband, took breakfast with them the next morning, and in the forenoon of the same day returned to the house of Capt.
Havens where we remained through the day in one

of his private rooms. He spent a great part of the day with us and appeared highly entertained with the relation of sea adventures and escapes. In the early part of the same evening Rock and myself took leave of Capt. Havens, and his nephew John Sawyer, who was intending to go to the house of his father the ensuing day, who had been a fellow prisoner with me, and went on board a small vessel bound to Saybrook point—set sail and arrived at Saybrook point about one o'clock the ensuing morning. We immediately left the vessel and repaired to a tavern near by and went to bed. Rock got up from his bed about day light, and went out. I kept in my bed until the sun had risen. When I arose I inquired of the landlord what had become of Rock. He did not know where he was. He had gone out. In a few minutes I looked into the street and saw Rock marching with a recruiting party at the head of which was a recruiting Serjeant—I inquired of Rock why he was there—he said he had enlisted. This mortified me, and I endeavoured to procure his release without success. I soon got on board a sloop bound to Norwich and arrived there the next day in the afternoon, where I spent the following night with the Capt. and after taking a good breakfast set off for Providence by land where I arrived the next day and the same evening arrived at the house of my father (32) in North Providence, much to the joy of my parents and not a little to myself—In a few days I visited my master Aaron Mason, from whom I had ran away when I went to New Bedford and shipped on board the Eagle. He appeared pleased to see me again and proposed my return under my indentures of apprenticeship which I declined, and the indentures were cancelled soon after. When I arrived at Providence from New York it was late in the month of Novr. 1778, and had been from my native land more than eighteen months and supposed myself pretty well satisfied with a sea faring life. I turned my attention to labouring on a farm. I went to reside with Obadiah Olney Esq. (33) of Smithfield, in the county of Providence, and commenced service with him on Christmas day 1778. I remained with him between two and three years and until one day in the haying season, being at work mowing grass, with two men who were stout and active, and my scythe not being in the best order I could not keep my end up with them. This

provoked me to such a degree that I threw my
scythe into a bush heap—the two men (Daniel
Clark & Stephen Scott) who were fellow labourers
with me, on observing me leave the field inquired
of me where I was going and whether or not I was
angry. I answered that I was not pleased with my
scythe, and that I was going to sea—upon this they
raised a laugh though I had by this time got some
distance from them towards the house. On arriving
at the house I eat some bread & cheese, and then
packed up my clothes. The girls of the house
laughed at my conduct, and Mrs. Olney inquired
where I was going. I gave her little, or no answer
but treated her with due respect. She had always
treated me like a mother and was an excellent and
worthy woman. I immediately went to Providence (34) and found a brig ready for sea mounting
sixteen carriage guns, if I now recollect correctly,
and commanded by Christopher Whipple Esq. (35)
I applied to him for a birth to go out in her on a
cruise privateering—he made some inquiries in a
good natured manner with respect to my ability in
such business. My answers were given much in his
own humour and I engaged with him at once. In

a day or two after entering on board we sailed from
Providence, and lay at Newport (36) a few days, and
then put to sea—on the morning of the fifth day
after our departure the weather was very thick but
cleared off after the sun had risen above the horizon.
And we soon found ourselves in company with two
british frigates—the Amphetrite (37) and Madea (38)—
the latter soon came up with and captured us (39).
Our crew were immediately taken from the Brig
and put on board one of the frigates, carried to New
York, and put on board the Jersey prison ship, our
commander excepted who was committed to a prison
in the city. When our crew were put on board the
frigate after capture it was sent into the cable-tier
with more than an hundred other American seamen
which they had captured, and if my recollection be
now correct, they were the crew of the Belsarius (40)
which sailed from Boston. Our situation in the
cable tier was uncomfortable almost beyond endur-
ance—we were so crouded that we could not either
sit or lie down. I was among them, but being
small, I crawled back on to the cable very near the
bulk-head where a man of common size could not
stow himself—here I stretched out—the following

night was one of extreme misery for my fellow prisoners, especially to the unfortunate men who had been in this floating hell for two or three weeks. Our crew were full of vigour and entertained the crew of the frigate with a number of our patriotic songs. Although entertained the loyalists were by no means pleased. The singing was excellent and its volumne was extensive—and yet extremely harsh to the taste of the captors. The guard frequently threatened to fire upon us if the singing was not dispensed with, but their threats availed them not. They only brought forth higher notes and vociferous defiance from the crew. The poetry of which the songs were many of them composed, was of the most cutting sarcasm upon the british and their unhallowed cause. I recollect the last words of each stanza in one song were, " For America and all her sons forever will shine." In these words it seemed to me that all the prisoners united their voices to the highest key, for the harmony produced by the union of two hundred voices must have grated upon the ears of our humane captors in a manner less acceptable than the thunder of heaven. For at the interval of time between the singing of every song

the sentinels would threaten to fire upon us and the
officers of the frigate would also admonish with
angry words. " Fire and be damn'd " would be
the response from perhaps an hundred voices at the
same instant. The singing would again be renewed
and louder if possible. In this manner the first
night was spent. The cowardly tyrants dared not
fire upon us, notwithstanding their repeated threats—
They were as often set at defiance sometimes in the
following words—" We dare you to fire upon us.
It will be only half work for many of the prisoners
are now half dead from extreme sufferings." The
hilarity of our crew begun to abate the second day,
their sympathies being called into action from the
dying situation of some of their unfortunate fellow
prisoners. It was discovered that two of them had
fallen down apparently dead. They were handed
up the hatchway and taken care of by the british.
The Surgeon resuscitated them after some time as I
was informed. Two only of the prisoners were
allowed to visit the upper deck at the same time.
The officers of the frigate being probably afraid of
us which arose from our turbulence. Many of the
prisoners while they were thus confined on board

the frigate, became so exhausted that they would
fall and lean against each other. In this situation
self preservation destroyed humanity. The leaning
or exhausted party would receive the points of sail
needles into any part of his body that could be
reached by the standing one. These operations
would provoke the cries of "murder." I will here
mention that the two boys who belonged to the
crew of the brig were not put into the Cable Tier—
of this however I am not certain. They were called
by the name of Smith. I hope that these young
men are now alive, and if they are and should ever
see this narative, I am sure they will confirm the
details of the capture of the brig, and subsequent
sufferings of her crew when prisoners. They were
from Plainfield, in the state of Connecticut, as they
informed me. They were cooks on board the brig,
were brothers, and well behaved. We were kept
on board the frigate three or four days in the direful
situation before mentioned when we arrived in the
port of New York and were put on board the Jersey
prison ship. (41) I shall now describe the prison
ship, and the discipline enforced by the british upon
the unfortunate prisoners—their treatment and suf-

ferings. The ship had mounted 74 guns in the
british navy, but was old and out of commission
and kept in the port of New York for the purpose
of confining captured seamen—had been dismantled
of her sails and rigging and moored in the East
river, but a short distance from the Long Island
shore. When our crew were put on board her, the
number of prisoners amounted to about 800. We
were all put between decks ev'ry night before dark,
the number being great our situation was here
extremely unpleasant. Our rations were not sufficient to satisfy the calls of hunger. (42) Although
the british had an hospital ship (43) near us for the
accommodation of the sick yet we had a great deal
of sickness on board the Jersey, and many died on
board her. (44) The sickness seemed to be epidemic
and which we called the bloody flux or dyssenterry.
After the prisoners had been driven below at dusk
of the evening and the boat had ceased conveying
the sick to the hospital ship, many of the prisoners
would become sick the fore part of the evening and
before morning their sufferings would be ended by
death—such was the malignancy of the disease.
My situation amongst others after being stowed

away for the night was on the larboard side of the
ship with our heads near the wall or side, and the
two boys before mentioned by the side of me. Thus
situated, but one gangway to the upper deck was
open, from which my place of rest was about 20
feet, and only two prisoners were allowed to visit
the upper deck at the same time in the night let the
calls of nature be never so violent, and there was no
place between decks provided us to satisfy those
calls. This induced an almost constant running
over me by the sick, who would besmear myself
and others with their bloody and loathesome filth—
The situation of the prisoners was truly appalling.
The place of interment for the dead prisoners was
not far off and completely within our view from the
Jersey (46)—Report said that one dead body was disturbed to bury another, the mortality was so great.
The cruel and unjustifiable treatment of the prisoners by the british soon produced the most demoral-
izing effects upon them. Boxing was tolerated
without stint. Pilfering food was another evil
which prevailed in some degree among the prisoners. During the short period I was on board one
of the most horrid scenes I ever witnessed occurred

from indulging this vice. A prisoner had pilfered
food from a mess, who complained of him to the
chief british officer on board. This officer decided
that the delinquent should be punished by all the
members of the mess who had suffered by his
pillage. The accused was tied across a water butt
on the upper deck—his posteriors were laid bare,
and a wooden instrument six feet long, one end
expanded and shaped much in the form of an oar
and used by the ship's cook to stir the burgoo (46)
when cooking it. The mess-mates who had suffered
by his pilfering, and six in number were arranged
around him and directed to inflict six strokes each
with the instrument aforesaid upon that portion of
the defaulter's body which had been laid bare.
The officer who directed this punishment being yet
present. Next, one of the mess took the instrument
in hand—(it was very heavy, and as much so as one
man could conveniently wield)—and inflicted six
strokes with the ponderous weapon, apparently with
all his might—the sufferer groaning at ev'ry stroke—
blood appeared before the first six had been administered—a second man took the instrument and with
no less mercy than the first inflicted six more

strokes—the blood and flesh flying ten feet at ev'ry
stroke—during this period the defaulter fainted, but
was resuscitated by administering water to him—
a third man took the instrument in hand and
inflicted six more strokes though not as severe as
the two first—The officer before mentioned then
interposed and observed to the enraged mess-mates
that they were too severe with their fellow. He
had again fainted. No more blows were given and
the horrible looking man was untied and fell down
on the deck. He was again resuscitated but still
lay prostrated on the deck, not being able to rise.
Beef brine was thrown upon his wounds but he
appeared to be senseless. He lay some time on the
deck, and about or near evening was taken below
by men more humane, and ev'ry attention was paid
him that their situation would admit. The sufferer
died in two or three days after his punishment as I
was afterwards informed. I had escaped from the
ship before his death. His punishment sickened
me, at the stomach, and the horrid, inhuman scene
has made an impression on my mind which can
never be effaced. I will mention another instance
of treachery and the cruelty which followed, although

to this I was not a witness, it having occurred after
I left the ship—The subjects of it were one of our
crew by the name of Spicer, a sailing master's mate,
and a boy—all three, prisoners. An American
vessel came into the port of New York as a cartel
for the exchange of prisoners. The agents came on
board the prison ship with the names of such prisoners as were to be exchanged. The mate above
alluded to was so fortunate as to be one of the
exchanged. He had a large chest on board and as
privately as he could, put the boy into the chest,
locked him in, and in this situation the boy was
carried on board the cartel—Spicer had seen the
boy stowed in the chest, and after he had been conveyed on board the cartel, the treacherous Spicer
communicated the affair to the commanding officer
of the prison ship. The cartel was immediately
boarded as she had not yet left the port, although
ready to leave, and the boy found and brought
back. Spicer paid for his treachery with the forfeit
of his life—When evening was coming on, and the
prisoners were going below for the night, he was
knocked down the hatchway to the bottom of the
steps below among those who had been awaiting his

fall, and who fell upon him, cut off his ears and mangled his body in the most shocking manner, and to such a degree that he died of his wounds in a day or two after.(47) I will mention another thing which added to the horror of this prison ship—this was filth. It was permitted to such an extent that ev'ry prisoner was infested with vermin on his body and wearing apparel. I one day observed a prisoner on the fore-castle of the ship, with his shirt in his hands, having stripped it from his body and deliberately picking the vermin from the plaits of said shirt, and putting them into his mouth. A number of the prisoners had told me before this time that many of them were in the habit of thus acting. I could not credit these statements, but in the case last mentioned the proof was demonstrated beyond all doubt. I stepped very near the man engaged with his vermin, and commenced conversation with him. I inquired for his name which he gave me. He also informed me that he sailed in a privateer from Marblehead, Massachusetts, and was on board her when taken. To my question, "How long have you been a prisoner on board this ship," he answered, after some hesitation, "two years and a half or eighteen months." He had been so sparingly fed that he was nearly a skeleton, and all but in a state of nudity. He had been so long on board this prison ship and so severely treated that 1 am convinced that when he conversed with me, he had lost the correct knowledge of the period of time he had been in captivity. This was only one case from perhaps an hundred of others similar. This man appeared in tolerable health as to body, his emaciation excepted. The prison ship was strongly secured, and in addition, was strictly and rigidly guarded. The discipline of the prisoners by the british was in many respects of the most shocking and appalling character. The roll of the prisoners, as I was informed, was called ev'ry three months, unless a large acquisition of prisoners should render it proper more often. The next day after our crew were put on board the roll was called, and the police regulations of the ship with respect to the conduct of the captives were read. I heard this. From these it appeared that ev'ry captive who should be detected undertaking to effect his escape from this "floating hell," either by swimming, taking the ships boat, or any other way, should suffer instant death, and should not even be taken on board alive. Notwithstanding all this, attempts were made after I had escaped, as I was afterwards informed from undoubted authority. The details of my own escape and that of William Waterman, who started with me from the ship, I shall give after I have mentioned the attempt of six others, and the tragical death of five of them in the undertaking. It appeared that about a week after myself and Waterman had left the "floating hell," and many of the captives concluding that we had reached the shore in safety, the six captives before alluded to were prompted to undertake the perilous enterprize. They had all got clear from the ship by nearly the same means and method that myself and Waterman had adopted and used—And after obtaining the watery element one of the party became alarmed after gaining the stern of the ship and the party about leaving it (he being the last to leave the stern,) exclaimed, "Oh! lord have mercy I shall be drowned." He was overheard by the officers who were on the night watch on the quarter deck. The ship's boat was immediately launched, and four of them were soon found swimming in the harbour,

and shot by the guard. (48) The fifth was found
near the ship and caught, with his hands upon the
boat when an officer struck one of them with such
severity that the bone was laid bare. The captive
persevered with his hold upon the boat—The unrelenting british useing their bayonets with all dex-
terity upon his body which they pierced in a number of places. Notwithstanding all this bloody
opposition, he gained the boat when one of the
guard begged for his life, but this interference was
untimely for the bayonets had been so freely used
that he was desperately wounded, and wherewith
died the next day. The sixth captive saved himself
by gaining the anchor which hung at the bow, and
suspended from the cathead of the ship. He clung
to the flukes of the anchor, which was under the
surface of the water, with his nose barely above the
surface. In this situation he eluded the vigilant
search of the pursuers for they were twice, within
two feet of his hiding place, and did not discover
him. After the pursneing party had given up pursuit and search, and hoisted their boat out of water,
saying they had killed all the damned rebel run-
aways, and became still, the survivor crawled upon

and stood upon the flukes of the anchor in an erect posture until day light dawned, and the prisoners had begun to get upon the upper deck, when he ascended the stem of the anchor, half chilled to death and naked, (the stem of course being of iron, and twelve feet long) to the stock of the anchor, and from thence over the bow of the ship to the fore-castle, and from thence sprang to the gangway with all his might and descended below, without being stopped or arrested by the guard who were stationed very near the hatchway. I will here mention the names of several of my fellow prisoners who after-wards stated to me the occurences which took place on board the Jersey after I escaped from it and here related, and who survived their captivity, and with whom I was well acquainted, and in whose veracity full reliance can be placed, viz, Benjamin Whipple, (49) who after the revolutionary war, removed to Albany in the state of New York, and was an officer in the house of Assembly of that state for some years. He formerly resided in Cumberland, in the state of Rhode Island. Benjamin Dexter, (50) also of Cumberland aforesaid, and Jabez Hawkins, (51) a distant family connection of mine.

Immediately after being put on board the Jersey, I began to meditate an escape from my captivity. This was an enterprize of great peril and extreme difficulty and could not be effected without swimming a great distance with any prospect of success. I will mention the impediments—near us lay a guardship for the apparent purpose of quelling any mutiny which might arise among the prisoners and to destroy, capture or drive away any vessel which should undertake our release. The hospital ship which I was informed had a guard on board her was also near us. On shore was a line of sentinels from the burying ground already mentioned and extending east on the banks of the cove towards Hurl-Gate, a mile and an half as near as we could calculate on board the Jersey—at the same time estimating the distance of the several curves which indented the shore. Others, more acquainted with distances on water, estimated the distance from the ship beyond the line of sentries, at two and an half or three miles. To get clear from the ship was a consideration of much moment. To leave the upper deck with any kind of safety was impossible. The *gunports* of the lower deck on which was no guard, was barred strongly with iron, and bolted to the sides of the ship. It was late in the season and the water cold, being late in the month of September or the beginning of Oct. (1781.) Notwithstanding all these difficulties I determined to undertake the hazardous enterprize. I communicated my intention to William Waterman, already mentioned, and invited him to accompany me. He was one of our crew, and did not hesitate to comply. I knew him to be a good swimmer. We tried others out of which to obtain one to go with us—we could not succeed. We were reminded that our lives would be in four fold jeopardy by the undertaking, and were strongly dissuaded from attempting it. The police regulations of the ship was mentioned which we had heard read—the great distance to swim—the certainty of being taken by the tories after we *might* get on shore—the treachery we might encounter were all urged in the most sympathetic colours by those with whom we communicated. But all to no purpose—our resolution had been taken. The second day of our captivity on board the Jersey, and after we had determined on escape by swimming, we (Waterman & myself) took the advantage of the

peals of thunder in a shower or storm (₅₂) that came
over us in the afternoon to break one of the gun
ports on the lower deck which was strongly barred
with iron and bolts as before mentioned—having
previously obtained from the cooks' room an old
axe, and crow bar from the upper deck for the purpose, in a private manner, and concealed them till
an opportunity should offer for use. The thunder
storm was opportune for our design, for when a peal
of thunder roared we worked with all our might
with the axe, & crow bar, against the bars and
bolts—when the peal of thunder subsided, we
ceased, without our blows being heard by the
british until another peal commenced—we then
went to work again, and so on until our work was
completed to our liking. The bars and bolts, after
we had knocked them loose, were replaced so as not
to draw the attention of our british gentry if they
should happen to visit the lower deck before our
departure. We also hung some old apparel over
and around the shattered gun port to conceal any
marks. Being thus and otherwise prepared for our
escape, the ship was visited by our Capt. Whipple
the next day after we had broken the gun port—to

him we communicated our intention and contemplated means of escape. He strongly remonstrated against the design—We told him we should start the ensuing evening. Capt. Whipple inquired, " How do you think of escaping." I answered, by swimming to that point, (at the same time pointing to a place then in our view on Long Island, in a north easterly direction from the prison ship.) We must do this to avoid the sentinels which are stationed on shore in the night. What, said Capt. Whipple, do you think of swimming to that point. Yes, we must to avoid the sentinels, I answered. Well, said Capt. Whipple, Hawkins, give it up. It is only throwing your lives away, for there is not a man on earth that can swim from this prison ship to that point as cold as the water is now. Why, how far do you think it is to that point? Why, I answered, Waterman and myself have estimated the distance at a mile and an half. Yes, said Capt. Whipple, it is all of *two* and an half miles—*you* cannot measure across water as well as I can—so you had better give it up for I have encouragement of getting home next week, and if I do, I will make it my whole business to get you all exchanged imme-

diately. Although Waterman was several years
my senior in age, the conversation was carried on
between Capt. Whipple and myself, for the reason
that Capt. Whipple was more acquainted with me
than with Waterman, but Waterman was present—
before our interview ended, Capt. Whipple said to
me, Hawkins, if you do start as you say, you *shall*,
and as there is one chance in a hundred for you to
get home, should you get to Providence, you must
go and see my mother (she resided there) and
inform her what my recent fate has been. This I
promised him I would do, and faithfully performed
it. Capt. Whipple was an excellent seaman, and
much the gentleman, and had a very large circle of
family connections in Rhode Island of the first
respectability. He was patriotic to the cause of
America to enthusiasm, and vigilant and perse-
vering. Notwithstanding all this he had been unfortunate in his sea adventures for from the commencement of the revolutionary struggle to the
period of which I am now mentioning, he had been
captured by the british on the high seas the fifth
time, and at each time he was commander of the
captured vessel. Capt. Whipple's advice had great

weight on our minds, but did not shake our purpose. We had not been on board the "Old Jersey" more than one hour before we began to plot our escape. We had been only three days on board when we (Waterman and myself) left it forever. We had been on board long enough to discover the awful scenes which took place daily in this "floating hell." Our preparations for leaving were completed by procuring a piece of rope from an old cable that was stretched under the forecastle of the ship and called "service" and wound around the cable to preserve it. We had each of us packed our wearing apparel in a knapsack for each, and made on board the Old Jersey. I gave some of my apparel to the two Smiths (boys before mentioned)—I stowed in my knapsack a thick woollen sailor jacket, well lined, a pair of thick pantaloons, one vest, two shirts, two pair of stockings, one pair of shoes, a pair of heavy silver shoe buckles, a pair of knee buckles, two silk handkerchiefs, four silver dollars, not forgetting a Junk bottle of rum which we had purchased on board at a dear rate. These were all stowed in my knapsack. Waterman had stowed his apparel and other articles in his knapsack. My knapsack was very heavy. It was fast'ned to my back with two very strong garters passing over my shoulders and under each arm, and fast'ned with a string at my breast, bringing my right and left garter in contact at or near the centre. Thus equipt we were ready to commit ourselves to the watery element, and to our graves as many of our hardy fellow prisoners predicted. The evening was as good an one as we could desire at that season of the year—the weather was mild and hazy, and the night extremely dark. It was arranged between Waterman and myself, after leaving the ship to be governed in our course by the lights on board the ships and the responses of the sentinels on shore, and after arriving on shore to repair near a dwelling house which we could see from the old Jersey in the day time and spend the balance of the night in a barn, but a few rods from said dwelling. Waterman was the first to leave the ship through the broken open gun port and suspended to the rope before mentioned by his hands and at the end behind him by several of our fellow prisoners whom we were leaving behind us, and with whom we affectionately parted with reciprocal good wishes.

He succeeded in gaining the water and in leaving
the ship without discovery from the british. It had
been agreed, if detection was about to take place
that he should be taken back again into the ship. I
had agreed to follow him in one minute in the same
manner. I left and followed him in half that time,
and succeeded in leaving the ship without giving
the least alarm to those who had held us in captivity—I kept along close to the side of the ship
until I gained the stern and then left the ship. This
was all done very slow, sinking my body as deep in
the water as possible without stopping my course,
until I was at such a distance from her that my
motions in the water would not create attention
from the enemy on board. After gaining a suitable
distance from the ship I hailed Waterman three
times. He did not answer me. It was my great
desire to fall in with him, but I have never seen him
since he left the old Jersey to this day. Nevertheless he succeeded in getting on shore and to his
home and friends (53)—his fate and success I have
since learned from James Waterman one of his
brothers. In the meantime I kept on my course,
without thinking that any accident would befal him

as I knew him to be an excellent swimmer, and no
faint hearted or timid fellow. I could take my
course very well from the light reflected from the
stern lanthrons of the prison, guard and hospital
ships, and also from the responses of the sentinels
on shore, in the words "all's well." These responses were repeated ev'ry half hour on board the
guard ship, and the sentinels aforesaid. These
repetitions served me to keep the time I was
employed in reaching the shore—no object occupied my mind during this time so much as my
friend Waterman, if I may except my own success
in getting to land in safety. I flattered myself that
I should find him on shore or at the barn we had
agreed to occupy after we might gain it. After I
had been swimming nearly or quite two hours, my
knapsack had broken loose from my back, which
had resulted from the wearing off the garters under
my arms in consequence of the friction from them
by swimming. This occurrence did not please me
much. I endeavoured to retain my knapsack and
contents by putting it under one arm, and thus
meant to reach the shore, with the use of only one
then in swimming, but soon found that this situa-

tion impeded my progress, and led me from my true course. I then pulled the skirt of my vest out of my knapsack, the other portion of the vest yet remaining within, took the skirt in my teeth and again proceeded to swim having thrown my knapsack over my shoulder—This reminded me of the manners of Reynard in conveying his stolen goose to his hiding place for a repast from his booty. I continued in this situation but a short time observing that I was again out of my true course—and my load cramped my neck, and I had now become chilled from the coolness of the water, having been in it more than two hours, and could not satisfy myself how far I had yet to swim to find land, beyond the chain of sentinels. Meantime I could see, or thought I could see something ahead more dark than it was around me, but how far was doubtful. My bundle was burdensome, and hindered my progress for I again put them under one arm and swam a short time with them—By this time I had become much chilled and benumbed from cold, but could swim tolerably well—In this situation I was much at loss in my mind how to act and what to do with my knapsack. I hesitated whether or not to

retain it longer in my possession or part with it forever—I soon determined on the latter and sent it
adrift. In this balancing state of mind and subsequent decision I was cool and self collected as perhaps at any period of my life. After I had parted
with my knapsack and contents, I set myself on my
true course still guided by the light from the ships.
Immediately the land sentinels sang again "all's
well." Thinks I, that is a lie, for I have lost my
apparel and bottle of rum. I was much relieved by
this last cry of "all's well" for the last sentinel who
responded was not far from my right and I had
passed him at some distance and was now beyond
all the guards stationed on shore—I then made for
the land. I soon found I was close in with the
shore: I attempted on this discovery to touch bottom, but could not, the shore being very bold. I
swam within twelve feet of the shore before I could
touch bottom, and in so doing, found I could not
stand I was so chilled—had "lost my land legs" to
use a seaman's phrase, but I moved around in shoal
water until I found I could stand, then slept on
shore—I had not sent my clothes adrift more than
twenty five minutes or so before striking the shore.

I was completely naked except a small hat on my head which I had brought with me from the old Jersey. What a situation this, without covering to hide my naked body—in an enemy's country, without food or means to obtain any—and among tories more unrelenting than the devil—more perils to encounter and nothing to aid me but the interposition of heaven. Yet I had gained an important portion of my enterprise. I had got on land after swimming in the water two hours and an half, and a distance of perhaps two and an half miles. The distance however I can by no means determine with any degree of accuracy, it may be more or less. The house which we had destined as our point of meeting, or arriving, when on board ship, and before alluded to, was forty or fifty rods from my place of landing. I discovered it and took my course for it— had gone but a short distance before I came in contact with a rock. I tumbled over it which nearly prostrated me. This sudden and unexpected impediment aroused me to anger, and I gave loose to some profane language, for which I relented on the spot. My overthrow broke the skin on several parts of my body—I rubbed the most injured bruises with my hands. The passion of anger, united with the shock my fall produced, seemed to quicken the circulation of my blood, and I seemed to feel much warmer than before. I got near the house and passed by it to the barn—opened one of its doors—found a place near the stanchions large enough to lie down in near a large body of hay—got into it—pulled some hay from that mentioned—covered myself with it and soon went to sleep. It was between two and three o'clock in the morning when I arrived at the barn, and after being in it a short time, called for my friend Waterman in great hopes of finding that he was in it, or within my hearing, for here it was that we had agreed to stay the remaining part of the evening and all the succeeding day. But much to my disappointment he answered not. I then concluded if he had been so fortunate as to reach the shore that he had made his way to a house near hurl-gate (54) on the Long Island shore, whither he had been directed by a young man he had conversed with but a short time before we left the ship and who was a prisoner on board. Waterman communicated this to me before we started but not in sufficient detail for me to

undertake to arrive to the place. He had not time
to inform or give me particulars in relation to this
route before leaving the ship—but calculated to do
so after our getting ashore. I slept in the barn
until late in the morning not calculating to leave it
until the following evening. About nine o'clock in
the forenoon of the day as I lay in my hiding place
and in the hay, a black girl came into the barn,
muttering because she found the door open, which I
had left in that situation when I came into the barn.
Her object seemed to be eggs. After rumaging
about some time she left the barn, and shut the door
in question. The day had been spent and night
coming on. After all was still around the house
and barn I left the latter. Hunger had by this time
created a craving for food. I undertook without
success to milk some of the cows which were in the
farm yard into my hat. They were so afraid of my
naked situation that I was not suffered to get near
them. If I attempted it, they would run and snuff
like deers. I then left the farm yard as soon as
I could, fearing that the noise of the cattle would
excite the attention of the inmates of the house. I
travelled an easterly course. The night was very

dark, and rain began to fall very soon in large drops, which when striking my naked back would make me cringe. I proceeded across fields and meadows without seeking for a road—after some time went through a gate, which passing, I thought my course was too much north or bearing to the west. On my left it seemed to be woods—on my right it appeared to be a champaigne. I was now in a road but left it, and on my right went into the fields and was pursuing my course east as I then supposed. In this ramble I found a melon yard and took two melons and went on—I could not open them, having no instrument that would effect it—continued walking, and it yet rained. When coming near a ditch, on hearing the chains on a fettered horse, became alarmed, fearing I was near an enemy, but on a closer examination, and approaching near, conceived a sentry box when the old white horse began to walk from me as fast as he could, which dispelled my fears, and I proceeded. I had understood that this part of Long Island was then infested with Hessian guards, but it seems none were here. After going some distance I came to a fence partly stone and partly wood—here I

broke my water melons and eat some of them but
they were unsavoury. The season for them had
gone by, and they had been bitten by the frost. I
threw the remaining part of them away. I yet kept
on my course again as I supposed, and gained a
road and soon came to a gate. On examination I
found it to be the same gate that I had passed and
before mentioned. This shewed me that my wan-
derings had been of no avail towards my desired
progress. Although bewildered, I took a course
directly contrary to my formerly supposed direct
course—wandered some hours, through fields, meadows and shrubs, sometimes going through thickets
of briers which tore my naked skin. I went through
a corn-field and found some corn which I plucked,
and hunger induced me to eat. The rain fell during
the greater part of the whole night, and sometimes
in torrents. The atmosphere was quite chilly, and
I was obliged to walk fast to keep from perishing.
Towards daylight, I found a barn, which I entered
and on the floor found a car or waggon laden with
salt hay. This barn was an object very desirable
for I had been weary for several hours, and at one
time was induced to lie down near the side of a

fence under some shrubs—after breaking a number
of small twigs from the surrounding shrubs and
placing them in the tops of those I had selected to
cover me from the falling rain—having done this I
gathered a quantity of fallen leaves and put them
on the boughs of the shrubs and among the twigs to
keep the pelting rain from my body—having put a
quantity of these leaves around the roots of the
shrubs, all wet I lay down on them to rest. I had
not lain long in this situation before I discovered
that my calculations to avoid the falling rain were
far from being realized, and that I must again put
myself in motion or inevitably perish. And some
time before entering the barn, the night being very
dark, without intending it, visited a grave yard, and
the first intimation I had of being in a congregation
of the dead, was my coming in contact with the
head and foot stones which had been set there in
memory of the departed. It was not untill I had
been prostrated several times by these monuments,
that I found myself thus situated. The skin on my
legs and other parts of my body had been broken
and severely bruised. These obstructions to my
progress induced a strict examination. If "the

darkness visible" rendered the sight of my eyes useless, I thought the touch of my hands might test my location. (55) I found the stones had characters on them, denoting inscriptions. This discovery created no fears from the dead—I had more to fear from the living. The barn last before mentioned and in which I entered, was partially filled with salt hay. I crawled into that part which seemed to have been filled—prepared a place to rest and stretched myself in it, and being wet the salt hay soon made a very lively impression on my fresh wounds, which I received from the briars and the monuments in the graveyard. The duration of the pain thus produced, was, however, short. I am inclined to think that the saline properties of the hay heal'd my scratches sooner than they otherwise would have been. It was nearly day light when sleep stole upon me. I slept soundly until after sun rising the following morning notwithstanding the rain poured down in torrents nearly the whole of the night—the sun appeared to have risen clear, and ev'ry appearance indicated a fine pleasant day. Soon after the sun had rose, a man came into the barn, and began to speak in the low dutch language, but his talk appeared to be all to himself. His object in visiting the barn appeared to be for unlading the hay from the car, for he soon began to pitch it off. Before he had finished, a neighbor visited him for the purpose of obtaining assistance to make a coffin, for, said the neighbor "that fellow must be buried to day"—"not to day," said I to myself, "for I am not yet dead." The conversation between the two men was carried on in the english language—in the course of which I learned that a young man had died the evening before very suddenly. The deceased appeared to be well the early part of the evening—eat his supper without intimating illness of any kind, and before nine o'clock the same evening died. These men both left the barn at the same time. I remained in the barn some time after this but left it early in the forenoon, but not from the side fronting the house and went into an orchard in quest of fruit, now being excessively hungry—found two or three half rotten pears—They were quite savoury, I having fasted ever since I had left the old Jersey, the corn and melons excepted. Apples I could not find. I then travelled south easterly, nearly in a direction with

the road. The weather fair and warm—saw a field
of potatoes directly ahead, and calculated to carry
some of them away with me, hoping I could find
fire soon and then would roast and eat them. But
I was soon frustrated in this, for on gaining the
patch of potatoes, a young woman started up who
had come to the place for the apparent purpose of
gathering them in a small basket—She immediately
saw me. I was of course naked, my head excepted.
She was, or appeared to be, excessively affrighted,
and ran towards a house, screeching & screaming at
ev'ry step, leaving her basket behind. Her fears
were gratuitous for I had not offered any violence
to her person, not even gentle gallantry. I ran with
more speed than herself in an opposite direction for
a glade of woods by the side of which ran a rivulet
or small bay—the water was still. I had before
discovered this on my right—I entered this wood
some distance fearing I might be pursued by the
tories. I had some fears that they would pursue
me with dogs, and armed myself with an heavy
club for defence from these canine loyalists—I had
further determined if pursuit should be made that I
would throw myself into a cove then in view—If I

should do this before being overtaken I felt well
assured that I could keep away from the tory crew
in that vicinity. I was not molested however by
this discovery. In sight of this potatoe patch were
several dwellings and a small meeting house, and
perhaps six or seven miles from N. York city. I
kept to the left of this cove and it seemed to run in
a north easterly direction, into the sound. I soon
found a bay on my right, and a road on my
left—the latter I dared not to travel. Hunger now
preyed upon me excessively, and my body weak—I
searched for something to eat, but in vain—except
some ears of corn which I plucked from a field that
day—It was poor food but sustained me—that day
and the following night, I had made no progress in
my journey. Early in the evening I crept into
another barn, and lay in a stuble upon unrotted flax.
This was a poor bed for a naked hungry boy, but I
tarried until morning and slept considerably. I
arose from my bed of flax after the rising of the sun.
I determined to proceed on my course, happen what
would. The course I had left the evening before I
resumed in the morning keeping in the fields
between the bay and road. I could see the farmers

at their labour in the fields. I then concluded to
still keep on my course and go to some of these
people then in sight. I was by this time almost
worn out with hunger. I slowly approached two
tall young men who were gathering garden sauce.
They soon discovered me and appeared astonished
at my appearance, and began to draw away from
me, but I spoke to them in the following words,
"dont be afraid of me, I am a human being."
They then made a halt, and inquired of me, " are
you scared "—" no," said I, but I thought I never
saw two men more operated upon by fear than they.
I soon moved to a low place in the ground to avoid
discovery by the people on my left who were upon
a rising ground, near the road. The two young
men advanced slowly towards me, and inquired,
" how came you here naked." I seated myself on
the ground and told them the truth respecting my
situation and history—in short, they said, " we wish
you were at home." This expression encouraged
my feelings that they were friends. One of them
asked, what do you want of us. I answered, I am
hungry, and want some old clothes—If you can help
me I pray you would. Well, said he, keep close

down from the sight of these folks up here, and I
will go and see my mamma and hear what she will
say about your request. I kept still on the ground.
They had a knife with them which I took in hand
and opened a water melon from the dry vines. The
brother, as I supposed he was, soon returned from
the house whither he had been to see his mamma—
He brought me two large pieces of bread buttered
and a pair of decent pantaloons, which I immediately put on, saying in the meantime you must go
by the barn, which was directly forward of me, and
my mother will give you a shirt. I eat my food
which he had bro't me in haste. It was delicious to
my taste—nothing ever tasted better to me. He
cautioned me that when I started for the barn, I
must keep out of sight (meaning that I had better
not be seen by those near me and whom I had
seen) of those people. For said he, if those people
see you they will take you back again to the Provost. I stepped nimbly to the barn in the manner
I had been directed, where I found an old lady with
a shirt on her arm on the south side of the barn—
the house stood north of it. She inquired whether
or not I had a father and mother alive—I told her I

had a mother alive when I left home and that my father was in the American army. Well, said she, I wish you was at home with your mother now. She then handed me two large pieces of bread well buttered which she had been holding in her hand. I had told her son that went to the house how long I had fasted and I presume he had communicated it to his mother when at the house for she cautioned me against taking too much food at that time, and I eat but one of my pieces of bread and butter which she gave me at the barn, and stopped. That is right, said she—still holding the shirt across her arm. She then told me I must go into the barn, take my pantaloons off and throw them out to her and she would take them with the shirt and hang them on a fence then in sight (pointing to it) and I will go a little back to a place where I cannot see you, and then you must come out and get them, and put them on—And if you are taken up you must swear you took them from the fence where they were hung out to dry. That will be no lie. I agreed to it. I was then about moving around the barn in sight of the house. The old lady caught hold of me, at the same time exclaiming "for God's

sake don't let that black woman of mine see you"
(the wench was washing in the stoop) "for she is as
big a devil as any of the king's folks, and she will
bring me out. And then we should all be put in
the Provost, and die there, for my husband was put
in there more than two years ago, and rotted and
died there not more than three weeks since." Her
grief was by this time so excited that she shed tears
profusely—in which I joined. After she had sighed
and sobbed for some time and partially dried her
tears, she observed, this will all do you no good at
last. I had told her where I wished to go—"you
must go to Oyster bay first and they can tell you,
but you cannot get there, for if you go down this
road to the ferry across this cove, there they are all
king's folks, and they will certainly take you up.
And if you go three and an half miles back to the
tide mills, Three hundred Hessians (56) are stationed
there on parol—but they will take you up for all.
Now if you were over this cove in that great road
you can see over on the other side, that would lead
you directly on the way to Oyster bay." I had by
this time become uneasy and wished to be under
way. For I thought myself well clad for a warm

day, but the old Lady again took me by the arm,
and stopped me, asking the last part of a thousand
questions to which I was bound to give answers.
At length I began to move toward the cove. Where
are you going, inquired the old lady. I am going
down to the cove and to swim across it, gain the
road you mentioned, and go on. She earnestly
entreated me not to undertake to swim across the
cove—no man had ever dared undertake to swim
across it. You cannot do it. Oh, said I, I can
swim across it—no, no—they call it a mile across.
I mentioned the manner which I should adopt to get
across the cove. She then said if I would go across,
that I could do better than to swim. She then
informed me where I could find a canoe and an
oar—the latter was hidden near the former, on the
bank of the cove in a thick bunch of bushes—these
you must steal and set yourself across and fasten
the canoe on the other side, and let the owner find
it. I found the canoe and oar, and crossed the cove
without accident, and left them as directed. This
lady and her two sons were dutch. And I was
informed by them that their residence was nine
miles from Brooklyn ferry. I had now been from

the old Jersey more than 60 hours, and no further
from her than before stated, and thought I had suffered enough for an whole year. It was now something late in the afternoon—after I had crossed the
cove, the weather warm, I travelled forward keeping the road except a suspicious character appeared
in sight. If this occurred I would be fixing the
fence on the road side, putting up the rails &c.
until they passed. This impeded my progress. I
came near the village of Jamaica, (57) when the sun
was about an hour above the horizon. Here was
trouble again—to pass the sentinels at Jamaica
safely and without suspicion would be difficult.
Here I was in great peril. The sentinels were so
near each other across the Island as to communicate
one with the other, as I was informed. On arriving
in view of the village I could plainly see the sentinels—two were stationed on either side of the road.
In this situation, went into a field near the road
side, and concealed myself in a bunch of bushes on
the side of a fence. What device to pursue with
success was a matter of much moment. While thus
devising ways and means to pass the sentinels, a
black or coloured man appeared with a small drove

of cattle which he had taken from some of the adjoining fields. Being thus situated I resolved to turn driver and assist the coloured man in getting his drove through the village. It was now near sun setting, and I set myself to driving with a stick in my hand. It may not be amiss to state that these sentinels were british—I passed them without their noticing that I feared or paid any attention to them. This device had the desired effect—I passed without being hailed or stopped by them. This was what was called the lower lines of the British. I was now in better spirits. Soon after I had passed the sentinels I left the drove of cattle in quick pace— the coloured man kept his eyes on me but said nothing. I conceived him to be a stupid fellow. I went on to what was called the last house. It was so called from its situation, there being no other for the space of seven miles east. It was occupied as a tavern, was large, and if I mistake not had been painted white. On arriving near this house I dare not enter it—left the road and entered into the orchard—seated myself and there remained until late in the evening intending to take up quarters in the barn when I could get to it without being observed by the inmates of the house, those around it or the barn. But there came up a shower of rain which my apparel could not resist. I laid myself under a fence for some time, and until all was quiet about the premises. This hap'ned as I supposed about nine o'clock in the evening. I then left my situation under the fence, crossed the road, went to the barn but could not enter, it being locked at ev'ry door. I then took a manger in a long open shed which was attached to the barn. This shed answered the purpose of a fence on the south side of the road the extent of its length. I search'd the manger the full length of the shed for materials of which to make me a bed, but in vain. I laid myself in the manger intending to remain in it until morning. In this I was frustrated. A carriage soon came to the house from the east, before which was a span of horses. Those persons who accompanied it determined to put up for the night. The horses were soon led to the barn for stabling. They were taken through the shed near that portion of it where I had taken quarters. One of the two men who led the horses had a lanthron lighted up which he set in the manger very near me, while the other was

employed unlocking the stable door. The former
soon discovered me from the light of his lanthron.
He exclaimed to his companion, "here lies some
person in the manger." "Who the devil is it?"
inquires the companion. "I dont know" (answered
the former) "for he is asleep." This snoring and
sleep was affected on my part to deceive them. It
was then concluded to awaken me from my slumbers, saying wake him up and let's see who he is.
One of them took hold and shook me and inquired,
Who are you? a friend. What do you do here?
I raised myself partially up, and in a reclining
posture, affecting to be in a state of intoxication
from an immoderate use of ardent spirits. At the
same time muttering in a sort of under tone, I came
in here to-get-out-of-the-rain. Where did you come
from, or where are you going. I am going-to-
Jamaica. And then fell back into the manger
apparently to them very drunk. One of the examinants observed, It is a boy as drunk as the devil
for he cant set up. Then (answers the other) lets
put up the horses and we'll take him into the house
and find who he is, for he may be here to steal
another horse, for we have had them stolen before

we got locks to our doors. On hearing this I thought I might get into more trouble by the ordeal of a further examination than to go immediately on through the desert plain (58) be it never so rainy. When my discoverers were about to leave for the purpose of putting the horses into the stable, one or both observed that I could not get away being so much intoxicated. But as soon as they had got into the stable with their light and horses, I nimbly left the shed the same way that I came into it—from the orchard—which was through a vacant place in the wall of the shed, where one of the boards was off from some cause or other, and near where I lay. I ran fast for some distance parallel with the fence, on the road as near as I could judge—it was cloudy and the night very dark but the rain had ceased. After I had ran some distance I came to a stop, and listened for any one who might be in pursuit, but I heard nothing indicating it. And concluding if pursuit were made that it would be toward Jamaica village whither I had told them I was going, and which I had passed—I immediately took the road and proceeded on east—nothing occurring to disturb my

journey except a light which appeared on my left
when I was about half way across the plain.—
Three times I undertook to approach it without
success. The third time my anger had been provoked to such a degree that I indulged in some
profane language. I had no fears, and even in that
period of my early life, I was no believer in ghosts
nor hobgoblins. I had been informed when travelling this road about three years before in company
with Sawyer and Rock that these plains were
haunted and that men had been seen upon it without heads and also with their throats cut—whether
or not the latter had heads on their shoulders we
were not informed. This information was given us
by the honest superstitious inhabitants living on the
road, and who entertained us in our transit from
New York to Sag-Harbour. This light that I have
mentioned appeared to be not more than a quarter
of a mile from the road, but must have been much
further and change of ground probably contributed
to my loosing sight of it in each effort I made to get
to it. (⁵⁹) After I gave up my light I took to the
road again and went on. I was soon over the
desert, and at a short distance discovered a barn on

my left which I went into quickly as the atmosphere indicated rain very soon. Three fourths of the roof of this barn appeared to be off—but I got under that portion of the roof which appeared to be on, found some straw under it and made myself a bed into which I crawled. I had no sooner done this than the rain fell in torrents. What a happy escape this, thought I. But my situation was dry. By this time it was at least as late as two o'clock in the morning. In crossing the plain my shirt had not been wet through by the rain—I got warm in a short time and went to sleep. My slumbers continued until the sun had risen the following morning. The sky was clear and the sun shone with his usual splendor after a heavy rain. After some time I arose from my place of rest, left the barn and went on in the road an easterly direction. I had not progressed more than a mile before I discovered a two horse waggon with a team of horses before it laden with salt hay, and moving towards me on the same road, and accompanied with armed soldiers. I soon gave them the road not being pleased with the costume of the soldiery. Their coats being red was to me a sure indication that they were the mer-

cenaries of Royal George. I had selected a spot
where I remained stationary, and in a short time
discovered another waggon with the same kind of
freight, and attended in the same manner as the
first. I remained in this place until twenty two
waggons had passed on by me and all accompanied
as the two first. (60) I kept still for some time and
not discovering any more of these or any other
things so unpleasant to me resumed my course. I
soon came to a spot (61) where one road bore to
the right and the other to the left—not knowing
which to take I halted. I had travelled here before
but could not remember which of these roads I had
taken. I remained standing near this place a short
time when a boy coming up I ventured to inquire
which road would lead me to Oyster Bay. This
was the place that the old Dutch lady who had
given me my shirt had told me the day before I
must go to. The boy directed me to take the left
hand road—I took it to my cost as I soon learned.
The old dutch lady had directed me to call at a gentleman's house which I should pass on my way to
Oyster Bay which she described. She confidently
told me that the gentleman who occupied it would

assist me if I would call and disclose to him my situation. After travelling some time on this left hand road I descried the house the old lady had described to me. I called at the door—a lady appeared. I inquired for the gentleman to whom I had been directed—the lady answered that her husband was not at home, and was not expected for several days, at the same time the lady required of me my business with her husband. I told her of my escape from the prison ship, and my destitute situation, and that a friend had told me I could get relief by calling and making known my situation. The lady sternly answered that I could have no relief from that house, and expressed astonishment that I should presume to call there for the purpose of obtaining it. She said if her husband were at home he would do nothing for me, but would be bound to take me up and send me back to the prison ship. She told me that they lived under the government of the King, with other expressions indicating toryism. I left the house in no comfortable mood, conceiving I had been irreverently treated by my lady. This was a large white house about four miles from the small village of Oyster

Bay. (62) I soon came in sight of the village but not without apprehensions for my safety. I stopped and hesitated whether or not to go into it, but after reflecting some time I decided to go into it, which I did deliberately. The sun was now about an hour and an half high in the afternoon. Before entering the village I regretted that I had neglected the right hand road. If I had taken it I was confident that it would have led me directly to Sag Harbour, the place of my intended destination on the Island. I had concluded to pass directly through the village as the road below it seemed to bear to the right. The weather was now more cool than it had been, and my wearing apparel was illy calculated to resist the cold. I walked leisurely along until I had got into the centre of the village when a rag muffin of a scoundrel whom I was afterwards informed was a mercenary tory came out of a sort of rendezvous or grocery, dressed partly in a british uniform and asked me where I was going. I answered that I was going home if I could get there. He then beckoned to a gang he had left behind him in the rendezvous or grocery, to come out and tell the sergeant to come out with a file of men. They soon burst out with guns and bayonets in their hands and surrounded me as though I had been a Wallace. They ordered me into the place or room from whence they came, and then began to propound questions to me, with respect to the place I had come from, where I was going &c. I answered them as well as I could and gave them a true state- ment in a minute manner giving the history of my last voyage at sea, my capture, escape from the old prison ship, and my subsequent sufferings. I dis- guised nothing which related to me. I thought truth better than falsehood. Although three years before in company with Sawyer and Rock I had successfully adopted a different course, but there were three of us then and better clad than I was at this time. Besides I concluded that my true his- tory would excite or invite the pity and compassion of my captors rather than their hatred or revenge. But in this I was disappointed. The imperial refugee sergeant put on a very authoritative air and said, let me see your hands. I then shewed him my hands. There, by G—d (said he) I thought when I first saw him he was a whale boat-man from the main—a robber—for his hands shew it plain enough.

How long since you rowed a boat. I answered,
that I could not tell exactly for I did not remember
how many days it was since I had left Newport,
and I had not rowed a boat since. It was fifteen
days or more since I had rowed a boat. The loyal
refugee serjeant then exclaimed with another important air, as follows, I believe you lie for I have
heard of your boasting of going through this place
in the day time to find a *place* to plunder at night,
and we will hang you to morrow. I then became
angry and not a little saucy. For I said I think
there must be some law even among refugees under
the english government, and you need not threaten
me with your gallows, for I do not fear it. Well
(said the high minded refugee to his gang of armed
men) we will take him to the guard house, and see
how he will look on the gallows tomorrow. By this
time many of the villagers had come in apparently
to look at me and witness my examination. After
my examination had closed and I had been ordered
to the guard house, a genteel looking young gentleman whom I had observed for some time, having
entered the room about the time I had entered it.
He had not said a word yet but seemed attentive to

what I had said—stepped forward and said to the
tory Serjeant, can I have liberty of asking him some
questions. Oh, yes, said the tory. I saw that this
young gentleman was regarded in a respectful manner by these refugee scoundrels. When he began
interrogating me all was as still as a death watch.
He said to me, you said you sailed from Providence.
Yes sir. With whom. With Capt. Christopher
Whipple. What in. In a privateer brig of sixteen
guns. He put many more questions to me in relation to our capture, captivity on board the prison
ship, escape from it, and subsequent conduct, to all
which I gave him true answers, so far as I was concerned. He then turned to my first examinants
and said, I have no question but he has told you
the truth, for I am acquainted in Providence, and I
know he could not have answered those questions
so just if he had been a stranger at that place. But
I suppose you will send him back to the prison ship.
If you will suffer him to go with me to my house,
and send a guard with him if you please, I will be
bound he shall return in a short time. For he must
be hungry after fasting forty eight hours, and must
suffer with cold in the dress he has now on. The

tory officer said, Yes, doctor, to oblige you, I will
send a sentinel with him, if you will not detain him
long. It was by this time about sun setting. I
went with the Doct. across the street to his house.
He directed the sentinel to stop in an entry at the
door, which he did. As soon as we had arrived to
an inner room of his house he gave directions to his
black woman to get me some victuals. This was
soon done and I partook heartily. The Doct. was
absent a short time, and returned, with a quantity
of wearing apparel, and said when you have done
eating, do you take these clothes and put them on
for you will suffer in those clothes. I will further
mention that on getting into the house, the Doct.
offered me ardent spirits or wine to drink which
I declined. He then offered me cider which I also
declined. He then urged me to drink either spirits
or wine—of the latter I finally drank a glass. When
I commenced augmenting my dress from his charity,
he observed, these damn'd rascals will send you
back to the prison ship, and that is the most they
can do with you. I need not tell you to despise or
disregard their threats, for I see you are not afraid
of them. He spoke low to me and close to my

elbow. He continued, these scoundrels are stationed here to protect our property as the pretence is, and they steal pounds from us where they save us pence. They will undoubtedly carry you back, and think they have achieved some great exploit. But if I could swim on shore from that abhorent place I would not stay a day there. I would try it again. And if you should get down the Island as far as here, do not come among these refugee scoundrels. If you had kept down the country road, and got six miles below here, there would have been three chances in your favour to one against you, if you had conducted right—by this time the sentinel halloed for me to come out. The Doct. answered, in a few minutes, and said to me, I suppose you must go, and do you remember what I have said to you. He then handed and gave me a silver dollar. I thanked him kindly and said it was all the pay I could return him. He shook me by the hand and replied, you are heartily welcome. Thus I left this patriotic and benevolent gentleman. I regret that I have forgotten his name. The sentinel at the door again hallo'd for me. I stepped out to him and into the street. The men and boys crowded around me in the street, and presented me with money, some a quarter of a dollar and others less. This notice from the people created surly looks in the refugee corps, who hurried me along. Then came out the serjeant and three more refugee scoundrels, who stationed me in their centre, and they marched me off in great triumph for the guard house about two miles distant, where we arrived about dark. The house occupied by the guard was a long low building with two square rooms in it with two outside doors. It appeared to have been used and built for a school house. The first room we entered was filled with the same kind of rag muffin rascals as those who had been my guard. I think it must have been a subaltern's guard for they were numerous and a drunken set of gamblers. I was a fine subject for this loyal set to vent their spleen at. They soon asked the serjeant what he had got there. He said, I think he is a whale boat boy from the *main*, looking for a place to plunder us at night, but he says he has run away from the prison ship and was taken in a privateer, and some think he tells the truth, but I dont. The doctor, (meaning the gentleman who was present at my

examination, and who had given me clothes, money
& food,) has questioned him and thinks he tells all
truth, and has a great deal of charity for him, and
has given him a suit of clothes all but a shirt and
trousers in which I took him. But the Doctor with
all his learning does not know ev'ry thing. Some
one of the refugees then said, Well, sergeant this
fellow will grace our gallows to morrow well, and
we will take care of him. I was then ordered into
the other room. The door and windows fast'ned,
and I ordered to lie down on a small quantity of old
straw, and an old blanket and to " lie damn'd still."
And as the partition wall between the room occupied by the sentinel who guarded me, and who was
in the room with me was only of one board in
thickness, with cracks through it into the guard
room, we could hear all that was said by those in
the guard room. After I had lain down on this
horrid couch and before the fleas which infested the
room had got through my clothes to my skin, I
heard several in the guard room say one to the
other, I will bet a bowl of sling that fellow gets
away from the sentinel, (calling him by name) before
morning, for he is a damn'd weasel looking curse,

and is saucy, for he called us refugees at the village
when he was first taken. The fleas soon commenced
giving me trouble as I thought by thousands running over my skin, rank and file. This flea attack
gave me a great deal of trouble. I moved about
and rose partly up to catch them in the dark—my
sentinel who was in the room with me would break
out in true refugee style, "lie still G—d damn you,"
with other profane and smutty language too indecent
to mention. I remonstrated against his unprovoked
cruelty, observing that "I was only fighting the
fleas"—for God's sake dont murder me for this.
The sentinel had already pricked me in several
places so severely that I plainly felt the fresh blood
run. I told him I would not try to escape, and
more than all there was no possible chance to
escape. I mentioned to the sentinel that there was
no honor in such cruelty to a prisoner. I will give
you honour G—d damn you if you stir again, was
his reply. I was obliged to bear the attacks of the
fleas without moving a limb, until this rascal was
releived. This next sentinel appeared to be humane
and a gentleman. I had a long conversation with
him as I could not sleep in consequence of the stabs

I received from the first sentinel, and the continued attacks of the fleas. I complained to the second sentinel of the treatment I had received from the first, which he condemned in the strongest terms, and said that " some men were born brutes." I fell to sleep the latter part of the night, the attacks of the fleas notwithstanding. Soon after the appearance of day-light I was sent off to the quarters of their refugee Col. a mile from the guard room, and escorted by a refugee corporal and file of men. Our course was not in a road but over the fields of grass on which was an heavy frost. On being ushered into the presence of the grave colonel a paper was presented to him by the intrepid corporal who commanded my escort, from the officer of the guard respecting me, which I was not allowed to read nor hear read. The Col. was a tall man of fine appearance by the name of Brown or Smith (I am not certain which of these names he bore.) The Col. and a gentleman present whom I understood was master of a wood vessel then about to sail for New-York, put me under another examination. To them I repeated all I had said the evening before to the then refugee examinants and to my benevo-

lent Doctor. After my examination was closed, the
Col. and master of the vessel went into an adjoining
room to take their breakfast. They soon commenced a conversation about me which I over-
heard. The Col. thought my story about leaving
the prison ship probable. Oh, yes, (answered the
master) your men's conjecture about his being a
whale boat robber is wrong, for he tells ev'ry thing
right about the prison ship. Well, (says the Col.)
you can take him back with you. Oh, yes (says the
master.) The door leading from the room I was in
to the room in which they were breakfasting was
open, and I heard ev'ry word of their conversation,
without any apparent idea from them that I heard
their dialogue. Before sitting down to his breakfast
the Col. came into the room in which I was under
guard, and spoke to one of my guard, (calling him
by his given name)—the man answered, yes, sir.
The Col. then said to him, you can take charge of
this boy—yes, answered the man. The Col. then
ordered the remaining portion of my escort back to
the guard house, and they immediately withdrew.
The Col. before returning into his breakfast room
directed a servant to give me some *breakfast*, which

was instantly set before me. I eat it in a short
time, and seated myself before the fire, took my
shoes off to dry them, and my feet which had
become very wet by crossing the frosty fields. I
was now guarded by a single sentinel, and he a
molatto, very tall, and appeared nimble and very
athletic. One of the servants about the house was
a black woman. Between this black woman and
the molatto sentinel there appeared to be an intimate acquaintance, as they were very sociable with
each other. The female servant went about the
house in quick time, sometimes in the kitchen and
sometimes in the room with the Col. and his companion waiting on their breakfast table and also out
of the back door into the yard and in the pantry
whither my molatto guard had gone to provide
himself with food which he began to eat. He had
set his musket near to the entrance of the pantry
door. When in the pantry he would frequently put
his head through the door to look for me. When
his black paramour visited the pantry he would
talk in gentle words to her. I had learned in a conversation held between the Col. and master of the
wood vessel that she was to get under sail that

morning immediately after breakfast, and it was in this vessel that I was to be conveyed back to New York. I had determined to effect my escape if possible and to make a violent and hazardous attempt. The sentinel had not yet finished his repast in the pantry. The wench was out of sight, in which room of the house, or whether or not she was in the yard I did not know. As soon as I had eaten my breakfast I had partly turned myself around from the front of the chair in which I was seated with my arms crossing the back and around one of the higher posts, and my face resting on them. I had watched the motions of the sentinel and fast'ned the buckles to my shoes. In this situation at the instant after the sentinel had put his head through the door of the pantry to observe me and had withdrawn it, I took my shoes in hand and very carefully arose from the chair and also taking advantage of the absence of the wench, lightly stepped across the room and through the outside door into the yard and from thence into a patch of standing hemp very near the yard of the house, and thence into an orchard and soon gained a copse of wood through a cornfield. All this

running I performed in my stockens, without my
shoes on. The corn in the field had not been har-
vested. I entered the wood some distance. The
under bushes were thick and I halted in them
several hours, keeping myself still. I soon had few
fears of a recapture except through the agency of
dogs. These last suspicions were the same that
I indulged after I had met the young woman in the
potatoe field two days before. I was not molested
nor pursued from any observations that I could
make. Here I lay several hours and cleaned my
stockens as well as I could from the dirt that stuck
to them in consequence of their use without shoes.
I put on my shoes and proceeded slowly on in an
easterly direction and keeping from the road, until
I had travelled more than six miles as near as I
could estimate the distance, meaning to observe the
caution given to me by the Doctor at the village of
Oyster Bay. After I commenced travelling on the
road I dared not call at any house during that day,
and the following night I slept in a barn. Early
next morning I left the barn and travelled forward
until my stomach began to crave food. After some
time I arrived at a house where I thought it would

do to call. It was small, and the door open, and a
woman sweeping near it. I stepped near her and
asked if I could get something to eat from the
house, and if she would furnish me with food I
would pay her well for it, and that bread and milk
would please me as well as any food she could give
me. She answered me in the affirmative. I went
in. Conversation soon commenced between us. It
was commenced on her part first, and by an interrogation, How far are you travelling. The answer
I gave her was, "to Sag Harbour, on a visit to see
my friends, and then to return to New York." This
was a part of the story with which Sawyer, Rock
and myself had so well succeeded in useing when
we had travelled from New York city to Sag Harbour down the island by land three years before. I
had not made a new story, not intending to use
anything fabulous on my journey. But on this
occasion I thought proper to feed my hostess with
something plausible. It had the desired effect.
For she soon replied by the observation "I suppose
you are not a rebel." This short sentence gave me
her cue. I answered, oh, no, I am going back as
soon as I can get ready, and my business through,

126   NARRATIVE.

to fight the rebels. " Well," (said my hostess) " do you think they (the rebels) will hold out much longer." "It seems to me they cant, for their cause is so bad, and I have heard they were almost subdued." " Oh, yes." " Well I thought they would from the first beginning of it." I finished eating my dish of bread and milk, which my hostess observing, brought me some bread and butter. I partook of it freely. I obtained this last dish from my lady in consequence of my supposed loyalty to the King. My loyalty pleased madam in the extreme. Having finished my repast, I offered to pay for it, but my hostess would not take a single copper from me. I was " so devoted to King George" and " a fine lad." I bade her good morning and resumed my journey. After leaving this benevolent mansion I could not avoid indulging some rude reflections about my loyal hostess. One was whether or not her loyalty had been so enthusiastic and outrageous as to prostrate more than one Liberty pole in the cause. Her calculations concerning the American cause were hardly true prophesy for in a few days from this time lord Cornwallis surrendered his entire army to our arms at Yorktown. (63) I travelled from ten till about one o'clock in the afternoon. I met Capt. Daniel Havens on horseback—he had no other person in company, and had several fine horses with him going west—with whom I had become acquainted three years before at his own house in the village of Sag Harbour. I knew him and addressed him by name. He did not know me, but soon recollected having formerly been acquainted with me after I had mentioned having been at his house in company with his nephew John Sawyer, and Rock. I related to him in a concise manner my late adventures, perils, sufferings &c. He then observed that he was going west, and that I must go to his house and make it my home until his return which would be the day after to morrow evening. And that he would procure a safe passage for me across Long Island sound to the main—that I must make myself known to his family, who would provide well for me &c that I must keep myself still in the house in order to secure my safety and that of himself and family. For (said he) there is people there who are constantly on the watch that you would not mistrust, who would do us mischief, and as it is past noon you cannot get there to day. It is twenty miles to my house, and you will want something to eat before you arrive to it. I answered, I am not hungry—a short time since I ate a hearty breakfast. He replied, so much the better, for you ought to travel seven miles before you stop—you can stop at the end of that distance in safety. At that distance is a tavern (64) kept by a Mr. Snow—the name you will see on the sign. There you must find the landlord and speak to him first if you see those about whom you may conclude are travellers, and tell him you want dinner. Inform him also where you have come from, and that I have sent you to his house. Here is a quarter of a dollar to pay for your dinner if he shall ask any pay of you for it, but I think he will not. I refused his money saying to him that I had got money. Well rejoined he, take it and keep your money—you may want it before you get home. I took the money, and went on travelling fast until I arrived at the tavern where Capt. Havens had directed me to call. It was now early in the afternoon—And as I passed the barroom I saw two gentlemen whose appearance did not please me much. I stepped by the door of the bar room to the kitchen and inquired of the inmates for the landlord. They informed me that he was in the back yard after wood. I siezed this opportunity to introduce myself to him. I found him alone, and in a low tone of voice did so in a few words, at the same time mentioned to him that I had been commended to him by Capt. Havens. He then told me to walk into the sitting room, saying dinner would be ready in a few minutes. I then mentioned my suspicions about the two gentlemen I had seen when passing to the kitchen. He made me easy about them. Before entering the room however, the landlord told me that if any suspicious persons should visit his house before I left it that he would give me a wink and I could follow him, (the landlord.) He then said I will go in with you. On going into the room where the two gentlemen were sitting, the landlord addressed them in the following language, here is a boy who says he is a run a way from the old Jersey, and wants dinner if you will consent for him to eat with you. Oh, yes, was soon the answer. The one was an elderly gentleman, the other young and son in law to the former. The landlord soon left the room to attend affairs about his house. I expected a long series of interrogatories from the gentlemen present, which I dreaded as I had been an old run a way and the repetition of my story had become irksome. I was in a hurry also. They soon began their interrogatories, and I had to relate all my adventures. After I had told my story, the old gentleman informed me that he was a brother or a cousin to a Mr. Snow who was or had been a clergyman in Providence, R. I. (65) I cannot now remember whether it was brother or cousin, but am more inclined to think the latter. We had eat our dinner when wine was set on the table and we sat to it an hour. In the mean time more company came into the bar room and the landlord gave me a hint to be off which I observed, and left the table and room. I was secretly followed by the two gentlemen—one of them gave me a crown, and the other a dollar and said, put it up and say nothing. I offered the landlord pay for my dinner—no, said he, not a copper—you are welcome. They all hoped I would get home without difficulty. The old gentleman took me by the hand and we took leave. I then went on my way in quick motion and took the road on the north shore of the Island, which was passable for people on foot and two miles nearer Sag Harbour than the carriage road. I travelled seven miles very quick. The sun had set and I called at a large farm house and inquired the distance to Sag Harbour. (66) I saw only an old lady about the house. Her appearance pleased me and I asked leave of her to tarry in her house through the ensuing night, the road not appearing very plain, and darkness coming on. She said I could stay in her house if I would behave myself well. But she soon commenced her examinations—this was dreadful to me—meantime she informed me that the male portion of her family had gone from home and were six miles off, and would not be at home for several days to come. They had gone from home to perform some kind of labour. She informed me that herself and that black boy (pointing to one then present) were the only members of the family then at home. The old lady again commenced asking me more questions and among them, "Where did you come from?" "I have ran away from the old Jersey prison ship." She then said, "if you have ran away from the prison ship you

may stay." I then went into the house and seated
myself. She put me many questions. I answered
all she put me as well as I could. She ordered the
black boy to prepare supper which he did all but
preparing the tea which was done by herself. It
was an excellent repast. I soon assumed drowsi-
ness. And after some time the black boy was
directed to light a second candle and I was conducted to an excellent bed. I was soon in sleep,
and remained in bed the next morning until I
heard the old lady and her black servant about the
house. I arose from my bed and went down from
the chamber. She was preparing breakfast. It
was soon ready and I was invited to take breakfast
with her which I did. The breakfast was also
excellent. I was about to resume my travel, when
the old lady took a handkerchief of her own and
tied up full of cakes and cheese and said to me, you
must take this with you when you go. I declined,
saying I had got money and would soon be at
Capt. Havens. "Well you will go over the sound
in the night and you will be hungry before you get
over, and you must take it." I took her handkerchief and contents, bid her good bye, with my

thanks for her kindness and generosity. I went on
in good spirits. In my morning travel I drew a
contrast between my hostesses the day and evening
before. The one was loyal to enthusiasm, and
prayed for the success of the British arms and the
subjugation of the people to their unhallowed
ambition, and the confiscation of the property of all
those patriots who had drawn the sword in defence
of their rights; the other patriotic to the cause of
civil liberty, and no sacrifices too great for the purpose of securing freedom and independence. In the
short space of eight hours both had treated me with
the most generous and unalloyed hospitality. The
former for the reason that, through fear her agency
might send me back into New York again into a
loathsome and dreadful captivity, I had avowed
myself to be in favour of the oppressive measures
of the british crown towards my bleeding and
suffering countrymen. The latter because I had
escaped from captivity and from the power of these
oppressors. I also concluded from an observation
which the latter made to me, after I had declined
her handkerchief and contents that she was well
acquainted with the mode of trade or traffic be-

tween the people of Long Island and those on the
main, and that she probably had been personally
engaged in it. The observation I allude to I will
repeat. It was in the following words, "you will
cross the sound in the night, and will be hungry
before you get over." My reader will here understand that I have before mentioned that the whole
of the territory on Long Island was under the controul of the british authority for nearly the whole
period of the revolutionary contest. The two bel-
ligerents carried on a smuggling trade with each
other during the contest. The gold currency of the
british was tempting to the patriotic merchants and
farmers of New England, and the fine fancy goods
of the british invited the cupidity of many patriotic
families in the aforesaid states—notwithstanding
the loyalty of the british the products from the
farms of freemen were not unsavoury to their tastes.
Hence the trade. The government authority used
constant means to destroy this traffic. (67) The
New England or continental governments employed
small armed vessels which by the smugglers and
others were sarcastically called "Shaving Mills."
The vigilance of the Shaving Mills constrained the

smugglers to cross the sound to or from the main in
the night.   Hence the old lady's words addressed
to me that I would cross the sound at night.   The
smuggling agents were many of them females.
This I learned by crossing the sound three times in
these smuggling packets.   A majority of the passengers were females on these occasions.   It was
four miles from the house where I had slept to the
village of Sag Harbour.   I soon travelled to it and
called at the house of Capt. Havens.   I mentioned
to his family that I had seen him the day previous
and delivered to them the message he had sent by
me.   There were no males about the House.   I felt
lonely.   The family did not know me and I had
been under the necessity of calling their attention
to the visit I had made three years before in company with Sawyer and Rock.   This circumstance
made them recollect me but I did not feel at home.
I went into the street rather mute and conversed
with no person.   While standing in the street,
sometimes walking slowly about, I saw a small
sloop lying at the dock.   I concluded that she was
a "Shaving Mill" or a smuggler but dare not
approach her for the fear of being questioned by

some one on board or near her. Thus being in the
street a female came in sight—she walked near me
and I felt confident that I had been acquainted with
her. I was well satisfied that she was the sister of
my old companion John Sawyer, and at whose
house Sawyer, Rock and myself had slept when I
had visited this place three years before. I addressed her by her name. She appeared surprised
and inquired how I was acquainted with her. I
then mentioned having slept at her house as before
mentioned, with her brother whom I inquired after.
I was then recollected by her. On my calling her
attention to the circumstance of having slept in her
house with her brother, the sympathies of her heart
were called into action and her tender emotions
very visible. She soon beckoned me to follow her
which I readily did. We walked into an ally or
lane between some buildings, and from the observation of any persons who might notice us in the
street. Here she soon informed me the cause of her
sympathies. They were excited by mentioning the
name of her brother and inquiries for and concerning him. After she had partially suppressed her
emotions, she informed me that he had died a tra-

gical death about three weeks before at sea. She
related to me the circumstances of her brothers
death. He had been employed at or near his home
ever since he had escaped from the Maidstone
frigate, and returned home with me, until the then
present summer when he had sailed in an American
privateer from the port of New London (68)—that
about three weeks before, he had been put on board
of a prize the privateer had taken, as one of the
prize crew, to navigate the prize into some American port. That after the prize had doubled Montauk point (69) bound in, the captured crew of the
prize had mutinied against the captors, subdued
and killed them—that her brother being aloft in
the rigging was shot and fell dead on deck—that
they had learned the fate of her brother from the
newspapers from the city of New York, whither the
prize had been taken by her crew after they had
retaken her. During this interview, my own sympathies were freely associated with the sister, for he
was a person dear to me no doubt in some degree
from having been my companion under severe trials
and perils. In addition to this he was active, intelligent and brave, far beyond his years. The gene-

rosity of his soul was unbounded, and his honesty
unsurpassed perhaps by any. I had also entertained strong hopes of a personal interview with
him again at Sag Harbour, or at least of learning
that he was alive and well, as I had felt great
interest in his fate. In an interview with this
female at the house of Capt. Havens she informed
me that the sloop of which I had been so cautious
would sail the following night for Stonington, (70) a
port situate on the *main*, in the state of Connecticut, and that she was going in it as a passenger—
that she had no doubt I could go across the sound
in it also. I mentioned that I did not know whether
or not the master would suffer me to take passage
in said vessel, and that Capt. Havens had requested
me to remain at his house until his return from the
west. The family heard this conversation, and did
not solicit my stay. My female friend replied that
she was sure I could obtain a passage as well as not.
These circumstances induced me to visit the sloop
and make my situation known to the master with a
request for a passage. I did so. The master agreed
to take me on board. I mentioned where I could
be found when the vessel would be ready to sail.

The master made me welcome, and invited me to
eat and drink with him, and to take a berth for
the night in his cabin. The female friend tarried
at the house where I had taken quarters until
evening, Capt. Havens being her uncle. Evening
came on and we were called for—went on board,
and the vessel set sail. I went into the cabin, took
a berth, and went to sleep. All hands and the
greater portion of the passengers kept the deck, a
majority of the passengers being females. I slept
sound until morning. On going upon deck, I found
the vessel lying at a dock, no sail in sight, and no
person on deck. I could not identify the place
where the sloop lay. One of the hands soon came
on board, and I inquired of him whether or not the
place we had arrived at was Stonington. He
smilingly answered, no, it is not Stonington. Have
you not seen this place before. I answered, not to
my knowledge. At this answer he laughed heartily, and said, you are just where you were when
you started last night—you look wild. I felt fool-
ish, and asked, what does this mean. Oh, not
much—we had a head wind and put back last
night—dont be uneasy, for we shall start again

to night, and we will carry you over safe and free from expence. You can stay on board to day or go to Capt. Havens, but you must be ready at sunset. Before this conversation I had stepped on shore, and as soon as I had done this the surrounding country and scenery appeared natural to me, and I fully realized that I was again at Sag Harbour. My mistake had occurred in consequence of my calculations that when I should awake from my sleep I should find Stonington or some other place on the main, and in addition to this, the bow of the sloop had been shifted on coming back to the dock, directly around from what it was when she had left it the evening before. Those who have had their heads turned by shifting the heads of vessels, being themselves on board, can readily account for this occurence. The person above mentioned kept around the sloop some time regulating the rigging. The rigging indicated that some confusion had resulted on board the evening before, after I had "turned in." I observed this, and mentioned to the man—that the *head wind* the vessel had met with the evening before was a "shaving mill." He laughed, and said, how do you know—you was

sound asleep, and we were damn'd still. Oh, I
dreamed it—another laugh with the following
words, you dream as though you had been here
before. I have, and started from here twice on the
same occasion and wish to start again. When was
this you started from here before. Three years ago
the first time, and last night the second. Oh, I
guess you are an old boy then, but did you ever get
across from here. Yes, the first time. Where did
you land. At Saybrook. (n) That was out of your
way. I found it out. Not wishing to pursue this
dialogue any further, I left him. I kept about
during the day, without any event occuring worth
mentioning. I left Sag Harbour the same evening
in the sloop, and arrived to the main the same
night. I had turned in the fore part of the night
and slept sound. The sloop landed at a lonely dock
or wharf. I was soon awakened by some one on
board—there were no buildings, or other craft than
the sloop in sight. The place seemed to be a cove
from the sound or the mouth of a river. If I remember correctly, the people on board called it Mystic
river. It was my opinion that this place had been
selected to facilitate smugling. On leaving the

sloop we went up a hill through a brush wood in a
foot path to a house on the top of the hill. The
passengers had heavy luggage but of what consistence or substance, I knew not, nor did I care.
When we arrived at the house the person whom I
viewed as the landlord, rose from his slumbers.
He and the passengers appeared to be well acquainted with each other. The master of the house
soon intimated to me that the night was far from
being spent, and that if it was my choice I could
have a bed. I readily accepted of his bed, and
soon repaired to it for fear of questions. I did not
soon sleep for a continued bustle was kept up below
stairs for some time, as I supposed bringing goods
from the sloop, and secretly stowing them away in
and around the house. When I arose in the morning the house was as still as a clock, and no person
in sight. The master of the house soon left his bed,
as well as others of the family—none of the crew of
the sloop or a passenger to be seen in or about the
premises. I mentioned that I would see some of the
crew of the sloop before I started, and pay my fare.
The man present said, " it is all square for the
master of the sloop told me over night that he

should not charge you a copper—neither do I."
The master of the house then said I had better
have some breakfast before I started. He then
spoke to some member of the family to provide
something for me to eat, in the meantime inquiring
of me, if I could eat some "Pop Robbin."(72) I
answered that I knew nothing of such a dish, but if
others had and could eat it, I could. It was soon
provided and set before me. It proved an excellent dish, of which I partook heartily. On inquiry
I found it was cooked from milk and flour—the
flour first thinly kneeded and then dropped into the
boiling milk with a large table spoon. Having
taken my breakfast I inquired the distance to Providence, and received for answer that it was rather
more than forty miles. I thanked my host and
took leave—steered my course towards Providence
and arrived within two miles of the city the same
day, on foot except a ride of ten or twelve miles on
a horse without a saddle. This occurred in consequence of a man overtaking me, himself on horseback, and leading another without a saddle which
he solicited me to ride. I paid for this treat
severely afterwards for several days, as it made

me very lame. As before mentioned I halted two miles from Providence. It was near a dwelling house and a barn near it.(73) I determined to go into and sleep in the barn through the night—went into the yard, and discovered a man near me. I asked leave of him to sleep in the barn. Why not sleep in the house, was the question. I answered to avoid interrogatories, at the same instant informing him from whence I had come, and how far I had travelled that day, and was weary. He then said, If that be the case you shall not sleep in the barn— you can as well sleep in the house as not, and you shall be as welcome as a lord if you have not a far thing in the world. I told him I had money plenty which had been given me. He then said, dont talk about that, but come with me to my own house— you shall be well used. I told him, I did not doubt that. This benevolent, warm hearted gentleman was a stranger to me before this but I now learned from him that his name was John Waterman.(74) After we had conversed some time and it seemed settled that I was to sleep in the house, and before walking into it, I mentioned to him that if he wished to inquire any thing of me with respect to

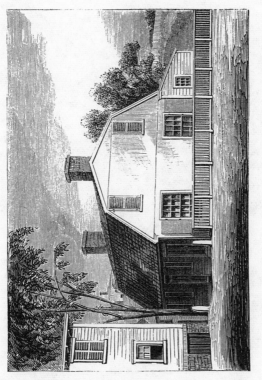

RESIDENCE OF THE BENEVOLENT JOHN WATERMAN.

my cruise I wished him to put me into a private room, and with as many others as he pleased. I would then relate all I knew with respect to it. But that he must be well aware that I had related my story over many times and that a repetition of it had become burdensome to me. I had before this told him the out lines of my story. And he then observed, if you sailed with Capt. Christopher Whipple in the Brig, I know your cruise has been short. He knew both Capt. Whipple and the Brig. We now went into the house and took supper. He then took me into another room where I related to him the substance of what had taken place in my cruise. He then said, I know you are tired and wish rest. He shewed me a bed and retired. In the morning after taking a good breakfast Mr. Waterman accompanied me into the city. He shewed me the residence of Mrs. Whipple, the mother of Capt. Whipple, whom I had left in New York, and went with me to her house. I was under particular obligation to Mr. Waterman for his politeness in this instance for he saved me much interrogation. After leaving Mrs. Whipple, we parted, and he offered me money which I declined taking from him. I went immediately over the great bridge(76) which connects the city—turned on my left to the north, conversing with some boys whom I knew with respect to my cruise. A gentleman by the name of Olney Winsor, (76) then a merchant in Providence and since cashier of one of her banks, who over-heard my conversation with the boys, inquired for William Waterman before mentioned, whom he said was a brother or cousin of his wife. I told him the enterprize he had been engaged in with me, and the manner I had left him. He, (Windsor,) then said, he is unquestionably drowned. I then went to Smithfield, to the house of Obadiah Olney Esq. whose service I had left about three weeks before, and again entered his service, where I remained for some time. Thus closes my sea adventures. I have written these for the perusal of my children, grand children and their decendants(77), not with any ambition to literary fame—in which view I wish the reader to appreciate the work.

Christopher Hawkins

NOTES.

(1) AARON MASON was the son of Aaron Mason by his wife Ruth, whose maiden name was Sanford, and was born in Swansey, Mass., on the 28th day of February, 1728–9. The father of Aaron, being a tanner and currier by trade, the son was brought up to the same occupation, and after his removal to Providence, R. I., he carried on the business at that place for many years. During the Revolutionary war, Mr. Mason was a member of the Town Committee, and exerted some influence in that body. In the year 1781 he was one of the Proprietors of Whipple Hall in Providence. As a citizen he enjoyed the respect of the community for his strict integrity, and for the Christian purity of his life. He died in Providence, on the 28th day of November, 1812, in the 83d year of his age. He was twice married, and had by his two wives, nine children, seven of whom survived him.

(2) CAPT. MOWRY POTTER was the son of Ichabod Potter, of Cranston, R. I., a tailor by occupation. His mother's

maiden name was Mowry. She was the daughter of a farmer of that name in Smithfield. She died in Vermont. Mowry, the subject of our sketch, was a native of Cranston. In the year 1776, he was master of a small sloop, and in June of that year, was on his way from Surinam to Providence when his vessel was captured by a British tender. The hands escaped in their boat. Capt. Potter died at sea, at the close of the Revolution, by being struck with the boom of a brig, while on his way to the West Indies. At the time of his death he was about fifty years of age. He had several children, who all survived him, and the youngest of them, a son, is still living.

(₂) In the early part of the Revolution, many privateers were fitted out at Boston and Providence to prey upon British commerce, and New Bedford, being the only port this side of the Chesapeake, that was not under control of the enemy, soon became a receptacle for the prize vessels taken by the Americans, and the town derived great benefit therefrom. This circumstance at length attracted the attention of Sir Henry Clinton, the British general, who, in the early part of September, 1778, despatched an expedition against it of about 4,000 men, under the command of General Grey. This force attacked the town, burnt about seventy vessels, between thirty and forty buildings, and destroyed public and private property to the value of $422,680.

(4) The SPHYNX was a British sloop of war, registered as a sixth rate, carrying 20 guns, and was built at Portsmouth, Eng., in the year 1775. Her length of gun deck was 108 feet; keel 89 ft. 7⅜ in.; breadth 30 feet, 1 in.; depth of hold 9 feet 8 in.; tons, 430. She was one of the fleet that was fitted out for the reduction of Charleston, South Carolina. She was commanded by Capt. Anthony Hunt, embarked from Cork, Feby. 12th, 1776, with troops under Cornwallis, and arrived in America in the month of May. In June following she bore a part in the attack made by Sir Peter Parker upon Sullivan's island, where the British met with so signal a defeat. On this occasion, the Sphynx got aground, and lost her bowsprit by running foul of the Acteon, one of her companions, while the Acteon herself became entangled in the mud, and was set on fire by her crew to save her from capture by the Americans. On the 30th November, 1777, the Sphynx captured the Eagle privateer belonging to Dartmouth, and on the first of December following, took the privateer Rover belonging to Salem. In 1778, she was commanded by Capt. Richard Græme and was on duty off the coast of Rhode Island. In the latter part of the year 1779, being then under command of Capt. Robert Sutton, she was captured after an engagement of an hour and a half, by the French frigate L'Ambuscade, in sight of Sir Hyde Parker's fleet at Barbadoes, and carried as a prize into the port of Martinique. She was afterwards retaken by Admiral Byron, and in 1782 was on home duty, her captain at that time being Thomas Totty, who became notorious for his

adultery with Ann, wife of Walter Nisbett, by reason of which her husband obtained a divorce. In 1788, the Sphynx was not in commission. In 1793, she was commanded by Capt. Richard Lucas, and in the year following, being then still under his orders, she engaged and captured the French 18 gun brig Trompeuse, off Cape Clear, on the coast of Ireland. In the year 1795, the Sphynx was commanded by Capt. C. J. M. Mansfield; in December of the same year, by Capt. George Brisac; in March, 1796, by Capt. J. W. Spranger; in February, 1797, by Capt. Andrew Todd; in March of the same year, by Capt. T. H. Coffin; and in September following, by Thomas Alexander. In April, 1799, she was commanded by Capt. W. Smith; and in June following, by Capt. James Oughton. In the year 1800, she was at Portsmouth, and in 1804, she was not in commission. She was broken up in the year 1811.

(s) "New York, December 22.—On Monday [Dec: 15] arrived his Majesty's Sloop of War the Sphynx, Anthony Hunt Esq; commander; she sailed from the Delaware the Beginning of November, as Convoy to the Harriot Packet, bound home to England, with Dispatches from Lord and General Howe, with Col. Cuyler, on board, and left her the 11th ult. 300 Leagues to the Eastward in Lat. 43, all well.

"The 30th of November, Capt. Hunt took the Eagle Privateer, belonging to Dartmouth, N. E. of 3 Carriage Guns, and 12 Swivels; and on the 1st Instant, he came up with, and also took the Rover Privateer, belonging to Salem; Neither of them had taken any British Vessels, tho' they were long from Port, and had but 69 Men on board both Vessels; one a Schooner the other a Sloop; the former Capt. Hunt ordered to be burnt, and the latter sunk, but the Crews were brought in with the Sphynx.

" The Eagle on her Cruize brought too a Brig from Liverpool for this Port, and ordered her to strike to the Congress; but by Means of some Threats used by the Liverpool Man, who had only one rusty Gun on board, the Rebel Crew were afraid to board the Brig, and it being in the Night, she got clear."

Gaine's New York Gazette and Weekly Mercury,
Monday, December 22, 1777.

(6) CAPT. ANTHONY HUNT, who was the first commander of the Sphynx, and who continued in command of her until the year 1778, was made lieutenant, April 2, 1757, and was commissioned as captain, January 10, 1771. He commanded the Sphynx at the siege of Charleston in the year 1776, and in 1782 was first captain of the Diligente, of 70 guns, at which time Sir Thomas Pye, Admiral of the White, had his flag on board her. Capt. Hunt died in England on the third day of December, 1795. At the time of his death, he was second captain of Greenwich Hospital.

Another officer of this name, perhaps a son of the former, was made captain in 1793, and was appointed to the Amphitrite of 24 guns, and commanded her when she was lost. In 1794, he was one of Nelson's officers at the siege of Bastia. In

1796, he commanded the Concorde of 36 guns, and while in her, being attached to the squadron of Sir J. B. Warren, assisted in the capture of the French frigate "La Virginie," on the 20th April, and the prize having been added to the English navy under the same name, Capt. Hunt was appointed to command her. The Virginie was a new vessel, mounting 40 guns, and was for years the fastest ship in the British service, and on account of her beauty, was used as a model for a long time. In 1798, Capt. Hunt sailed in the Virginie to the East Indies, with Earl Mornington, Governor General of India, as a passenger. Capt. Hunt died at Calcutta, in Bengal, Aug. 10, 1798. The following epitaph was inscribed on a very handsome tomb erected to his memory in the burial ground at Calcutta, where his remains were interred:—"Underneath lie the remains of Capt. Anthony Hunt, Late Commander of His Britannic Majesty's ship La Virginie, and Post Captain in the Royal Navy, who departed this life at Calcutta in Bengal, on the 10th day of August, 1798, after a short illness, in the twenty eighth year of his age; and who, at this early age, had acquired great honours in his profession, and the esteem and regard of all who had the honour of his acquaintance. By his death, the Navy has lost one of its brightest ornaments, and Society one of its most valuable members, for he lived greatly beloved and respected, and died universally regretted."

(7) The "CAT-O'-NINE-TAILS," or, as it is more briefly called, the "CAT," was a whip, having sometimes five, but usually

nine knotted cords. With this instrument the soldiers and
sailors were punished. This punishment was often of the
most cruel kind. When inflicted by an expert, the thongs of
the instrument would tear the skin in strips from the flesh,
causing the blood to flow in streams from the unhappy
sufferer.

The earliest instance of this mode of punishment which we
have been able to discover, was in the case of George Dawson, a private in the 85th regiment, who, in the year 1763,
received 300 lashes with a " cat-o'-nine-tails " at the halberts.
The cat was used very freely during the Revolution, not only
in the English navy, but in the American. It has been
abolished by the latter for some years, but was in use among
the former as recently as 1862. In that year there were
31,602 lashes administered in the navy and 5,999 in the army.
In some vessels, well known and much avoided by the
sailors, the lash was at that time in constant use. The
names of these vessels were the Odin, the Neptune, the
Mars, and the Bachante. The cat is, however, getting into
disuse, as a general thing, in the English service since the
Act restricting corporal punishment to a maximum of fifty
lashes. Its effect, in most cases, was to ruin a good man and
render a bad one incorrigible.

An amusing anecdote relating to this mode of punishment,
is well worth recording here. A captain of a British frigate,
though of unquestioned bravery, had a natural antipathy to a
cat, and could never hear the dismal noise of that animal

without evincing much uneasiness. On one occasion, while
at sea, one of his sailors, who had been ordered a flogging,
saved his back from chastisement by presenting to his commander the following petition,—

> " By your honor's command,
>   A culprit I stand ;
>   An example to all the ship's crew ;
>   I'm pinion'd and stript,
>   And condemn'd to be whipt,
>   And if I am flogg'd, 'tis my due.
>
> A *cat*, I am told,
>   In abhorrence you hold—
>   Your honor's aversion is mine.
>   If a cat with *one* tail,
>   Makes your stout heart to fail,
>   Pray save me from one that has *nine*."

(8) The *Highlands of Navesink*, are located in the county
of Monmouth, New Jersey, extend along Sandy Hook bay for
nearly five miles, and are much noted. The range is from
three to four hundred feet in height, comes boldly down
to near the water's edge, and is covered with a forest, in
which deer and other game find a covert.

Near the southern termination of the Highlands is Beacon
Hill, on which the " Highland Light Houses" so called, are to
be seen. They were erected during the administration of
John Quincy Adams, and are the first beacons seen by vessels
entering the port of New York. Latterly they have been

fitted up with new and improved lights of French construction, which are seen by the mariner at a distance of 25 miles.

About a mile north of Beacon Hill is a locality known as Gravelly Point, where deep water is found near the shore. This is the spot where the British army embarked after the battle of Monmouth, and where the unfortunate Capt. Joshua Huddy, of the American army, was barbarously murdered by a party of Loyalists under command of Capt. Richard Lippencot, in the month of April, 1782.

The proximity of this part of the county to New York, rendered it in the revolution peculiarly liable to the incursions of the British troops. Many of the inhabitants, although secretly favorable to the American cause, in order to secure their property from marauding parties of refugees from vessels generally lying off Sandy Hook, were compelled to feign allegiance to the Crown.

(o) During the revolutionary war, the city of New York being under the control of the enemy from September, 1776, to November, 1783, her harbor was consequently the great rendezvous of the British fleet. The enemy's ships rode in triumph in the bay, brought their prizes hither, and passed all seasons of the year here in safety.

During the war of 1812, however, not so much as a cock boat belonging to that nation ventured to show its prow near Sandy Hook, a distance of no less than 27 miles from the city, although numbers of their armed cruisers were sailing upon the coast. The erection of the fortifications around New York inspired such a terror to the invincible navy of England, that upon merely hearing of the erection of these works, those gallant tars, even with their first rate line of battle ships, did not dare approach within sight of the outermost of them.

(10) The ASIA was a British ship of the line, registered as a third rate, carrying 64 guns, and was built at Portsmouth, Eng., in the year 1764. Her dimensions were as follows: Length of gun deck, 158 feet; keel, 129 feet 6½ inches; breadth, 44 feet 6 inches; depth in hold, 18 feet 10 inches; tons 1,364. In 1774, she was at Portsmouth, and was commanded by Capt. Richard King. She was soon after placed under the orders of Capt. George Vandeput, and was on the American station at the very commencement of the Revolutionary struggle, having been sent out by Admiral Graves pursuant to the suggestion of Lieut. Governor Colden, who thought the presence of a man of war in New York harbor would be the means of preserving order among the people, who were then much disaffected towards the mother country. The Asia arrived in the month of May, 1775, but instead of meeting the expectations of the authorities, her appearance here, overawing the populace, had the contrary effect of rendering the excitement only the more intense. To such a degree did it arise that it became necessary to remove the troops from the barracks to her for safety, and while the embarkation was going on, several of the soldiers deserted from the service,

having been induced to this course by offers of large rewards, accompanied by liberal promises of protection. On the 13th day of July following, one of her boats was seized and set on fire, and another which had been ordered by the authorities to be built to replace the former, was secretly cut in pieces before it was fairly completed, thereby rendering the substitution of another necessary, which was, however, secured against any future attempt at destruction. On the 23d day of August, the sons of Liberty, under Capt. Isaac Sears, removed all the guns from the battery under Fort George, in spite of a severe fire from the Asia, then lying off the city. This cannonade caused a return from the shore, in consequence of which she had one of her men killed. The conduct of the Asia upon this occasion rendered her still more obnoxious, and to such a height did this feeling arise, that a boat which took a supply of milk to her was burnt on its return to the shore, while a country sloop which carried her some provisions met with the same fate. In consequence of threats having been made to burn the city, the public records were placed in the Duchess of Gordon, another vessel that had arrived, and when threats were made of boarding and capturing that ship, the records were moved to the Asia, and she continued to be their custodian until her departure from the city. While the Asia lay in our harbor, she was the common receiving ship of all the tories of consequence, and among those who sought her protection were William Tryon, Governor of New York, and Rev. Myles Cooper, President of Kings, now Columbia College, both of whom had become distasteful to the people by the unpopularity of their sentiments and acts. In the month of January, 1776, her commander declared his intention to cannonade and burn New-York, but was defied by General Lee, and wisely forebore to carry his threat into execution. While the Asia lay in the East river, about this time, she had on one occasion, under the cover of her guns, a British sloop, laden with provisions. The American troops were then suffering much from want of proper clothing and the necessaries of life, and Captain Nathan Hale, whose subsequent fate is well known, formed the bold design of capturing this sloop and bringing her and her cargo into the harbor of New York. He soon found some kindred spirits, and at dead of night, the time agreed upon, the little band of adventurers rowed silently, in a small boat, to a point near the sloop, dropped their oars, and there waited for the moon to go down. As soon as it was dark, and all was still save the voice of the watchman upon the deck of the Asia, they pulled away for the sloop, sprang aboard, hoisted sail, and brought her into port with her crew in the hold, and without the loss of a man. This exploit, so happily conceived, and so successfully executed, was long and loudly applauded, and the daring leader distributed the goods of his prize, to feed the hungry and clothe the naked troops. The Asia was one of the vessels which under command of Sir Peter Parker, were ordered to bear a part in the battle of Brooklyn, but owing to the tide, were unable to render much service. After the defeat of the

Continental forces, she and two other vessels went up the North river, but were roughly handled by the American battery at Powle's Hook. A ship, so noted and detested, naturally attracted the attention of Capt. Silas Talbot, who made an attempt on her destruction by means of a fire ship. From near Fort Washington, he proceeded cautiously along, at two o'clock on the morning of the 16th of September, and soon brought up alongside of the enemy with his craft in a blaze, but lingering too long he was badly burned, although he effected his escape to the Jersey shore in safety. The Asia managed to extricate herself from the impending peril, and returned to the city at daylight the next morning, but, in the language of the papers of the day, "*she came down much faster than she went up, she and her consorts having narrowly escaped destruction by four of our fire ships that ran in among them.*" While the Asia was stationed off New York, she also very narrowly escaped being blown up by means of an ingenious American contrivance. Several barrels of gunpowder were put on board a small vessel which is said to have purposely thrown herself in the way of one of the Asia's tenders. In one of the barrels was an alarum or piece of clock work, which being wound up previous to its being put into the barrel, was arranged to go off at a distant period, and by means of a musket lock attached to it, would fire the gunpowder which surrounded it. This barrel, on being taken into the magazine of the Asia, would have set fire to the whole store, and thereby blown up the vessel. This

scheme, although ingeniously conceived, was frustrated however by the sagacity and prudence of Captain Vandeput, and
the terrors of one of the American prisoners who was on
board the ship at the time, and in the secret. In the month
of January, 1777, being then still under Vandeput's orders, the
Asia sailed from Newport for England, with General Clinton
on board. A frigate accompanied her on the voyage. On
her arrival home, she was immediately put into dock for refitment and repair, and when she came from the dock, Vandeput again took command of her, and sailed in her to the East
Indies, where she had been ordered on duty. In May, 1781,
she was in St. Augustin's Bay, Madagascar, homeward bound
from the coast of Africa, where she had been serving. In the
year following, she was again in active service, sailing from
Portsmouth under the orders of Capt. Richard Rodney Bligh,
and was one of the fleet under Admiral Lord Howe, which
sailed for the relief of Gibraltar and had a partial action with
the combined French and Spanish fleets off Cape Spartel, on
the coast of Barbary, on the 20th day of October of that year.
In the following month she was cruising under Bligh off the
Irish coast, was afterwards at St. Helens, and in the year 1786
was undergoing repairs at Chatham. In March, 1793, Capt.
John Brown was appointed to command her, and he was succeeded in October, 1794, by Capt. John McDougall. The Asia
was at the Assault of Fort Bourbon, afterwards Fort George,
by Vice Admiral Sir John Jervis on the 20th March, 1794, on
which occasion she was ordered to cover the landing of the

troops, but in consequence of the incapacity of her pilot, she was unable to reach her station or bear the part assigned her in the operations of the day.   In June, 1795, she was the flag ship of Rear Admiral Thomas Pringle; in May, 1796, Capt. Robt. Murray was appointed to command her; in 1798 she was still under his orders, as she was also in 1800.   In the latter year she was at Halifax, and was the flag ship of Vice Admiral Vandeput, her former commander.   In the year 1801 she was under the command of Capt. John Dawson.   In the latter part of 1803 she was not in commission, and being soon after condemned as unfit for further service, she was accordingly broken up in the course of the succeeding year.

Mr. Hawkins is in error in regard to the Asia being the vessel in which he was confined as a prisoner.

GEORGE VANDEPUT, the commander of the Asia while she was on the American station, was the son of Sir George Vandeput, who in 1747 was engaged in the memorable contest with Lord Trentham, afterwards Earl Gower, for the representation of Westminster—a contest by which his large fortune was considerably impaired.   Sir George, who was the son of Peter Vandeput, and grandson of Sir Peter Vandeput, was made one of the five searchers of the port of London, by patent dated April 20, 1777.   His first wife was Francis, daughter of Baron Augustus Schutz, of Shotover House, near Oxford; she died at Chelmsford, May 21, 1771.   His second wife was a Miss Philadelphia Grey, to whom he was married August 19, 1772. Sir George died June 17, 1784.

His son, the subject of this sketch, served as a midshipman on board the Neptune, at the siege of Quebec under Saunders, and was appointed a lieutenant Sept. 24, 1759. After the peace, he was sent to Senegal as commander of a guard-vessel stationed there, and on his return he was made commander April 17, 1764. On the 20th day of June 1765, he was raised to the rank of captain and appointed to the Surprize of 24 guns. In the year 1767, he moved to the Carysfort, of 28 guns, a new frigate just launched. He was afterwards on duty for three years in the Mediterranean sea, and in 1770 was apppointed to the Solebay, of 28 guns, cruising for the same period of time on the home station. He subsequently commanded the Thames of 32 guns, and in 1774 was appointed to the Asia of 64 guns, and ordered to North America. He remained here about three years, returning in the beginning of the year 1777, and on his arrival home his vessel was ordered into dock for refitment and necessary repair. He continued in command, however, and when she came from the dock, he sailed in her to the East Indies, where he remained some years. In the beginning of 1781, he returned to England, with a fleet of East India ships under his convoy, and after being a short time unemployed, he was at the beginning of the ensuing year appointed to the Atlas of 98 guns, then newly launched. As soon as his ship was ready for sea, he was ordered to join the Channel fleet, which, in the month of September, proceeded to the relief of Gibraltar. In the skirmish which took place with the combined fleets of France and Spain, on the 20th of October, and at which Capt. Vandeput was, of course, present, the Atlas had two men killed, and three wounded. On the return of the fleet, he quitted this command, and peace following soon after, he was appointed to the William and Mary yacht. At the commencement of the ensuing summer, he moved to the Princess Augusta, a vessel of the same description, and shortly afterwards proceeded in her to the Elbe, for the purpose of conveying thither, Prince Edward, the fourth son of King George the third. Capt. Vandeput held the last mentioned command till he was advanced to the rank of a flag officer, which took place on the 1st February, 1793, in consequence of which he became Rear Admiral of the Blue. Soon after this he hoisted his flag on board the Saturn of 74 guns. On the 12th April, 1794, he was made Rear Admiral of the Red, and on the 4th July following, was advanced to the rank of Vice Admiral of the Blue. In May, 1795, he was in the Jupiter of 50 guns, and was appointed to command a squadron or division in the armament which the irruption of the French into Holland rendered it indispensably necessary to keep stationed in the North Sea. On the 1st June he was advanced to Vice Admiral of the White, and in the interim moved his flag into the Leopard, a ship of the same force with the Jupiter. He was subsequently at Plymouth, in the absence of Sir Richard King, and, in 1796, was on the coast of Portugal. In 1797, he moved to the Resolution, of 74 guns, and proceeded in her to Halifax, Nova Scotia, having been invested with the North American command, which he filled with diligence and credit. In 1799, he was advanced to the rank of Admiral of the Blue, and subsequently moved his flag to the Asia, of 64 guns. He continued on the Halifax station till his death, which occurred at Halifax in the month of March, 1800. He was succeeded in office by Vice Admiral Sir William Parker, bt.

Admiral Vandeput was a plain, unaffected, manly character, and was well acquainted with his profession. He was also a judicious critic in the arts, and a great admirer of pictures, particularly those on nautical subjects. In private life, he was esteemed for good sense, intelligence, and moral worth.

The family of Vandeput was descended from an ancient stock in the Netherlands, and was founded in England by Henry Vandeput, of the city of Antwerp, who fled from his native country to escape the persecution of the duke of Alva.

(11) CAPT. POTTER, notwithstanding the glaring exhibition he had given of his cowardice and of his unfitness to command, seems nevertheless to have retained the confidence of his employers, as we find by the following extract:

"PROVIDENCE, June 29.—On Thursday [26th] Captain Mowry Potter, in a sloop, arrived here from Gaudaloupe, after a passage of 25 days." *Pennsylvania Packet, July* 16, 1782.

(₁₂) THE MAIDSTONE belonged to the British navy, was registered as a sixth rate, carried 28 guns, and was built in the
year 1758. In 1759, she was under command of Capt. Dudley
Digges, carried 200 men, and was one of the fleet under Sir
Edward Hawke, participating in the action off Belle-isle,
November 20th of that year, when the French under M. Conflans sustained such a signal defeat, having four capital ships
destroyed, one taken, and the remainder so disabled, that the
naval power of France was for some years effectually crushed.
We next hear of the Maidstone, in 1764, when she was commanded by Charles Antrobus, and when she lay in the harbor
of Newport for several months. Here she gave great dissatis-
faction to the people by her arbitrary course of impressing
seamen from vessels entering the harbor, as well as in taking
them from the boats and small craft in the bay. On one occasion she boarded the brig Africa, which was entering the
port, and pressed her entire crew into the British naval service. The atrocity of this act roused at once the public indig-
nation, and a mob of 500 men and boys, exasperated by the
affair, seized one of the boats of the Maidstone from the
wharf where it lay, pulled it on shore, and after dragging it
through the streets to the common in front of the Court
House, consigned it to the flames, amid the shouts of an
immense crowd which the occasion had brought together.
This movement was so secretly concocted and so suddenly
carried into effect, that the public authorities had no opportunity to interfere. In 1771, the Maidstone was on the Ports-

mouth station as she was also in 1774. In the year 1775, she
was under the command of Capt. Alan Gardner, and continued under his orders for three years. On the 15th day of
December, 1777, she arrived in New York from England with
a large convoy, having on her passage hither taken no less
than four American vessels. On the 9th March, 1778, she was
spoken with by another British vessel in lat. 38, long. 62, and
had then taken 5 prizes and burnt them. On the 21st April
following, she took the sloop Greenwich, of 12 guns and
50 men, having the day previous taken and burnt another,
and on the 24th of the same month she captured the brig
Ranger, a valuable prize, owned by Capt. Tracey of New
London. On the 3d November following, while cruising off
the Chesapeake, eastward of Cape Henry, she discovered the
French frigate Lyon of 40 guns (12, 6, and 4 pounders), Capt.
James Mitchell, and made chase for her, and about 3½ o'clock
the next morning, succeeded in getting along side. An action
commenced, which was maintained with great spirit on both
sides for upwards of an hour, when the Maidstone, having
received much injury to her sails and rigging, was reluctantly
compelled to heave to and repair damages. At noon the same
day, she again brought her opponent to action, and at 10
o'clock P. M., compelled her to surrender. The Maidstone, of
a crew of 190, had 4 killed and Capt. Gardner and 8 of his
men wounded. The Lion had a crew of 216 men, of which
there were 8 killed and 18 wounded. She was a valuable
prize, being crowded with merchandize, having about 1500

hhds. of tobacco on board. In this engagement both ships were very considerably damaged in their masts, sails and rigging, and when the Lyon struck, she had several feet of water in her hold.

The Maidstone was cruising on the American station for nearly all the period of the Revolution, and made many captures of American vessels, causing many a brave man a long and painful confinement on board the British prison ships. In 1782, she was under the orders of Capt. William Parker. In the year 1786, she was at Woolwich, and in 1788, she was commanded by Henry Newcome. She was under the orders of Capt. Matthews in 1798, and she appears to have been broken up in the course of the following year. Her place was supplied by another vessel bearing the same name, but carrying 32 guns.

(13) This word is probably used in the sense of "hand money;" something like the "king's shilling," which was given to the new recruit upon his enlisting in the army, and which was supposed to bind the bargain. It is derived, probably, from the active verb "cope," to cover, to spread, etc.; one definition of which, but now obsolete, is "to reward, to pay," as in Shakspeare—

"In lieu whereof,
Three thousand ducats due unto the Jew,
We freely *cope* your courteous pains withal."
Merchant of Venice, Act IV., Scene I.

(14) At the time spoken of, there were no less than four ladies in Providence by the name of Crawford, all of whom were, or had been, married. The one referred to by our author as the person with whom the boy Jacob Good had resided, was most probably the widow of Joseph Crawford. This gentleman was born in the year 1712, and died January 1, 1776, at the age of 64 years, 7 months, and 20 days. He was the owner of a large landed estate in Providence. His widow, whose maiden name was Susannah Bernon, was born in 1715, and resided in Providence to her death, which occurred on the 18th day of February, 1802, at the age of about 87. She had an independent fortune, and the boy Good was most likely a servant in her employment.

(15) ALAN GARDNER was born in Uttoxeter, in Staffordshire, England, April 12th, 1742. His father, William Gardner, was an Irishman by birth, and was bred to the profession of arms, and rose to the rank of Lieut. Colonel in the 11th Regiment of Dragoons. He came from Coleraine, and settled in England, where he married two wives, by the second of whom he had no less than twelve children. Alan, the subject of this sketch, after receiving all the benefits that could be derived from a provincial education, was destined for a naval life. He commenced his career as a midshipman on the 1st day of May, 1755, on board the Medway of 60 guns, Capt. Peter Denis, and belonged to that ship when she took the Duke d'Aquitane. He was afterwards in the Dorsetshire, of 70 guns, under the

same commander, and was in that vessel when she took the
French 64 gun-ship Raisonnable. He was also in the Dorsetshire in the general engagement off Belle-isle, between the
English and French fleets, commanded by Sir Edward Hawke
and Marshal de Conflans, on the 20th November, 1759. He
was made lieutenant, March 7, 1760, and while acting in that
rank on board the Bellona, Capt. Robert Faulkner, was present
at the capture of the French ship Le Courageux, of 74 guns,
after a desperate struggle, on the 14th Aug., 1761. He was
made commander, March 12th, 1762 ; was promoted to the
rank of captain, May 19, 1766, and shortly afterwards appointed to the Preston, of 50 guns, the flag-ship of Rear-
Admiral Parry, who was sent out as Commander-in-Chief of
the Jamaica and Windward Island station. This was a period
of peace, in which few opportunities offered for distinction,
and we have therefore nothing to record of Capt. Gardner
during the time he continued in the Preston, which was about
two years. Towards the end of the summer of 1768, he moved
into the frigate Levant, of 28 guns, and continued on the
Jamaica station till 1771, when he returned to England. He
remained unemployed until 1775, when he was appointed to
the frigate Maidstone, of 28 guns, and sent out, probably at his
own request, to his former station, the island of Jamaica.
The American Revolution having broken out, Capt. Gardner
was ordered, in the Maidstone, to cruise off the coast of
America. On the 3d day of November, 1778, he captured, off
Cape Henry, the French ship Lyon, of 40 guns, and 216 men,

after an obstinate engagement. On this occasion he had 4 men killed and 8 beside himself wounded of a crew of 190. On the 22d of December following, he arrived at Antigua with his prize, and shortly afterwards was promoted to the Sultan, of 74 guns, as successor of Capt. Wheelock, who had died a short time before. In the action off Grenada of Byron with D'Estaing, July 6, 1779, he was present and fought his ship with great bravery, having 16 of his men killed and 39 wounded. Capt. Gardner soon after this was ordered with his vessel to Jamaica, and in the following year he returned to England with a convoy. After remaining a short time out of commission, he was, towards the end of the year 1781, appointed to the Duke, of 98 guns, one of the ships ordered to reinforce Sir Geo. Rodney's fleet in the West Indies. He arrived at his station, and by his gallantry contributed very materially to the victory won on the 12th of April, 1782, over the Count de Grasse. In this engagement Capt. Gardner's ship was next to the Formidable, the flag-ship of Lord Rodney, and was the first to break the French line, thereby deciding the fortune of the day. During one period of the action, the Duke, the Formidable and the Namur, had to sustain the fire of eleven of the enemy's ships, and their loss of men was proportionately great. On board the Duke, there were 13 men killed and 60 wounded, and among the latter were one of the Lieutenants, the Master and the Boatswain. Having returned to England, Capt. Gardner was on the 8th Sept., 1785, appointed Commander-in-Chief on the Jamaica station. He hoisted his board pennant on board the Europa, of 50 guns, James Vashon, Captain, and continued at Jamaica for three years, when he returned to England, and in 1790 was appointed to the Courageux, of 74 guns. On the 19th of January of that year, he was made a Lord of the Admiralty, and in the same year was chosen one of the representatives in Parliament from the borough of Plymouth. On the 1st February, 1793, he was promoted to the rank of Rear Admiral of the Blue, and the war with France having now broken out, he was sent to the West Indies, whence he returned in September following with a large fleet of merchantmen under his convoy, and the following year he was made Rear Admiral of the White. In the engagement by Lord Howe with the French fleet, on the 1st June, 1794, a day which has since been, and ever will be memorable in the annals of Great Britain, Admiral Gardner commanded the Queen, of 90 guns, and how effectually he contributed to the glory of that day, is stated in the despatches of the Commander-in-Chief. Here he lost his captain, the brave John Hutt, also three of his lieutenants, a midshipman, and had 36 men killed and 67 wounded. For his services on this occasion, he was appointed Major-General of Marines, and raised to the rank of Vice Admiral of the Blue, and his name was included in all the votes of thanks and congratulations from public bodies on the sharers of that hard-fought action. In common with his colleagues, he was presented by the king in person with a gold chain and medal, and honored with the title of a baronet of Great Britain. On the 1st June, 1795, the anniversary of the glorious victory, he was appointed Vice Admiral of the White, and on the 23d of the same month was second in command in the engagement of Lord Bridport with the French fleet off Port L'Orient. At the general election in 1796, Admiral Gardner was returned member of parliament from the city of Westminster, and having moved his flag to the Royal Sovereign, of 110 guns, he soon after commanded a squadron in the Channel. On the 14th February, 1799, he was made Admiral of the Blue, and in the following year appointed commander-in-chief of the Irish coast. On the 23d December, 1800, he was created a peer of Ireland, by the title of Baron Lord Gardner, of Uttoxeter, and a short time before his death he had command of the fleet in the Channel. Lord Gardner died at Bath, in England, on the 30th day of December, 1808, in the 67th year of his age, and was succeeded in his titles by his eldest son, Hon. Alan Hyde Gardner, since also an admiral in the British navy.

(16) JAMES VASHON was the youngest son of Rev. J. V. Vashon, Rector of Eye, etc., and was born about the year 1742. He entered the navy as a midshipman under Sir George Cornwall, in 1756, and in 1777 was lieutenant in the Maidstone, under Capt. Alan Gardner. He became Commander, August 5, 1779, and in 1780, was in the sloop Alert, and in the latter part of that year captured and carried into Jamaica, two schooners, besides the American letter of marque Race Horse, from Beverly. He was made Captain, April 12, 1782, and in

the following year commanded the Sybil, of 28 guns, at
Jamaica. He was subsequently appointed to the Europa, of
50 guns, the flag-ship of Alan Gardner, on the same station, in
which ship the gallant Capt. Duff, who fell at Trafalgar, was
his first-lieutenant. During the Spanish and Russian armaments, Captain Vashon commanded the Ardent, of 64 guns,
and at the commencement of the war with the French
Republic, the St. Albans, of the same force. In that vessel he
proceeded to Gibraltar with the fleet, under Lord Hood, and
returned thence with a convoy, after which he escorted the
trade to the West Indies. In the summer of 1795, he moved
into the Pompée, of 80 guns, stationed in the channel. On the
15th June, 1797, he returned to Spithead, in consequence of a
most dangerous conspiracy among his crew, which was, however, discovered before it was ready for execution. A court
martial was immediately assembled to try six of the principal
mutineers; when the charges having been proved in the
clearest manner against four of them, they were sentenced to
suffer death. On the 28th two of these unhappy men were
executed on board the Pompée, and the other two received
the Royal pardon. In the spring of the year 1799, Captain
Vashon moved into the Neptune, of 98 guns, and was sent to
reinforce the fleet in the Mediterranean, under Earl St. Vin-
cent, on which station he remained, however, but a few
months. Early in 1801 he took command of the Dreadnought,
a new 98 gun ship, and after cruising for some time in the
channel, proceeded off Cadiz, and to Minorca, where he con-

tinued until the summer of the following year. Toward the
latter part of 1803, he was in the Princess Royal, of 98 guns,
stationed at the mouth of the Southampton river, to guard
that place, and the west end of the isle of Wight, in case of an
invasion. He was promoted to Rear Admiral of the White,
April 23, 1804, and in 1805 was raised to Rear Admiral of the
Red, and about the same time, appointed to command the
naval force on the coast of Scotland, under the general orders
of Lord Keith. He proceeded to Leith, where he hoisted his
flag, and remained there till the latter part of the year 1808,
when he was relieved by Sir Edmund Nagle. Previous to his
relinquishment of the above command, the only one, we
believe, enjoyed by him as a flag-officer, the Masters and
Brethren of Trinity House, at Leith, unanimously conferred on
him the freedom of their corporation, and presented him with
an elegant silver snuff-box, with the following inscription
engraved upon the lid:—" Presented to James Vashon, Esq.,
Vice Admiral of the Blue, by the Trinity House of Leith,
November, 1808."   In the year 1806, he was made one of the
Commissioners of Naval Enquiry ; April 28th, 1808, promoted
Vice Admiral of the Blue; and June 4, 1814, raised to Admiral
of the White. Admiral Vashon died at Ludlow, in Shrop-
shire, England, Oct. 20, 1827, at the age of eighty-five years.
His funeral was attended by Earl Powis, Lord Clive, Hon. R.
H. Clive, Rear Admiral Balland, Col. Bromley, and others.
An excellent portrait of deceased, engraved in mezzotinto by
John Young, from a painting by George Watson, is extant.

Admiral Vashon left one son, Rev. James Volant Vashon, A. M., Rector of Sharpe, in Worcestershire.

(17) ABIGAIL HAWKINS, the wife of Hezabiah Hawkins, and the mother of our hero, was a native of Rhode Island, and was born in the town of Smithfield, in the year 1745. Her maiden name was Abigail Patt. Her father was for many years a resident of Smithfield, but finally moved to Newport, Herkimer Co., N. Y., and died there. After the war Mrs. Hawkins moved with her husband to Newport, N. Y. They belonged to no church, but were nevertheless very worthy people, and were much esteemed for their integrity. Mrs. Hawkins died in Newport, N. Y., about the year 1805. She had 13 children, all of whom lived to be men and women.

(18) We think Mr. Hawkins is in error in regard to the name of this officer, as we do not find it among any list of English naval officers which we have examined. We find

T. Sal. Richards appointed lieut. Nov. 12, 1777.
Richard Leggett   "   "   " 30, 1778.
Richard Raggett   "   " Dec. 15, "
and Richard Retalick   "   " Sept. 6, 1779,
but we find no *Richard Richards*.

(19) The frigates of the Revolutionary time were usually vessels varying from 600 to 1000 tons, and rarely carried on their main deck batteries, guns of a metal heavier than 18

pounders. There was usually no spar deck, but the forecastle and quarter deck were connected by gangways, with gratings to cover a part, or even all of the intermediate space. The armaments above were light sixes, nines or twelves, according to the respective rates, but were commonly of trifling amount. The Maidstone carried 28 nine-pounder guns.

($_{20}$) Prize money was usually divided into eight equal parts, and was distributed in the following proportions : captains to have three-eighths, unless under direction of a flag-officer, who in that case was to have one of the said three-eighths; captains of marines and land forces, sea lieutenants, etc., one-eighth ; lieutenants of marines, gunners, admirals' secretaries, etc., one-eighth; midshipmen, captain's clerk, etc., one-eighth ; ordinary and able seamen, marines, etc., two-eighths.

($_{21}$) Burgoyne's surrender on the 17th of October, 1777, was an event at once startling and incredible to the British public. It was the severest blow which their army in America had yet sustained, and coming as it did, at the most critical moment in the fortunes of the colonies, it had the important effect of determining France to ally her arms and influence with the cause of American liberty. Those who have had an opportunity of reading the British newspapers, magazines and letters of that day, will easily recognize in the incredulity of the crew of the frigate Maidstone, as related by our author, a fair example of the sanguine expectations and confidence which was universally felt in the success of Gen. Burgoyne and his army.

(22) POINT JUDITH is a noted cape on the southern coast of Rhode Island. Many vessels have been driven ashore and wrecked upon this dangerous point. It derives its name from the sister of a Mr. Thacher, whose daughter was the mother of Rev. Thomas Payne, of Weymouth, father of the Hon. Robert Treat Payne, Judge of the Supreme Court of Massachusetts. The tradition is that in former times Judith Thacher, with her father, were on board a small vessel which got aground on that point and came very nigh being wrecked. The lady rendered great service, whereby the vessel was saved, and in remembrance of this, the crew called the point after the Christian name of Miss Thacher, by which name it has ever since been known. Point Judith farm belonged to the Sewell family, and was the largest estate confiscated by Rhode Island at the end of the Revolution. It was confiscated on account of the toryism of the owners, who resided in England.

(23) The COLUMBUS was one of the frigates which were purchased by Continental Congress in pursuance of Resolutions of Oct. 13th and Oct. 30th, 1775. She was placed under the command of Capt. Abraham Whipple, and was one of the squadron under Commodore Ezek. Hopkins, which made a descent in Feb., 1776, on New Providence, one of the Bahama Islands, taking the town of Nassau, and capturing nearly 100

cannon, besides a large quantity of other stores. This was the
first expedition of the infant American navy, and was very
successful, the vessels all returning with their booty in safety.
On the return of the Columbus, she was one of the vessels
that made an unsuccessful attack on the British ship Glasgow,
Capt. Tyrlingham Howe, off Block Island. The Columbus
was afterwards placed under the command of Capt. Hoysteed
Hacker, and was under his orders at the time spoken of by
our author. She is believed to have had a gun-deck battery
of eighteen long nine pounders. She was a clumsy, crank
ship, and did not prove herself a very good sailer.

CAPT. HOYSTEED HACKER was a native of Rhode Island. In
1762, he sailed with Capt. Joseph Crawford of Providence, in
the privateer Revenge, which vessel was captured on its
cruise by a French frigate. In the year 1770, he commanded
a packet, and in the month of April took as a passenger from
Newport to Providence, the late President of the Rhode
Island Historical Society, John Howland, Esq., then a boy
of 13, and on his way to Benjamin Gladding of Providence, to
whom he had been apprenticed to learn che business of hair
dressing. At the time when Congress was organizing a navy,
attention was called to Capt. Hacker. He was appointed by
that body a lieut., Dec. 22, 1775, and on the 10th Oct., 1776,
was commissioned as captain. In command of the sloop
Providence, of 12 guns, he captured a number of valuable
prizes. In November, 1776, he took a ship from England

bound to Quebec, with 12,000 suits of clothing, 4,000 stands of arms, besides a quantity of powder and other warlike stores. In 1778, he commanded the Columbus, and in endeavoring to get to sea, was chased on shore at Point Judith, on the 29th March, by the frigate Maidstone, and the next day his vessel was burnt by the enemy. In the spring of 1779, he captured the British sloop Diligent, off Sandy Hook, after a sharp action. In July of the same year, he was engaged in the Penobscot expedition, where his vessel, the Providence, was lost. In 1781, he commanded the private armed ship Buccanier, and sailed from L'Orient in France, Nov. 3, arriving at Boston in December following. After the war, Capt. Hacker took up his residence in the city of New York, where he kept a boarding house for a few years, and until the death of his wife in 1794. He was for a long time and until his death, a pilot for vessels sailing through Hellgate. He was one of the original members of the New York State Society of the Cincinnati, having been admitted at its organization. He died in the month of July, 1814. His wife died Feb. 4, 1794, and was buried in Trinity church yard in this city. A tombstone was erected to her memory, and it is still to be seen in that cemetery. The stone, which is a plain one, bears the following inscription : " *In Memory of Mary Hacker, Wife of Capt. Hoysteed Hacker, who departed this Life, 9th Feb'ry, 1794, aged 43 Years.*"

(24) NEWPORT, April 2.—" Last Friday night [March 28] the

Rebel frigate Columbus, of upwards of 20 guns, attempting to pass the Narraganset passage, she was early discovered and warmly saluted by his Majesty's ship Somerset; whose guns apprising the Commodore that a vessel was attempting to get out, he immediately dispatched the Maidstone and Diamond frigates to intercept her at the passage. They were soon judiciously disposed for that purpose, which the rebels discovering, they thought it most prudent to run her ashore upon the Main. The wind suddenly falling, prevented the frigates from destroying her till towards evening, when it was effected by the Lieutenant of the Maidstone, who boarded her under a very severe fire from the shore. An armed galley which was sent from hence, was particularly useful in covering the boats."

Pennsylvania Ledger, Saturday, April 25, 1778.

PROVIDENCE, April 4.—" On Friday night, last week, [March 28] Capt. Hacker, in the ship Columbus, attempting to pass the enemy's shipping in the Bay, to proceed to a neighboring fort, whither her guns and stores were to have been transported by land. A brig, bound for the West Indies, that had sailed the same evening, was perceived by the enemy's upper ship, which fired signal guns, when two frigates immediately got under way, and intercepted the Columbus off Point Judith. Capt. Hacker finding it impracticable to pass them was reduced to the necessity of running the ship on shore near the point, where her sails and the greatest part of her rigging were saved. Next day the

frigates and a galley drew near, and began a brisk fire from
their cannon and musquetry; it was returned from the shore
with such effect, that a boat, full of men, which the enemy
had sent to fire the ship, was beat off, and it is thought with
some loss, as several of the hands were seen to fall. Towards
evening the galley, under cover of the frigates, ran in and set
fire to the hull, which was burnt. We sustained no loss of
men, though the firing continued several hours. The brig
above mentioned got safe to sea."

Gaine's New York Mercury, Monday, May 18, 1778.

(25) CAPT. JOHN BURROUGHS HOPKINS was a native of Rhode
Island, and was born on the 14th day of September, 1742. He
was the son of Commodore Ezek Hopkins, the commander-
in-chief of the American navy, and was a nephew of Stephen
Hopkins, who was at one time Governor of Rhode Island,
and subsequently one of the signers of the Declaration of
Independence.

Capt. Hopkins was one of the prominent leaders in the
destruction of the British schooner Gaspee, in Narragansett
Bay, on the night of the 9th June, 1772. In the year 1776, he
commanded the ship Cabot, and was in the expedition against
New Providence. In an action with the British ship Glasgow,
that took place on this cruise, he was severely wounded. In
the month of October following, he was appointed to the
frigate Warren, of 32 guns, one of the two vessels ordered by
Congress in 1775, to be built at Providence. He continued in

command of her until the Penobscot expedition in 1779, when Dudley Saltonstall was appointed. Capt. Hopkins was made Captain of the Cabot by resolution of Congress, Dec. 22, 1775, and Captain of the Warren by resolution of Oct. 10, 1776.

He died at his residence in North Providence, R. I., on the 5th day of December, 1796, at the age of 54 years, 3 months, and 21 days; and his remains were interred in the Hopkins' Burial Ground, at that place. His widow died about the year 1820.

(26) GOVERNOR'S ISLAND was called by the Indians, Pagganck, and by the Dutch, Nooten Eylandt, or Nut Island, on account of the quantity of nuts found there. It became afterwards a perquisite attached to the office of Governor of the province of New York, from which circumstance it derives its present name.

It is situated in the harbor of New York, 3,200 feet South of the Battery, and covers about 70 acres of ground. It belongs to the United States government, and is used as a military station. On the N. W. point of the island is Castle William, a round tower, 60 feet in height, and 60 feet in circumference, with 3 tiers of guns; on the summit of the island is Fort Columbus, in the form of a star, mounting 105 heavy cannon; and on the S. W. part is a battery commanding the entrance through Buttermilk channel.

The above fortifications, when fully garrisoned, would require 800 men. There are extensive barracks, with houses for the officers, occupied by a small garrison.

(27) It is really surprising what extreme ignorance is displayed by Englishmen in regard to the history and geography of this country. Even among the higher classes, where one would, from their rank and pretension, naturally expect some intelligence shown, we find, on the contrary, the most glaring exhibitions of a truly pitiable lack of the most ordinary points of information. Even at this day, in this enlightened age, we see numerous instances of this, of not only occasional, but we may truly say, of almost every-day occurrence.

One of Britain's own distinguished sons, well and favorably known for his high sense of justice as well as for his high attainments, in alluding to this subject, expresses himself with as much candor as lamentation, in the following emphatic words:

" There is a newspaper published in London, read by everybody, but I have marveled at the ignorance which it has betrayed of the geographical features of this territory. In one article recently, there was a river of 580 miles of internal navigation, to which the largest river in this country is a mere rivulet, and it was made to turn up hill any number of miles into another river, and these two rivers cemented, were made to fall into a third river, into which neither really pours a drop of water. Now, there is a real danger in the ignorance of what, for want of a better term, I may call the ruling classes of this country—there is a real danger from their *total ignorance of everything relating to America*, and you may get into difficulties from this ignorance, which may cost much national dishonor to escape from. If I were a rich man, I would *endow a professor's chair at Oxford and Cambridge, to instruct the undergraduates of those Universities in American history.* I would undertake to say, and I speak advisedly, that I will take any undergraduate now at Oxford or Cambridge, and I will bring him to a map of the United States, and ask him to put his finger on *Chicago,* and I will undertake to say that he does not go within *a thousand miles* of it. Yet Chicago is a place of 150,000 inhabitants, from which *one to two millions of people in our own country are annually fed.* These young gentlemen know all about the geography of *ancient Greece* and *Egypt.* Now, I know I shall be pelted with Greek and Latin quotations for what I am going to say. When I was at Athens I sallied out one summer morning to seek the famous river Ilissus, and after walking some hundred yards or so up what appeared to be the bed of a mountain torrent, I came upon a number of Athenian laundresses, and I found they had damned up this famous classical river, and were using every drop of its water for their own sanitary purposes. Why, then, should not these young gentlemen, who know all about the geography of the Ilissus, know, also, *something about the geography of the Mississippi?*

Richard Cobden's Speech to his constituents at Rochdale,
November 23d, 1864.

(28) The FLY, or more properly, the VLIE MARKET, was erected in the year 1706, in what was then called by the

Dutch, Smee's Vlie, or Smidt's Vley, and by the English as
Smith's Vly or Meadow, a name occasioned by the fact that
the ground for some distance about there was formerly a salt
meadow, and also from the fact that a blacksmith in early
times carried on an extensive business in the locality. The
market was located in that part of the Vlie now known as the
lower end of Maiden Lane, but at that day called by the name
of Fly or Vlie Market-street. It was, in its best days, a place
of great resort, being for many years the principal market in
the city, and was at one time bounded by the residences and
places of business of many of the most respectable citizens.
At the lower end of the market were the ferry stairs leading
down to the river, where the boats from Brooklyn took in and
landed their passengers, and discharged their market freight.
These boats were large, stout and clumsy, and were rowed by
negroes, one of whom usually gave notice of the boat's
departure by blowing a conch shell, at the same time calling
the attention of the people by shouting the words, "*over*,
over," repeatedly, in a stentorian tone. The ferry-master, in
1777, was John Van Winkle, and the fare at that time was six
pence for each foot passenger. The Vlie Market was enlarged
in 1736, further enlarged in 1772, and was demolished in or
about the year 1822.

(₂₉) CAPT. DANIEL HAVENS.—Of this gentleman we know
but little, save what the narrative tells us of his humanity,
and by inference, of his loyalty. On the 31st January, 1779,

he assisted in capturing, at the wharf at Sag Harbor, L. I., where she then lay, the brig Ranger, a refugee privateer, of 12 guns, that had long infested the Sound, and had taken many prizes, besides plundering the coast. On the following day, in company with others, he made a bold but unsuccessful attack on seven vessels which had put into that port. In the year 1785, he was master of the brig America, and went on a whaling voyage in her to the Brazil Banks, returning to Sag Harbor early in the month of June, with 300 barrels of oil— a remarkable success at that time.

A committee appointed in the winter of 1863–4, to terrace the old Burying Ground adjoining the Presbyterian Church at Sag Harbor, L. I., and remove the front tier of the graves of the oldest occupants, removed among others, the remains, tombstone, etc., of Capt. Daniel Havens. The inscription on the stone read as follows: "*Died, May 25th*, 1789, *Capt. Daniel Havens, in the* 40*th year of his age*." As near as can be ascertained, he belonged in Moriches, (in Brookhaven township.) He lived in Sag Harbor, on the main street, on the site now (1864) occupied by the heirs of Capt. Oliver Steele ; and had two sons, named Paul and Merritt.

(30) SHELTER ISLAND lies at the east end of Long Island, in Suffolk county, about 100 miles from New York city. It is about five miles from east to west, and seven from north to south. It is a fruitful spot, containing about 8,000 acres, and was incorporated in 1788. A considerable number of cattle,

sheep and poultry, are raised here. The place contained, in
1810, about 200 inhabitants, of whom 34 were electors. In
1858, its population was 386.

The name of *Sawyer* was a common one in the town at the
time spoken of in the narrative.

(31) This was, probably, John Polhemus' Tavern, which
was near the celebrated tavern of J. J. Snedeker.

(32) HEZABIAH HAWKINS, the father of our author, was born
in Rhode Island, on the seventeenth day of September, 1740.
He resided in the town of North Providence, now Smithfield,
and was, by occupation, a ship carpenter. He was a soldier
during the revolutionary war, and served in the army for
seven years. In 1779, he was a private in Col. Angell's regiment, and was also a private in the Rhode Island regiment,
February 1st, 1781. After the war he moved to Newport,
Herkimer Co., N. Y., and died there in the month of October,
1817, at the age of seventy-seven years.

(33) OBADIAH OLNEY was the eighth child of Capt. Thomas
Olney, and was born in Providence, R. I., on the 14th February, 1710. He was by occupation a farmer, and was a man
of high respectability. His first wife was Deborah Smith, to
whom he was married November 9, 1734, and by whom he
had one son. She died in Smithfield, April 13th, 1735. Mr.
Olney's second wife was Lydia Hawkins, to whom he was

married January 12th, 1737, and by whom he had seven children. This lady died in Smithfield on the 29th day of August, 1805. Obadiah Olney died in the same town on the 12th day of March, 1798, in the 88th year of his age. He left one son and six daughters surviving him. Mr. Elisha Olney, a grandson of Obadiah, still lives on a part of the old homestead, and is now 74 years of age.

(34) PROVIDENCE, the chief city and one of the capitols of Rhode Island, is situated at the head of the navigation of Narragansett Bay. It is the oldest town in the State, having been settled by Roger Williams and his company in the year 1636, and presented the first instance of a community, established on principles of perfect religious toleration. The origin of its name is explained in a curious deed, dated Dec. 20, 1661, executed by him: "Having a sense of God's merciful providence unto me in my distress, I called the place Providence." During the Revolution, Providence abounded with privateers, which were generally successful in eluding the British cruisers that swarmed upon the coast, and in making prizes of merchantmen, transports and small vessels of war. Many of the resources of the American army and navy were obtained by means of these privateers, and most of the foreign merchandize in the country was introduced through their agency. Moreover, by touching the pockets of British merchants, much was done towards influencing the English Government to acknowledge the independence of these States, and to conclude

peace with them. Privateering was, besides, almost the only business in which American merchants could employ their vessels, and private interest as well as patriotism concurred in urging them to pursue it vigorously.

NORTH PROVIDENCE, a township in Providence county, R. I., north of the town of Providence, and separated from the State of Massachusetts on the east by the Pawtucket river.

(35) Capt. CHRISTOPHER WHIPPLE was in the year 1773 one of the owners of the sloop Two Pollies, which in October was sent with a cargo of goods to the Mississippi river for disposal to the settlers there, and which was boarded, while there, by some Spanish soldiers, who, under force of arms, took possession of the vessel, and stole a part of her cargo. Capt. Whipple subsequently applied for compensation for the loss he had incurred. In the year 1775, the Council of Safety, of Rhode Island, ordered two vessels to be chartered, manned and equipped, to protect the trade of the colony, and appointed Christopher Whipple to command the smaller one, but he declining, Capt. John Grimes was appointed in his place. In the year 1776, Capt. Whipple commanded the privateer brig Putnam, and about October captured a ship bound from Nova Scotia to Jamaica, laden with fish, boards, spars, etc. In January, 1777, he was on his way from Turks Island to Newport, in a vessel richly laden. He was pursued by two British cruisers, and in endeavoring to escape from them, he was compelled to run his vessel on Point Judith shore, when

the enemy seized his ship, set it on fire, and departed. Capt. Whipple having in the meanwhile obtained assistance, the fire was extinguished, and a part of the cargo saved. He afterwards applied to the General Assembly of Rhode Island for relief for the losses he had sustained on this occasion.

(36) The harbor of Newport, for several years previous to actual hostilities, was occupied by his Majesty's ships. They were stationed there to enforce the revenue laws, and to sustain the authority of the king. After the destruction of the sloop Liberty in the harbor, in 1769, and when the hostility of the colonies to the acts of the British ministry became more fully developed, the number of these vessels was increased, until, at length, a whole squadron of men-of-war were stationed in the bay. In the spring of 1776, however, the enterprise of American sailors made the harbor so hot a berth for the British, that they were obliged to abandon it in haste, and during the following season, a large number of privateers were fitted out from this port and Providence, which captured from fifty to one hundred valuable prizes. Early in December, a British fleet and army took possession of the harbor, and though threatened by D'Estaing's French fleet in 1778, maintained their hold upon the place until the autumn of 1779, when Sir Henry Clinton recalled them to New York, in anticipation of an attack upon that city by the allied military and naval forces of America and France. On the 10th day of July, 1780, the large and powerful fleet, under the Chevalier

de Ternay, and an army under Count de Rochambeau, arrived at Newport, and remained there until near the close of the war.

(37) The AMPHITRITE (so named from Amphitrite, the goddess of the sea, who was the daughter of Oceanus and wife of Neptune,) was a coppered line-of-battle ship, belonging to the British navy, registered as a sixth-rate, carrying 24 guns, and was built in the year 1778. In the month of October, 1779, she was under the command of Capt. James Montague, and was cruising off the coast of Spain. In 1780, she was under the orders of Capt. Robert Biggs, and was one of the squadron that sailed for America, under Rear-Admiral Thomas Graves, on the 17th day of May of that year. In the year following, she sailed from Sandy Hook in Admiral Graves' fleet for the Chesapeake. In October, 1782, in company with another vessel, she took two brigs with lumber, a ship with silks from Bilboa, and a privateer schooner, as well as retook two brigs from Virginia, laden with tobacco. She returned to England at the restoration of peace, and was wrecked in the Mediterranean sea, in the year 1793, by striking upon a sunken rock. Her crew were saved. At the time of her loss, she was under the command of Capt. Anthony Hunt.

CAPT. ROBERT BIGGS, who commanded this vessel at the time spoken of by our author, was made Lieutenant, August

7th, 1761 ; raised to Commander, January 10, 1771; and
obtained post rank, March 18, 1778. In 1771, he commanded
the Grace, an armed cutter, and in 1774, the sloop Favorite,
of 16 guns. He was afterwards in command of the Lively, of
20 guns, and remained in her till she was taken by the French
in 1778. In 1780, he was appointed Captain of the Amphitrite, of 24 guns, and ordered to America. He was a Rear-
Admiral of the White in 1795, and a Vice-Admiral in 1799.
He died at Catisfield, Hants, on the 11th day of July, 1803.
At the time of his death, he was senior Vice-Admiral of the
White squadron.

(38) The MEDEA (so named from Medéa, the daughter of
Æetes, King of Colchis, and wife of Jason,) was a coppered
line-of-battle ship belonging to the British navy. She was
registered as a sixth rate, carried 28 guns, and was built
in the year 1778. She came to America in 1781, arriving
at New York in the month of July, and shortly afterwards sailed from Sandy Hook for the Chesapeake, in the
fleet of Thomas Graves, Rear Admiral of the Red, at which
time she was commanded by Capt. Henry Duncan. In the
month of August, being in company with the frigate Amphitrite, she took the American frigate Belisarius, of 20 guns,
and soon after captured the Brig Mariamne, of 16 guns. In
the month of December following, she made a prize of the
privateer Black Princess, of 24 twelve-pounders and 170
men, commanded by the noted McCarty. She afterwards

sailed for England, bearing despatches thither from Rear
Admiral Graves. In 1782 she was under the orders of Capt.
Erasmus Gower, and was sent to India, where she was used as
a store-ship to the army of Gen. Sir Eyre Coote, in his expedition to Pondicherry. On the 29th September she sailed for
Bengal, and had as a passenger Gen. Coote, who was seeking
a change of air for the recovery of his health, then much
impaired. On the 16th January, 1783, she captured the
French ship Chaser, of 20 six-pounders; and subsequently, by
a bold attack, made a prize of the Vryheid, a Dutch East India
ship, pierced for 64 guns, but mounting at the time only 32.
Previous to taking the Vryheid, the Medea had, on the
3d February, very narrowly escaped capture herself, the cover
of night, together with a thick haze which prevailed at the
time, being all that saved her from two French frigates off
Pondicherry, that got within hail of her before she discovered
them. In the month of July, the Medea was dismantled and
converted into a flag-of-truce, and ordered to convey a part of
the council of Fort St. George up to Cuddalore, to treat with
De Bussy, the French general, as to terms of pacification,
Capt. Gower being commissioned by Sir Edward Hughes to
act in the same capacity in regard to the naval department,
between himself and Mons. de Suffrein. In December, the
Medea left India, and on her voyage home, she encountered,
off the Western Islands, a dreadful gale, in which she lost her
main and mizzen masts, and was otherwise so materially
damaged, as to be in the most perilous condition. Her masts

went overboard, whereby 36 of her crew employed aloft were instantly precipitated into the sea, but were, with one exception, eventually rescued. After being refitted as well as circumstances would admit, and when the gale had somewhat moderated, she again proceeded on her course to England, and arrived at Spithead without further accident, on the 7th day of January, 1784. In the year 1786 the Medea was undergoing repairs at Portsmouth, and in 1788 was not in commission. She appears to have been broken up or otherwise disposed of previous to the year 1798.

CAPT. HENRY DUNCAN, who commanded the Medea at the time spoken of by our author, was made Lieut., September 21, 1759, promoted Commander, May 26, 1768, and raised to the rank of Captain, Feb. 7, 1776. In August, 1777, he was the first Capt. of the Eagle, of 64 guns, the flag-ship of Lord Howe, and co-operated with Sir William Howe in his operations on the Delaware. In August, 1778, he was on duty in this vessel off the coast of Rhode Island in presence of the French fleet. In 1781 he commanded the frigate Medea, of 28 guns, and while cruising off the Delaware in the month of August, he fell in with and captured the Belisarius, a frigate of 20 guns and 147 men, Capt. James Munro; and soon after made a prize of the Brig Mariamne, of 16 guns, Capt. Christopher Whipple. In June, 1782, he was second Captain of Admiral Lord Howe's flag-ship Victory, and was cruising in the North Sea; and in October following, was at the relief of Gibraltar.

At the age of 66, after a life of hard service, it fell to his lot to achieve a victory, which excited the gratitude of his country, and gained him the honors of the British peerage, by patent, Oct. 30, 1797. Capt. Duncan died at Cornhill, Durham County, England, on the 4th day of August, 1804, while on his way from London to Edinburgh, at the age of about 73 years.

(39) Among the American vessels taken by the British at this time, and noticed in the papers of the day, appear the following :

"The BELISARIUS, of 24 guns, Capt. *Munro*, from Salem, captured by his Majesty's frigates, the Amphitrite, Medea, and Virginia privateer belonging to Messrs. Shedden & Goodrich.

"The BRIG MARIAMNE, Capt. *Whipple*, of 16 guns, by his Majesty's frigate, the Medea."

Gaine's N. Y. Gazette, Mon : Aug. 20, 1781.
Rivington's Gazette, Wed : Aug. 22, 1781.

The BRIG MARIAMNE, on her arrival at the port of New-York, was sold at public auction; and for the gratification of the reader, we here present a copy of the advertisement of sale, taken from one of the papers of the day :

"PUBLIC AUCTION,
by McAdam, Watson & Co.
This day at 1 o'clock at the *Coffee House*,
Will be Sold,
The valuable *privateer prize Brig Mariamne*, with all her tackle and apparel as she now lies at Hallet's Wharf, mounts 12 carriage guns, well found in every necessary store, a prime sailor, a new vessel, and well calculated for a privateer or merchantman. Inventory to be seen on board, or at their office."

Rivington's Gazette, Wed : Aug. 22, 1781.

(₄₀) The "BELISARIUS" was a new and beautiful American privateer ship, frigate built, and of the newest construction. She was of about 500 tons burden, and mounted 20 nine-pounder guns. On her figurehead was a representation of the famous Roman general from whom she took her name, and the decorations about her stern, quarter-galleries, etc., were emblematic of that great and virtuous character. She was very roomy, and her accommodations were excellent, having a spacious ward-room and steerage, with state-rooms adjoining. She was commanded by Capt. James Munro, and was fitted out, and bound on a five months' cruise against the enemies of the United States. She sailed from the port of Boston, on the 13th May, 1781, on her first cruise, and was captured about the middle of August following, by the British frigates Amphitrite, Capt. Robert Biggs, and Medea, Capt. Henry Duncan, who were sailing in company with the privateer ship Virginia, Capt. Hazard, belonging to Messrs. Shedden & Goodrich, of New York. Previous to her capture, the Belisarius had taken as prizes, a schooner, a brig laden with rum, sugar and coffee; and also another schooner, laden with salt. Being a very fine vessel, a swift sailer, and in every respect well fitted for her purpose, she was, soon after her capture, converted to the King's service, and placed under the charge of Capt. Richard Graves, a relative of Thomas Graves, Rear-Admiral of the Red, then in command of the fleet. We find the following call for seamen to man the Belisarius, when about to sail under

Royal colors, published in the government papers of the day:

"All Gentlemen Volunteers,

WHETHER ABLE OR ORDINARY,

WHO are willing to serve their King and Country, and enrich themselves with the Treasure of their Enemies, on Board

HIS MAJESTY'S SHIP

BELISARIUS,

one of the most elegant and perfectly well appointed Frigates of her size in the universe, carrying 24 Six and Nine Pounders, commanded by

RICHARD GRAVES, Esquire,

are desired to repair on Board the said ship, at the KING'S YARD; where every able Seaman will receive a Bounty of Three Pounds; and every ordinary Seaman or able bodied Landsman, Forty Shillings, be entered into present Pay, and receive the most generous Encouragement.

The Ship is fitting out with all expedition.

GOD SAVE THE KING."

Rivington, Aug. 29, *to Sept.* 12, 1781.

The Belisarius, after being turned against her former friends, cruised along the coast for the remainder of the war, doing great damage to the Americans by capturing their vessels, and subjecting their crews to imprisonment. In January, 1782, she took the Venus, with a valuable cargo; and in May following, captured the sloop Chance, of 12 guns and 60 men, from Providence, Capt. Daniel Aborn; also, the brig Sampson, from New London, of 16 guns and 120 men, Capt. D. Brooks; and likewise the sloop Swordfish, from Warren, Conn., commanded by Capt. Charles Collins, and laden with lumber. In June of the same year, she ran a large privateer brig of 18 tons ashore near New London, and in the same month captured the Pilgrim, a privateer from New England, mounting 18 guns, Capt. H. Crary, having 100 men on board. In Feb., 1783, while returning from a cruise to St. Augustine, she fell in with two privateers, one of which was the Tartar, carrying 20 nine-pounder guns, and the other the Alexander, of 22 nine-pounders. An engagement took place, in which, although the Belisarius became much injured in her bowsprit and fore-mast, yet she beat her two opponents, causing the Alexander to flee for safety, and bringing the Tartar safely into the port of New York. In this action the Belisarius had three of her men killed and four wounded. The Belisarius remained under the command of Capt. Graves until the restoration of peace, when she was sold in the country, as were also others of the British privateer ships.

CAPT. JAMES MUNRO, who was the first commander of the frigate Belisarius, was, we believe, a native of Rhode Island. On the 7th June, 1776, he arrived in Providence from a cruise, in which he had retaken two sloops from Edenton, N. C., laden with lumber. These vessels had been taken by the Acteon frigate, and were then on their way to Antigua, to be adjudicated. Capt. Munro sent his prizes to Hispaniola. In 1778 he commanded the private ship of war Blaze Castle, of 24 guns, and while on a cruise in May of that year, was captured by the British frigate Unicorn, and he and his crew taken to Halifax, Nova Scotia, where they were confined in the jail of that place. In the month of September following, Capt. Munro was exchanged, and returned home. We next hear of him in May, 1779, when he arrived in Providence from South Carolina, having while on a cruise been taken by Capt. Chambers, of the privateer brig Gayton, from Jamaica, and carried to New Providence, but treated with humanity, and subsequently released. In 1779 he commanded the brig Saratoga, of Providence, and on the 25th August of that year, in company with the ship Argo, Capt. Silas Talbot, captured the British privateer cutter Dublin, Capt. Phœnix Fagan, of 14 guns, and on the next day took the brigantine Chance, bound from London to New York, with a valuable cargo of provisions and stores for the British army in America. While on this cruise, Capt. Munro retook a privateer schooner, of eight guns, formerly the Harlequin, of Salem, and a schooner from Connecticut, loaded with lumber. These prizes were all brought safely to port. On the 28th of the same month, he was captured by the British, and placed on board one of the prison-ships at New York. His stay there, was, however, but short, for on the 6th October following, he made his escape, in company with a number of others, and arrived safe again at Providence, on the 19th of the same month. In 1780 he commanded the ship Gen. Washington, owned by John Brown, of Providence, and sailed in her from that port on the 18th May, on a cruise, from which he returned on the 27th July. This vessel was shortly after commanded by Capt. Silas Talbot, and while under him was taken by Admiral Arbuthnot's fleet, and named the Gen. Monk, and in 1782 was retaken by the Hyder Ally, Capt.

Barney, of Baltimore, when her old name was restored to her. In the year 1781, Capt. Munro commanded the Belisarius, a new frigate just launched at Salem, and sailed in her from Boston on the 13th May, on a cruise, an account of which will be found in our sketch of that vessel. In August following, he was captured by the enemy, and taken to New York, where he was confined with his crew on board the prison-ship Jersey. Of his subsequent history, we have, unfortunately, no account, nor are we able to give the time of his death. Capt. Silas Talbot, who knew him well, and who was with him in action, says *" he was a brave man, and as honest as he was brave."*

CAPT. RICHARD GRAVES, who commanded the Belisarius while she was in the British service, was the son of a clergyman, and the youngest of four brothers, all born in Derby County, England, who went to sea at an early age, and after long service, became post captains in the English navy. The subject of our sketch was made Lieutenant, Dec. 24, 1775, and was promoted to the rank of Captain, Aug. 29, 1781. During the Revolution, while on his way to New York, with despatches, in the Swift, a leaky brig of 16 four-pounders and 35 men, with four feet water in her hold, and her pumps choked, he engaged a vessel, of 18 six-pounders and 120 men, which he beat off, although twice aboard of each other during the action. When beaten back, in an attempt to carry the Swift by boarding, his opponents left thirty of their pistols on the deck of the British vessel. The Swift was too much water-

logged to make pursuit, even had her force been such as to
have warranted Capt. Graves in so doing, and the Blonde
frigate, Capt. Berkeley, which fell in with her on the following day, was obliged to keep her company until she arrived at
the entrance of New York harbor, when she sunk. In this
action, Capt. Graves received a severe wound. In August,
1781, he was appointed to the Belisarius, a new frigate, just
captured, and his services while in her will be found in our
sketch of that vessel. On the termination of the war, the services of Capt. Graves being no longer required, he, with many
other gallant officers, was obliged to retire from active duty,
since which time he was not afloat. On the 18th June, 1804,
he was raised to the rank of a Rear-Admiral; and much against
his own will, and much to the shame and disgrace of the
British government, was placed upon the superannuated list.
Our officer married Louisa Carolina, daughter and sole heiress
of Sir John Colleton, bart , and had by this lady one son and
three daughters. His son, Samuel Colleton Graves, Esq., who
was lieutenant-colonel of the West Norfolk regiment of local
militia, and a member of the society of the Middle Temple,
was the author of several political pamphlets, published under
the signature of " Ulysses." Of his daughters, the eldest
became the wife of T. Radcliffe, Esq. The second was the
lady of Baron Vandersmissen, who was a lieutenant-colonel of
" *artillerie au cheval* " in the service of the king of the
Netherlands, and also a chevalier of the Legion of Honor and
of the order of Wilhelm. The third daughter was united in

Dec., 1819, to her relative, Lieutenant-Colonel Sir James R. Colleton, bart. Capt. Graves was still living in 1824, and resided at that time in Brussels. His wife died on the 25th day of December, in the year 1822.

(41) The "JERSEY." The first vessel by this name which we read of in English history, was one which, in 1666, was commanded by Francis Digby, second son of George, the second earl of Bristol, and which, on the 15th Sept. of that year, drove ashore and burnt four French vessels on their own coast, one of the vessels being a frigate, mounting thirty guns. In the year 1688 this ship was still in service, being then commanded by Capt. Beverley, and doing duty in the Channel fleet. On the 26th December, 1701, a frigate, carrying 48 guns and 226 men, and called the Jersey, a successor to the vessel just named, sailed from Spithead for America, having as a passenger to New York, Edward Hyde, by courtesy styled Lord Cornbury, who had just been commissioned by the king as governor of that colony, and was then on his way to assume the duties of the office. On the 3d May, 1702, the frigate arrived at her destination, and while the governor was yet on ship board, several merchants and others who were then in exile, delivered to him the original addresses by which Col. Nicholas Bayard and Capt. John Hutchins had been convicted of high treason, and for which they had been condemned to suffer death. While the Jersey frigate lay in the port of New York, the small pox raged fearfully in the city, and many per-

sons died of the disease. To such an extent did the epidemic prevail, that in ten weeks' time no less than 500 persons, of each sex and of all ages, became victims to the fell destroyer. Among these deaths were some men of note, and among these was Capt. Robert Stapleton, of the Jersey, a man who was as popular in his deportment as his character was above reproach. This lamented officer died on the 25th September, 1702, and Robert Rogers, the 1st lieut., succeeded him as Commander of the frigate, then the guard-ship of the colony. Unlike his predecessor, Rogers was unpleasing. Tenacious of his opinions, he hated contradiction. He was, moreover, negligent in his duties, and perhaps even indolent and incompetent. Several vessels, laden with provisions on account of the crown, lay at this time in Pennsylvania and Carolina, and Rogers was ordered to convoy them to Jamaica, their place of destination. Instead of proceeding at once to the duty, he delayed his departure from time to time, excusing himself at one time that the ship was unrigged; at another, that he wanted powder; and when that was supplied, that he needed something else; and again, when, through his negligence, some of his crew had deserted and fled to Long Island and Rhode Island, he complained that he had not a complement of men to make his vessel serviceable. Finally, winter coming on, and cold weather setting in, he was compelled to move at last into Kipp's Bay, where he was laid up the whole season by reason of the ice in the East river. At length he went to Philadelphia, but he refused to obey the governor's orders to stop at Carolina, whereby great loss was incurred by the crown; and having, before his departure, arbitrarily impressed seamen from merchant vessels into his service, his course in that matter ruined the entire summer trade of the colony. Though clearly amenable to law, the governor having no adequate power over his majesty's ships, was unable to arrest his course, or punish him as he deserved; and Rogers did, therefore, pretty much as he pleased. In November, 1704, John Nanfan, late Lieut.-Governor of the colony, having incurred some obligations which he found himself unable to meet, and dreading arrest and imprisonment, fled with the few clothes on his back, leaving all his other effects behind, and sought refuge on the Jersey, and in a miserable and impoverished condition, was taken by her to England, whither the frigate, much to the joy of the people, immediately sailed, bearing despatches from Lord Cornbury to the Lords of Trade in London. We next hear of this vessel in 1708, at which time she was under the orders of Captain (afterwards Admiral) Edward Vernon, and was one of three sail of the line which under the command of Capt. John Edwards, sailed in that year to the West Indies, to reinforce the squadron under Sir Charles Wager, then admiral on that station. The Jersey arrived there on the 24th July, but on account of the approach of the hurricane season, she does not appear to have been ordered to sea till January, 1709. The reinforcement of which she formed a part, had been sent out in consequence of intelligence that a powerful squadron, under that enterprising and successful French officer, Du Guai

Trouin, was likely to attack the British commerce and posses-
sions in that quarter; but the alarm which this intelligence
excited having now subsided, Sir Charles dispatched several
vessels of his fleet to cruise against the enemy, and among
them was the Jersey; and her captain, while on this service,
distinguished himself greatly, not only for his activity and
enterprise, but for his vigilance and success. The first month
he was at sea, he captured a Spanish sloop laden with tobacco;
retook from the French a Guinea ship, with 400 negroes on
board; captured a strong 400-ton merchant ship, of 20 guns,
laden principally with cocoa and wool; and took, off the
northern coast of Cuba, a small vessel of 100 tons, laden with
sugar and indigo. In May, 1711, while on a cruise to the
windward of Jamaica, he fell in with and captured a French
ship of 30 guns, and a crew of 120 men, and on the 20th Feb.
of the following year, ran another of 20 guns on shore, where
she went to pieces. The Jersey, however, while on this station, was chiefly employed as one of the squadron of Commodore Littleton, in ascertaining the force, and watching the
movements of the enemy in the port of Carthagena, and was
thus engaged until the peace of Utrecht, when she returned to
England. Of her subsequent history, we have unfortunately
no account. We have been, perhaps, rather prolix in our
account of this frigate, but considering that she was the first
of her name that sailed in our waters, that she lay even in our
harbor, and is therefore connected with our history, she has
an interest which we conceive will procure for us the leniency

at least, if not the absolute pardon, of our readers. This frigate was succeeded by another of the same name which we read of in 1727, as carrying 50 guns and 677 men, and the latter vessel was the immediate predecessor of the Jersey, so well known as a prison-ship. Having thus given some account of what we may be permitted to call the *ancestry* of the subject of our memoir, we will now direct our attention to the vessel, which at this time comes more immediately and particularly in our line of duty. The Jersey of our Revolutionary history, so noted, so detested, and in the zenith of her career of shame by many a brave man so feared, was originally a British line-of-battle ship, and probably no ship in the English service, or in the service of any other country, was the cause of more distress than she, or was the scene of more brutality and squalid wretchedness. She was built in the year 1736, on the bottom of the 50-gun frigate, and was the successor on the New-York station of the 48-gun frigate before mentioned. She was registered as a fourth-rate, carried 60 guns, and bore for her figurehead the image of a lion. Her first service appears to have been about the year 1738, when she was one of the fleet under Sir John Norris, stationed in the Channel. In the year following she was under the command of Capt. Edmund Williams, and was on duty in the Mediterranean sea, being one of the fleet stationed there under Rear-Admirals Nicholas Haddock and Sir Chaloner Ogle, to protect the commerce of Great Britain from the aggressions of the Spaniards, and the year after she returned to England.

Intelligence having been received about this time that a strong
squadron of Spanish ships of war were at Ferrol, waiting for
orders to proceed to the West Indies, Sir John Norris sailed
shortly after with a powerful fleet, of which the Jersey was
one, to dispute their voyage, but after various fruitless efforts,
he was at length compelled, by contrary winds, to lie inactive
at Torbay the greater part of the summer. Finally, having
received advice that the French and Spanish squadrons had
sailed in company, the design against Ferrol was thereupon
abandoned. In this expedition the Jersey occupied the centre
division in line of battle, which division was under the command of Sir John Norris himself. We next hear of the Jersey
in January, 1741, at which time she was on duty in the West
Indies, having been one of the ships sent out there from St.
Helen's, on the 26th October, 1740, under Sir Chaloner Ogle,
to reinforce the fleet of Edward Vernon, the commander on
that station. At this time she was under the orders of Capt.
Peter Lawrence, and had a crew of 400 men. In the unsuccessful expedition against Carthagena, by Admiral Vernon,
which took place in the month of March, 1741, the Jersey was
one of the fleet coöperating with the army under Gen. Went-
worth, and in the attack upon that place on the 9th of the
month, she was in the van division in line of battle. On this
occasion she was the flag-ship of Sir Chaloner Ogle, and was
under the immediate orders of the commander-in-chief. In
the month of March, 1743, Capt. Harry Norris was appointed
to command her, and in Jan. and Feb., 1744, she formed one

of the fleet of Sir John Norris, his father, having joined him in the Downs. After this, Capt. Norris was promoted to the Prince Frederick of 74 guns, and Charles Hardy, subsequently Governor of New York, was made Captain of the Jersey in his place. On the 9th June, 1744, this officer was appointed Governor of the island of New Foundland, with the port of Placentia, and all its dependencies, a position which he filled, however, only to the termination of the year. On his return home, some of the ships of his convoy having been captured by the enemy, his conduct became the subject of a court-martial, which was held on the 2d February, 1745, and which terminated in his honorable acquittal. Capt. Hardy continued in command of the Jersey, and during that year we find him on duty in the Mediterranean sea, in the fleet stationed there under William Rowley, Vice-Admiral of the White. While thus employed, he distinguished himself by the following very gallant exploit: On the 26th July, while on a cruise off Gibraltar, when near the Strait's mouth, he fell in with the D'Esprit, a French ship, mounting 74 guns. An engagement at once ensued, which continued from half-past six to nine in the evening, when the D'Esprit, being much disabled, having lost her foremast and bowsprit, and 20 of her crew killed, bore away for Cadiz to refit, and is said to have sunk the next day. The Jersey, being also much crippled, was unable to pursue her opponent, and accordingly proceeded to Lisbon, to repair damages. In the years 1746 and 1747, Capt. Hardy served in the Mediterranean, under Henry Medley, Rear-Admiral of the

White, but whether he continued in command of the Jersey to the termination of the war, is somewhat uncertain. In the year 1756, upon a rupture with France, we find the Jersey again fitting for sea, she having then a crew of 420 men. In the year 1757 she was placed under the orders of Capt. John Barker, and in the month of May she was one of the squadron that was sent out from England to the Mediterranean, under the command of Henry Osborne, Admiral of the Blue, with instructions to cruise between Cape de Gatt and the Spanish port of Carthagena, to prevent the French fleet, then at Toulon, from proceeding to North America, to the relief of Louisburgh, against which the English had sent an expedition. She was, therefore, present on the 28th February, 1758, at the capture of the Foudroyant, of 80 guns; the Orphée, of 64; the Oriflamme, of 50; and the Pleiade frigate, of 24 guns, composing the squadron of M. du Quesne, at the time he attempted so unsuccessfully to reinforce M. de la Clue, who had slipped out of the port of Toulon, and was then with his fleet blocked up by Admiral Osborne, in the harbor of Carthagena. In 1759 the Jersey composed one of the fleet under Admiral Boscawen, which was engaged in watching the movements of M. de la Clue, who had returned to Toulon, and was then seeking an opportunity to proceed to Brest to join the grand fleet, commanded by M. Conflans, at that port. To prevent the junction of these fleets, and to endeavor to discomfit that of M. de la Clue, were the principal objects of Boscawen's expedition. He accordingly cruised off Toulon for some time, and in order to force the French admiral to an engagement, he used every stratagem and offered every provocation that his ingenuity could devise. Finding, however, that no artifice could move De la Clue from his purpose, Boscawen determined to put his patience to a stronger test and a more decisive trial. He accordingly gave orders for the Culloden, of 74 guns, Capt. Smith Callis; the Conqueror, of 74 guns, Capt. Robert Harland; and the Jersey, of 60 guns, Capt. John Barker, to proceed to the entrance of the harbor, and either cut out or destroy two of the enemy's frigates, then moored there under cover of the batteries. The execution of this hazardous and daring attempt was entrusted to Capt. Callis, who had, on a previous occasion, successfully conducted a similar enterprise with singular intrepidity. On the present occasion, he behaved with equal skill and gallantry; but the strength of the enemy's position rendered all his efforts wholly ineffectual. When the English ships approached those of the enemy at the mouth of the harbor, the former were immediately assailed by a heavy fire, not only from the ships and fortifications, but from several masked batteries on both sides of the entrance. The English supported this unequal contest for upwards of three hours with great obstinacy, when Capt. Callis, seeing no probability of success, and finding his own ship almost entirely disabled, was at length compelled to desist, and having made the signal for recall, his ships were towed off by the boats of the fleet. In this arduous service, the Culloden had 16 men killed and 26 wounded; the Conqueror

2 killed and 4 wounded; and the Jersey 8 killed and 15 wounded. These ships being all very much cut up in sails and rigging, the Admiral thought it prudent to repair to Gibraltar to have them refitted. Of Boscawen's subsequent engagement with the French fleet on the 18th August, 1759, resulting in the complete defeat of the latter, and the glorious victory of the former, as the Jersey was not one of the vessels engaged, it is needless to enlarge, further than to say that the result of the action effectually dispelled the magnificent schemes for the invasion of England, with which the French minister had for some time before amused the military ardor and romantic spirit of his countrymen. On the promotion of Smith Callis to the rank of a flag-officer, Capt. Barker succeeded him in the Culloden, and at the close of 1759 or the fore part of 1760, Andrew Wilkinson succeeded Barker in the command of the Jersey. Under Capt. Wilkinson, the Jersey sailed from England on the 28th May, 1760, and formed one of the fleet in the Mediterranean, under Vice-Admiral Sir Charles Saunders, until near the termination of the war, when she again returned to England. In the year 1766, William Dickson was commissioned to the Jersey as Captain to Sir Richard Spry, who was appointed Commodore and Commander-in-Chief of the small squadron in the Mediterranean. Sir Richard hoisted his broad pennant on board, and continued in her until the year 1768, when she returned home. John Orde, afterwards Sir John Orde, bt., and Vice-Admiral of the White, served on this cruise as a junior officer, under Capt.

Dickson, with whom he commenced his naval career in 1766. In the latter part of the year 1768, we find the Jersey stationed at Plymouth, where she was probably undergoing repairs. On the 3d day of June, 1769, Hon. John Byron, grandfather of the poet, was appointed Governor of New Foundland, and two days after, he hoisted his flag on board the Jersey, then still under the command of Capt. Dickson, and sailed in her to that colony. Soon afterwards she again returned to England, when she was laid up, and we hear nothing more of her for some time. Having become old and much impaired, the Jersey, at the commencement of the American revolution, was deprived of her armament and converted into a hospital ship. She was placed under the command of William A. Halstead, and sailed on the 6th May, 1776, from Spithead, for Boston, in company with numerous transports conveying Hessian troops, the whole fleet being under the command of Commodore William Hotham, who had his broad pennant hoisted on board the Preston, a 50 gun ship. This fleet arrived in America shortly before the battle of Brooklyn. After the Jersey reached the port of New York she seems to have been used for a while as a store ship, and subsequently as a hospital ship again, in which latter character she figures from about the year 1777 to the winter of 1779–80, during which period she was anchored in the East river, off the Fly market, and not far from a private pier known then as Tolmie's wharf, so called from Normand Tolmie, the lessee, who was, at that day, a prominent resident of the city. During the winter of 1779–80 she was converted into a prison-ship; and after being a while thus employed, she was at length moved to the Wallabout, where she was moored with chain cables, and where she remained in the capacity of a prison-ship to the termination of the war. Her appearance at this time was anything but inviting. She had been dismantled of her sails, and stripped of all her rigging, and her only spars were the bowsprit, a derrick for taking in supplies, and a flag-staff at the stern. Her lion figure-head had been taken away to repair another ship, and her rudder was unhung. Her port holes had all been closed, and strongly fastened, and two tiers of small holes were cut through her sides. These holes were about 20 inches square, and about ten feet apart, and each one was guarded by two strong bars of iron crossing each other at right angles, thus leaving four contracted spaces which admit-ted light by day, and served as breathing holes by night. Stripped of every ornament, nothing remained of her but an old, unsightly, rotten hulk; and her dark and filthy exterior perfectly corresponded with the scenes of misery, despair and death that reigned within. On the decease of Halstead in May, 1778, David Laird was appointed to fill his place as com-mander of the Jersey; and Laird, on his return to Europe in the early part of 1781, was succeeded by John Sporne; but whether the latter officer continued in her during the remaining time she was used as a prison-ship, we have been unable to ascertain. On the 9th day of April, 1783, all the prisoners on board the prison-ships in New York were released, and the

Jersey was then broken up and abandoned where she lay. The dread of contagion deterred any one from visiting her, although she remained there for years exposed to public view. Finally, as if ashamed of her late so horrid career, and unwilling any longer to be seen by a world whose humanity she had outraged, she drifted into deep water, where worms destroyed her bottom, and she at last sunk to rise no more. Off the western shore of Long Island, deeply imbedded in the mud flats of the Wallabout, she lies, her planks covered with the names of her martyred victims, and the only vestige of her now to be seen is a beam preserved for curiosity at the Naval Lyceum, in Brooklyn. Such is the last of the Jersey, that ancient ship, once so famed, so execrated, so feared; and now there is none so poor to do her reverence. But she has gone. She has *cast her last anchor.* She has *fought her last battle.*

WILLIAM ANTHONY HALSTEAD, the first commander of the Jersey, while she lay in the harbor of New York, was made lieutenant on the 20th May, 1756, and was raised to the rank of commander on the 25th June, 1773. He died at New York while in command of his vessel, on the 17th day of May, 1778, and was succeeded by David Laird.

DAVID LAIRD was made lieutenant on the 2d day of July, 1762. He was raised to the rank of commander on the 18th day of May, 1778, and appointed by Lord Howe to the command of the Jersey, to succeed William A. Halstead, then just deceased. He continued in her until the early part of the year 1781, when he returned to England. A short time after the peace of 1783 he arrived at New York in command of a merchant ship, and moored his vessel at a wharf at or near Peck slip. A number of persons, who had been prisoners on the Jersey at the time he commanded her, and had suffered by his cruelty, assembled on the wharf to receive him, but he deemed it prudent to remain on ship-board during the short time his vessel was here. He was made captain on the 1st December, 1787, and was still living in the year 1804.

JOHN SPORNE.—Of this officer we know nothing further than that he succeeded Laird in command of the Jersey, and that he still commanded her in February, 1781, he being at that time a lieutenant. The date of his commission we do not know. He seems, after the peace, to have died, or left the service, as his name does not appear on any list of British naval officers which we have examined.

(42) The following extracts from the narratives of other prisoners will show, not only the character and quantity of the food furnished them, but also give some idea of the privations and sufferings endured by those who were confined on board this loathsome hulk :

JOHN VAN DYK, who was a prisoner in May, 1780, says :

"We were put on board the prison-ship Jersey, anchored off Fly market. This ship had been a hospital ship. When I came on board, her stench was so great, and my breathing this putrid air, I thought it would soon kill me, but after my being on board some days I got used to it, and as though all was a common smell. * * * On board the Jersey prison-ship it was short allowance; so short, a person would think it was not possible for a man to live on. They starved the American prisoners to make them enlist in their service. I will now relate a fact: Every man in the mess of six took his daily turn to get the mess's provisions. One day I went to the galley and drew a piece of salt boiled pork. I went to our mess to divide it. I held the pork in my left hand, with a jack knife in my right, to mark it in six parts—the second time came out right. I cut each one his share, and each one of us eat our day's allowance in one mouthful of this salt pork, and nothing else. One day, called pea day, I took the drawer of our doctor's (Hodges of Philadelphia) chest, and went to the galley, which was the cooking place, (like a poor Pil Garlick), with my drawer for a soup dish. I held it under a large brass cock; the cook turned it. I received the allowance of my mess, and behold! brown water and fifteen floating peas—no peas on the bottom of my drawer—and this for six men's allowance for 24 hours. The peas were all on the bottom of the kettle; those left would be taken to New York, and, I suppose, sold. One day in the week, called pudding day, three pounds of damaged flour; in it would be green lumps, such as their men would not eat, and one pound of very bad raisins—one third raisin sticks. We would pick out the sticks, mash the lumps of flour, put

all, with some water, in our drawer, mix our pudding, and
put it in a bag, with a talley tied to it with the number of our
mess. This was a day's allowance. We, for some short time,
drew half a pint of rum for each man. One Captain Lard,
who commanded the ship Jersey, came on board. As soon as
he was on the main deck of the ship, he cried out for the boatswain. The boatswain arrived, and, in a very quick motion,
took off his hat. There being on deck two half hogshead
tubs where our allowance of rum was mixed into grog, Captain Lard said, 'Have the prisoners had their rum to-day?'
'No, sir,' answered the boatswain. Captain Lard replied,
'Damn your soul, you rascal, heave it overboard.' The boatswain, with help, upset the tubs of grog on the main deck.
The grog rum ran out of the scuppers of the ship into the
river. I saw no more grog on board. I stood at the time
within twelve feet of the tubs of grog—saw the grog, run
through the scuppers of the ship. * * * Every fair day a
number of British officers and sergeants would come on board
ship, form in two ranks on the quarter-deck, facing inward—
the prisoners in the after part of the quarter-deck. As the
boatswain would call a name, the word would be, 'pass,' as
the prisoners passed between the ranks, officers and sergeants
staring them in the face. This was done to catch deserters,
and if they caught none, the sergeants would come on the
main deck, and cry out, 'Five guineas' bounty to any man
that will enter his majesty's service.' Shortly after this party
left the ship, a Hessian party would come on board, and

the prisoners had to go through the same routine of duty again."

EBENEZER FOX, (whose portrait we present to the reader,) was a prisoner during the spring and summer of 1781. He says:

" The first thing we found it necessary to do, after our captivity, was to form ourselves into small parties called '*messes*,' consisting of six men each, as, previous to doing this, we could obtain no food. All the prisoners were obliged to fast on the first day of their arrival; and seldom on the second could they procure any food in season for cooking it. No matter how hungry they were, no deviation from the rules of the ship was permitted. All the prisoners fared alike; officers and sailors received the same treatment on board of this old hulk. Our keepers were no respecters of persons. We were all 'Rebels.' The quantity and quality of our fare was the same for all. The only distinction known among us was made by the prisoners themselves, which was shown in allowing those who had been officers previous to their capture to congregate in the extreme after-part of the ship, and to keep it exclusively to themselves as their places of abode. The various messes of the prisoners were numbered; and nine in the morning was the hour when the steward would deliver from the window in his room, at the after-part of the ship, the allowance granted to each mess. Each mess chose one of their company to be prepared to answer to their number when it was called by the steward, and to receive the allowance as it

EBENEZER FOX.

was handed from the window. Whatever was thrust out must be taken; no change could be made in its quantity or quality. Each mess received daily what was equivalent in weight or measure, but not in quality, to the rations of four men at full allowance: that is, each prisoner received two-thirds as much as was allowed to a seaman in the British navy. Our bill of fare was as follows: On Sunday, one pound of biscuit, one pound of pork, and a half of a pint of peas. Monday, one pound of biscuit, one pint of oatmeal, and two ounces of butter. Tuesday, one pound of biscuit, and two pounds of salt beef. Wednesday, one and a half pounds of flour, and two ounces of suet. Thursday was a repetition of Sunday's fare, Friday of Monday's, and Saturday of Tuesday's. If this food had been of a good quality and properly cooked, as we had no labor to perform, it would have kept us comfortable, at least from suffering. But this was not the case. All our food appeared to be damaged. The bread was mouldy and filled with worms. It required considerable rapping upon the deck before the worms could be dislodged from their lurking places in a biscuit. As for the pork, we were cheated out of it more than half of the time; and when it was obtained, one would have judged from its motley hues, exhibiting the consistence and appearance of variegated fancy soap, that it was the flesh of the porpoise, or sea-hog, and had been an inhabitant of the ocean rather than of the sty. But, whatever doubts might arise respecting the genera or species of the beast, the flavor of the flesh was so unsavory that it would have been rejected

as unfit for the stuffing even of Bologna sausages. The peas
were generally damaged, and, from the imperfect manner in
which they were cooked, were about as indigestible as grape-
shot. The butter the reader will not suppose was the real
' Goshen;' and, had it not been for its adhesive properties to
retain together the particles of the biscuit that had been so
riddled by the worms as to lose all their attraction of cohesion,
we should have considered it no desirable addition to our
viands. The flour and the oatmeal were often sour, and when
the suet was mixed with it we should have considered it a
blessing to have been destitute of the sense of smelling before
we admitted it into our mouths; it might be nosed half the
length of the ship. And last, though not the least item among
our staples in the eating line—our beef. The first view of it
would excite an idea of veneration for its antiquity, and not a
little curiosity to ascertain to what kind of an animal it originally belonged. Its color was of dark mahogany, and its
solidity would have set the keen edge of a broad-axe at defiance
to cut across the grain, though like oakum it could be pulled
into pieces, one way in strings, like rope-yarn. A streak of
fat on it would have been a phenomenon, that would have
brought all the prisoners together to see and admire. It was
so completely saturated with salt, that after having been
boiled in water taken from the sea, it was found to be considerably freshened by the process. It was no uncommon thing
to find it extremely tender; but then this peculiarity was not
owing to its being a prime cut from a premium ox, but rather

owing to its long-keeping—the vicissitudes of heat and cold, of humidity and aridity it had experienced in the course of time ; and of this disposition to tenderness we were duly apprised by the extraordinary fragrance it emitted before and after it was cooked. It required more skill than we possessed to determine whether the flesh, which we were obliged to devour, had once covered the bones of some luckless bull that had died from starvation, or of some worn-out horse that had been killed for the crime of having outlived his usefulness. Such was our food; but the quality of it was not all that we had reason to complain of. The manner in which it was cooked was more injurious to our health than the quality of the food ; and, in many cases, laid the foundation of diseases, that brought many a sufferer to his grave, years after his liberation. The cooking for the prisoners was done in a great copper vessel that contained between two and three hogsheads of water set in brick work. The form of it was square, and it was divided into two compartments by a partition. In one of these the peas and oatmeal were boiled; this was done in fresh water ; in the other the meat was boiled, in salt water taken up from along side of the ship. The Jersey, from her size and lying near the shore, was imbedded in the mud ; and I do not recollect seeing her afloat during the whole time I was a prisoner. All the filth that accumulated among upwards of a thousand men were daily thrown overboard and would remain there till carried away by the tide. The impurity of the water may be easily conceived, and in this water our meat was boiled.

It will be recollected, too, that the water was salt, which caused the inside of the copper to become corroded to such a degree that it was lined with a coat of verdigris. Meat thus cooked must, in some degree, be poisoned; and the effects of it were manifest in the cadaverous countenances of the emaciated beings who had remained on board for any length of time. The persons chosen by each mess to receive their portions of food, were summoned by the cook's bell to receive their allowance; and when it had remained in the boiler a certain time, the bell would again sound, and the allowance must be immediately taken away. Whether it was sufficiently cooked or not it could remain no longer. The food was generally very imperfectly cooked; yet this sustenance, wretched as it was, and deficient in quantity, was greedily devoured by the half starved prisoners. No vegetables were allowed us. Many times since, when I have seen in the country a large kettle of potatoes and pumpkins steaming over the fire to satisfy the appetites of a farmer's swine, I have thought of our destitute and starved condition, and what a luxury we should have considered the contents of that kettle on board the Jersey." * * * "About two hours before sunset, orders were given to the prisoners to carry all their things below; but we were permitted to remain above till we retired for the night into our unhealthy and crowded dungeons. At sunset, our ears were saluted with the insulting and hateful sound from our keepers, of ' *Down, rebels, down,*' and we were hurried below, the hatchways fastened over us, and we were left to pass the night amid the accumulated horrors of sighs and groans, of foul vapor, a nauseous and putrid atmosphere, in a stifled and almost suffocating heat. The tiers of holes through the sides of the ship were strongly grated, but not provided with glass; and it was considered a privilege to sleep near one of these apertures in hot weather, for the pure air that passed in at them. But little sleep, however, could be enjoyed even there; for the vermin were so horribly abundant, that all the personal cleanliness we could practice, would not protect us from their attacks, or prevent their effecting a lodgment upon us. * * * The long detention of American sailors on board of British prison-ships was to be attributed to the little pains that were taken by our countrymen to retain British subjects, who were taken prisoners on the ocean during the war. Our privateers captured many British seamen, who, when willing to enlist in our service, as was generally the case, were received on board of our ships. Those who were brought into port, were suffered to go at large; for, in the impoverished condition of the country, no state or town was willing to subject itself to the expense of maintaining prisoners in a state of confinement; they were permitted to provide for themselves. In this way, the number of British seamen was too small for a regular and equal exchange. Thus the British seamen, after their capture, enjoyed the blessings of liberty, the light of the sun, and the purity of the atmosphere, while the poor American sailors were compelled to drag out a miserable existence amid want and distress, famine and pestilence. As every principle of justice and humanity was disregarded by the British in the treatment of their prisoners, so likewise every moral and legal right was violated in compelling them to enter into their service. We had obtained some information in relation to an expected draft that would soon be made upon the prisoners to fill up a complement of men that were wanted for the service of his majesty's fleet. One day, in the latter part of August, our fears of the dreaded event were realized. A British officer, with a number of soldiers, came on board. The prisoners were all ordered on deck, placed on the larboard gang-way, and marched in single file round to the quarter-deck where the officers stood to inspect them and select such ones as suited their fancies, without any reference to the rights of the prisoners, or considering at all the duties they owed to the land of their nativity, or the government for which they had fought and suffered. The argument was, 'Men we want, and men we will have.' We continued to march round, in solemn and melancholy procession, till they had selected from among our number about three hundred of the ablest, nearly all of whom were Americans; and they were directed to go below under a guard, to collect together whatever things they wished to take belonging to them. They were then driven into the boats, waiting alongside, and left the prison-ship, not to enjoy their freedom, but to be subjected to the iron despotism, and galling slavery of a British man-of-war; to waste their lives in a foreign service, and toil for masters whom they hated. Such, however, were the horrors of our situation as prisoners, and so small was the prospect of relief, that we almost envied the lot of those who left the ship to go into the service even of our enemy. * * * The food given the imprisoned rebels, as the British called them, was not only deficient in quantity, but even the scanty portion dealt them was such as would scarcely be tolerated by the meanest beggar, being generally that which had been rejected by the British ships, as unfit to be eaten by the sailors, and unwholesome in the highest degree, as well as disgusting in taste and appearance. * * * Many were *actually starved to death*, in hope of making them enroll themselves in the British army."

Revolutionary Adventures of Ebenezer Fox, 1st ed., p. 98–135–138.

THOMAS ANDROS, who was confined as a prisoner during the fall of 1781, says :

"Our water was good, could we have had enough of it. Our bread was bad in the superlative degree. I do not recollect seeing any which was not full of living vermin; but eat it, worms and all, we must, or starve."

Old Jersey Captive, p. 17.

ANDREW SHERBURNE, who was on board during the winter of 1781–2, says :

"The ship was extremely filthy, and abounded with vermin. A large proportion of the prisoners had been robbed of their clothing. The ship was considerably crowded; many of the

men were very low spirited; our provisions ordinary, and very
scanty. It consisted of worm-eaten ship bread, and salt beef.
It was supposed that this bread and beef had been condemned
in the British navy. The bread had been so eaten by weevils,
that one might easily crush it in the hand and blow it away.
The beef was exceedingly salt, and scarcely a particle of fat
could be seen upon it."

Memoirs of Andrew Sherburne, 1st ed., p. 107 ; 2d ed. p. 110.

THOMAS DRING, (whose portrait is here for the first time presented
to the public,) was a prisoner in 1782. He says:

"During my confinement in the summer of 1782, the
average number of prisoners on board the Jersey, was about
one thousand. We, as prisoners, were allowed each day for
six men, what was equal in quantity to the rations of *four*
men at *full allowance.* That is, each prisoner was furnished
in quantity with two-thirds of the allowance of a seaman in
the British Navy, which was as follows:

On Sunday.....1 lb. of biscuit, 1 lb. of pork, and half a pint of peas.
" *Monday* ....1 lb. of biscuit, 1 pint of oat meal, 2 ounces of butter.
" *Tuesday* ...1 lb. of biscuit, and two lbs. of beef.
" *Wednesday* .1½ lbs. of flour, and two ounces of suet.
" *Thursday*...The same as Sunday.
" *Friday* .....The same as Monday.
" *Saturday* ...The same as Tuesday.

Hence, as prisoners, whenever we had our due, we received, as they said, two-thirds of the ordinary allowance of
their own seamen; and even this was of a very inferior

CAPT. THOMAS DRING.

quality. We never received any butter; but in its stead, they gave us a substance which they called sweet oil. This was so rancid, and even putrid, that the smell of it, accustomed as we were to everything foul and nauseous, was more than we could endure. We, however, always received and gave it to the poor, half-starved Frenchmen who were on board, who took it gratefully, and swallowed it with a little salt and their wormy bread. Oil of a similar quality was given to the prisoners on board the Good Hope, where I was confined in 1779. There, however, it was of some use to us, as we burnt it in our lamps, being there indulged with the privilege of using lights until nine o'clock at night. But here, it was of no service, as we were allowed on board the Jersey, no light or fire, on any occasion whatever." * * * " Terrible indeed was the condition of most of my fellow captives. Memory still brings before me those emaciated beings, moving from the Galley, with their wretched pittance of meat; each creeping to the spot where his mess were assembled, to divide it with a group of haggard and sickly creatures, their garments hanging in tatters around their meagre limbs, and the hue of death upon their care-worn faces. By these, it was consumed with their scanty remnants of bread, which was often mouldy and filled with worms. And even from this vile fare, they would rise up, in torments, from the cravings of unsatisfied hunger and thirst. No vegetables of any description were ever afforded us by our inhuman keepers. Good heaven! what a luxury to us would then have been even a few potatoes, if but the very leavings of the swine of our country." * * * "So much of the water as was not required on deck for immediate use, was conducted into butts placed in the lower hold of the hulk, through a leathern hose, passing through her side near the bends. To this water, we had recourse, when we could procure no other. When water in any degree fit for use, was brought on board, it is impossible to describe the struggle which ensued in consequence of our haste and exertions to procure a draught of it. The best which was ever afforded us, was very brackish, but that from the ship's hold was nauseous in the highest degree. This must be evident, when the fact is stated, that the butts for receiving it had never been cleaned since they were placed in the hold. The quantity of foul sediment which they contained, was therefore very great, and was disturbed and mixed with the water as often as a new supply was poured into them; thereby rendering their whole contents a substance of the most disgusting and poisonous nature. I have not the least doubt, that the use of this vile compound, caused the deaths of hundreds of the prisoners; when to allay their tormenting thirst, they were driven by desperation to drink this liquid poison, and to abide the consequences." * * * "The quarter-deck covered about one-fourth part of the upper deck, from the stern; and the forecastle extended from the stern, about one-eighth part of the length of the upper deck. Sentinels were stationed on the gangways on each side of the upper deck leading from the quarter-deck to the forecastle. These gang-

ways were about five feet wide, and here the prisoners were allowed to pass and repass. The intermediate space from the bulk head of the quarter-deck to the forecastle, was filled with long spars or booms, and called the Spar Deck. The temporary covering afforded by the spar deck, was of the greatest benefit to the prisoners, as it served to shield us from the rain and the scorching rays of the sun. It was here, also, that our moveables were placed while we were engaged in cleaning the lower decks. The spar deck was also the only place where we were allowed to walk, and was, therefore, continually crowded through the day, by those of the prisoners who were upon deck. Owing to the great number of the prisoners, and the small place afforded us by the spar deck, it was our custom to walk, in platoons, each facing the same way, and turning at the same time. The derrick, for taking in wood, water, etc., stood on the starboard side of the spar deck. On the larboard side of the ship was placed the accommodation ladder, leading from the gangway to the water. At the head of this ladder, a sentinel was also stationed. The head of the accommodation ladder was near the door of the barricado, which extended across the front of the quarter-deck, and projected a few feet beyond the sides of the ship. The barricado was about ten feet high, and was pierced with loop-holes for musketry, in order that the prisoners might be fired on from behind it, if occasion should require.   *   *   *
The prisoners were confined on the two main decks below. My usual place of abode being in the Gun Room, on the centre

deck, I was never under the necessity of descending to the
lower dungeon, and during my confinement, I had no disposition to visit it. It was inhabited by the most wretched in
appearance of all our miserable company. From the disgusting and squalid appearance of the groupes which I saw ascend-
ing the stairs which led to it, it must have been more dismal,
if possible, than that part of the hulk where I resided.
* * * As soon as the gratings had been fastened over the
hatchways for the night, we generally went to our sleeping-
places. It was, of course, always desirable to obtain a station
as near as possible to the side of the ship, and if practicable,
in the immediate vicinity of one of the air-ports, as this not
only afforded us a better air, but also rendered us less liable
to be trodden upon by those who were moving about the
decks, during the night. But silence was a stranger to our
dark abode. There were continual noises during the night.
The groans of the sick and the dying; the curses poured out
by the weary and exhausted upon our inhuman keepers; the
restlessness caused by the suffocating heat and the confined
and poisoned air; mingled with the wild and incoherent
ravings of delirium, were the sounds which, every night, were
raised around us, in all directions. Such was our ordinary
situation; but at times, the consequences of our crowded condition were still more terrible, and proved fatal to many of
our number, in a single night. * * * A custom had long
been established, that certain labor which it was necessary
should be performed daily, should be done by a company,

usually called the 'Working Party.' This consisted of about twenty able-bodied men, chosen from among the prisoners, and was commanded, in daily rotation, by those of our number who had formerly been officers of vessels. The commander of the party for the day, bore the title of *Boatswain*. The members of the Working Party received, as a compensation for their services, a full allowance of provisions, and a half pint of rum each, per day, with the privilege of going on deck, early in the morning, to breathe the pure air. This privilege alone, was a sufficient compensation for all the duty which was required of them. Their routine of service was, to wash down that part of the upper deck and gangways where the prisoners were permitted to walk; to spread the awning, and to hoist on board the wood, water, and other supplies, from the boats in which the same were brought along side the ship. When the prisoners ascended the upper deck, in the morning, if the day was fair, each carried up his hammock and bedding, which were all placed upon the spar deck or booms. The Working Party then took the sick and disabled who remained below, and placed them in the bunks prepared for them upon the centre deck; they then, if any of the prisoners had died during the night, carried up the dead bodies, and laid them upon the booms. After which, it was their duty to wash down the main decks below; during which operation, the prisoners remained upon the upper deck, except such as chose to go below, and volunteer their services in the performance of this duty. Around the railing of the hatchway leading from the centre to the lower deck, were placed a number of large tubs for the occasional use of the prisoners during the night, and as general receptacles of filth. Although these were indispensably necessary to us, yet they were highly offensive. Nevertheless, on account of our crowded situation,. many of the prisoners were obliged to sleep in their immediate vicinity. It was a part of the duty of the Working Party to carry these tubs on deck, at the time when the prisoners ascended in the morning, and to return them between decks in the afternoon. Our beds and clothing were kept on deck, until it was nearly the hour when we were to be ordered below for the night. During this interval, the chests, etc., on the lower decks being piled up, and the hammocks removed, the decks washed and cleared of all incumbrances except the poor wretches who lay in the bunks; it was quite refreshing, after the suffocating heat and foul vapours of the night, to walk between decks. There was then some circulation of air through the ship; and for a few hours, our existence was, in some degree, tolerable. About two hours before sunset, the order was generally issued for the prisoners to carry their hammocks, etc., below. After this had been done, we were allowed either to retire between decks, or to remain above until sunset, according to our own pleasure. Everything which we could do conducive to cleanliness having then been performed, if we ever felt anything like enjoyment in this wretched abode, it was during this brief interval, when we breathed the cool air of the approaching night, and felt the luxury of our evening pipe. But short indeed was this period of repose. The working party were soon ordered to carry the tubs below, and we prepared to descend to our gloomy and crowded dungeons. This was no sooner done, than the gratings were closed over the hatchways, the sentinels stationed, and we left to sicken and pine beneath our accumulated torments, with our guards above crying aloud, through the long night, ' *all's well*.'"

Dring's Recollections of the Jersey Prison-ship, pp. 43–92.

The following impromptu lines are too appropriate to omit in this connection:

> "In yonder ship, 'tis strange to tell,
> Each night they cry out, ' All is well!'
> Though sick and sad doth there abound:
> Some with consumption, some with wound;
> And other evils far too long,
> Thus to describe in transient song:
> Then, why do they bawl, with ruffian-note,
> And strain the lungs, and stretch the throat;
> When all's *not well*, we clearly know—
> If *well above*, they're *sick below*."

ALEXANDER COFFIN, JR., who was a prisoner in the year 1782, and again in 1783, says:

" I was sent on board the Jersey prison-ship, where I found about 1,100 American prisoners; amongst them several of my own townsmen, and all the prisoners in the most deplorable situation. I soon found that every spark of humanity had fled the breasts of the British officers who had charge of that float-ing receptacle of human misery; and that nothing but abuse and insult was to be expected; for the mildest language made use of to the prisoners was, ' *You damn'd Yankee;*' and the most common, ' *You damn'd rebellious Yankee rascals.*' This language, at length, became so familiar to our ears, however insulting it was at first, that we took no more notice of it than we did of the whistling of the wind passing over our heads. Many of the prisoners, during the severity of winter, had scarcely clothes sufficient to cover their nakedness, and but very few enough to keep them warm. To remedy these inconveniences we were obliged to keep below, and either get into our hammocks or keep in constant motion, without which precautions we must have perished. But to cap the climax of infamy, we were fed (if fed it might be called) with provisions not fit for any human being to make use of—putrid beef and pork, and worm-eaten bread, condemned on board their ships of war, was sent on board the Jersey to feed the prisoners; water sent from this city in a schooner called (emphatically called) the Relief! water which I affirm, without the fear of refutation, was worse than I ever had, or ever saw, on a three years' voyage to the East Indies; water, the scent of which would have discomposed the olfactory nerves of a Hottentot; while within a cable's length of the ship, on Long Island, there was running before our eyes, as though intended to tantalize us, as fine, pure and wholesome water as any man would wish to drink. The question will very naturally be asked, Why, if good water was so near at hand, it was not procured for us instead of bringing it, at considerable expense

and trouble from the city? It is impossible for any one, but
those who had the direction of the business, to answer that
question satisfactorily : but the object in bringing the water
from New-York was to me, and the rest of the prisoners, as
self-evident as the plain and simple fact that two and two make
four : because the effects that water had on the prisoners
could not be concealed, and were a damning proof why it was
filled in New-York. On the upper gun deck of the Jersey,
hogs were kept in pens by those officers who had charge of
her for their own use ; they were sometimes fed with bran ;
the prisoners, whenever they could get an opportunity, undis-
covered by the sentries, would, with their tin pots, scoop the
bran from the troughs and eat it, (after boiling, when there
was fire in the galley, which was not always the case,) with
seemingly as good an appetite as the hogs themselves.
* * * There being so many prisoners on board the Jersey,
and others daily arriving, two or three hundred of us were
sent on board the John transport, which they had converted
into a Prison-ship, and where the treatment we received was
much worse than on board the Jersey. We were subjected to
every insult, every injury, and every abuse that the fertile
genius of the British officers could invent and inflict. For
more than a month we were obliged to eat our scanty allowance, bad as it was, without cooking, as no fire was allowed
us ; and I verily believe that it was the means of hastening
many out of existence. One circumstance I think deserves
particular notice, as it was a most singular one: A young

man of the name of Bird, a native of Boston or its neighbour-hood, was one evening, with others, playing at cards to pass away the time. At about ten o'clock I retired with my cousin to our hammock; we had but just got asleep when we were called by one of the card party, who requested us to turn out, for that Bird was dying: we did turn out, and went to where he lay, and found him in the agonies of death; and in about fifteen or twenty minutes he was a corpse. It was mentioned to the sentry at the gangway that one of the pri-soners was dead, and the body was soon hurried on deck. The impression Bird's death made on our minds is still fresh in my recollection: that he was poisoned we had no doubt, as his body had swelled very considerably, and two hours be-fore he was, to all appearance, as well as any of us. Many, shortly after, went off in the same manner, and amongst them my cousin, Oliver C. Coffin. I did but just escape the same fate: I was taken ill before I left the Prison-ship, and my legs began to swell; but being exchanged, or rather being bought off, I made out to reach my father's house in a most deplorable situation. I was attended in my sickness by a noted tory physician, Dr. Tupper, who declared to my mother, that noth-ing could have saved my life but having, as he expressed him-self, a constitution of iron; for that he knew of nothing that could have affected me in the manner in which I was affected but poison of some kind or other. Is it possible then, after all these facts, for any person to form any other opinion than that there was a premeditated, organized system pursued to destroy men whom they dare not meet openly and manfully as enemies, in that base, inhuman and cowardly manner. It is an old adage, and a very true one, that the brave are generous, and the coward savage and cruel; and it was never more completely exemplified than in the conduct of the British officers in this country during the revolution. Their cruelties here, and in India, have become proverbial."

Interment of the Martyrs, p. 29–30, *and* 32–34.

> " No waters laded from the bubbling spring
> To these dire ships these little tyrants bring—
> By plank and ponderous beams completely wall'd
> In vain for water and in vain we call'd—
> No drop was granted to the midnight prayer,
> To *rebels* in these regions of despair !—
> The loathsome cask a deadly dose contains,
> Its poison circling through the languid veins ;
>   ' Here, *generous* Briton, generous, as you say,
>   ' To my parch'd tongue one cooling drop convey,
>   ' Hell has no mischief like a thirsty throat,
>   ' Nor one tormentor like your *David Sproat.*'
>   *   *   *   *   *   *
> On every side dire objects met the sight,
> And pallid forms, and murders of the night,—
> The dead were past their pain, the living groan,
> Nor dare to hope another morn their own.
>   *   *   *   *   *   *
> Hunger and thirst, to work our woe, combine,
> And mouldy bread and flesh of rotten swine,
> The mangled carcase, and the batter'd brain,
> The doctor's poison, and the captain's cane,
> The soldier's musquet, and the steward's debt,
> The evening shackle, and the noon-day threat.
>   *   *   *   *   *   *
> Such food they sent to make complete our woes,
> It look'd like carrion torn from hungry crows ;

Such vermin vile on every joint were seen,
So black, corrupted, mortified and lean,
That once we try'd to move our flinty chief,
And thus address'd him, holding up the beef;
  ' See, Captain, see ! what rotten bones we pick,
' What kills the healthy, cannot cure the sick :
' Not dogs on such by *Christian* men are fed—
' And see, good master, see, what lousy bread.'

  ' Your meat or bread (this man of death replied)
' 'Tis not my care to manage or provide—
' But this, base rebel dogs, I'd have you know,
' That better than you merit we bestow :
' Out of my sight !'—nor more he deign'd to say,
But whisk'd about, and frowning, strode away."

FRENEAU.

(43) There were at this time two Hospital-ships lying near the Jersey, one of which was the SCORPION, and the other the STROMBOLO. They were used for the reception of the sick from the prison-ship, and of the many unfortunate beings who entered those vessels as patients, but very few ever left them alive. There was also another hulk lying at a short distance from the Jersey, named the HUNTER, which Capt. Dring, to whom we have before referred, thinks was used as a store-ship and depot for the Medical department.

The SCORPION was originally a sloop of war, and had mounted 14 guns. In 1759 she was at the reduction of Quebec, under Saunders, and in 1772, was on duty in the Mediterranean. In the following year, she was under the orders of Hon. G. K. Elphinston. In 1776, she was commanded by John Tollemache; in the year following, she composed one of Lord

Howe's fleet in America, and in 1779, she was one of the squadron of Sir George Collier, that anchored off New Haven, Conn., and burnt the towns of Fairfield, Norwalk and Greenfield. In 1780 she was used as a prison-ship, and lay in the North river. Among those who were confined in her at that time, amounting to about 300, was the celebrated Philip Freneau, who has left us a poetical account of his treatment and sufferings while a prisoner. On the 6th December of that year, she was offered for sale by the Naval Storekeeper at New York, but found no purchaser. She was soon after fitted up as a hospital-ship, and moved to the Wallabout, where she was used in that capacity to the end of the war.

The STROMBOLO was originally a fire-ship. In the year 1759, she was commanded by Richard Smith, and was at the siege of Quebec. In 1763 she was under the orders of W. Pattison, and was on duty in the Mediterranean. She came to America in 1776, in the fleet of Commodore William Hotham, and in company with the Jersey hospital-ship, then so called. In 1777 she was commanded by James Reid, and in 1778 by Richard Aplin. In the latter year she was in the fleet of Lord Howe, off the coast of Rhode Island, in presence of the French fleet. She was afterwards stationed in the North river, and used as a prison-ship. She was under the command of Jeremiah Downer from Aug. 21st to Dec. 10th, 1780, during which time she had never less than 150 prisoners on board, and frequently over 200.

SILAS TALBOT gives the following incident as occurring on board this vessel, while she was used as a prison-ship :

"The prisoners confined on board the *Strombolo* prison-ship, anchored in the North river, having been irritated by their ill treatment to rise one night on the guard, the commander being on shore, several, in attempting to escape, were either killed or wounded. The captain got on board just as the fray was quelled, when a poor fellow lying on deck, bleeding, and almost exhausted by a mortal wound, called him by name, and begged of him, '*for God's sake, a little water, for he was dying!*' The captain applied a light to his face, and directly exclaimed—'*What! is it you, d—n you?—I'm glad you're shot!—If I knew the man that shot you, I'd give him a guinea!—Take that, you d—d rebel rascal!*'—and instantly dashed his foot in the face of the dying man!!"

Historical Sketch of the Life of Silas Talbot, p. 127.

On the 6th December, 1780, the Strombolo was advertised for sale, but no purchaser appeared. Soon after this, she was fitted up as a hospital-ship, and moved to the Wallabout, where she was used as such to the close of the war.

The HUNTER was originally a sloop of war, mounting ten guns, and had a pink-colored stern. In 1764 she was commanded by John Henshaw, and in 1774 by Jeremiah Morgan. On the 6th Dec., 1780, she was advertised for sale by the Naval Store-keeper, but no purchaser was found. She then lay in the North river. She was subsequently moved to the Wallabout, where she was in service as before mentioned.

The following is a copy of the advertisement of the sale of these hulks, to which we have referred :

"Naval Store-keeper's Office, Dec. 4, 1780.

NOTICE is hereby given, that on Wednesday, the 13th instant, will be offered for sale at this office at twelve o'clock, the Hulls of his Majesty's sloops the SCORPION and HUNTER, and of the STROMBOLO fire ship, now lying in the North River.

WIL. FOWLER."

Rivington's Royal Gazette, Wed., Dec. 6, 1780.

There were, during the Revolution, other vessels at different times used as prison-ships and hospital-ships, in addition to these, such as the Whitby, Frederick, Glasgow, Prince of Wales, Falmouth, Good Intent, Hope, Chatham, Kitty, John, Scheldt, Clyde, and others, but as they do not properly come under our notice at this time, we must pass them by, with this mere mention of their names.

In order that the reader may form some idea of the treatment on board the hospital-ships, and the sufferings and deaths therein, we append the following extracts, to which we invite attention. The scenes occurring in one or two of these vessels, may be taken as a fair example of what took place in all :

PHILIP FRENEAU (who was on board the Scorpion in 1780,) thus speaks of her :

"Thou, Scorpion, fatal to thy crowded throng,
Dire theme of horror and Plutonian song,
Requir'st my lay—thy sultry decks I know,
And all the torments that exist below !
The briny wave that Hudson's bosom fills

Drain'd through her bottom in a thousand rills :
Rotten and old, replete with sighs and groans,
Scarce on the waters she sustain'd her bones ;
Here, doom'd to toil, or founder in the tide,
At the moist pumps incessantly we ply'd,
Here, doom'd to starve, like famish'd dogs, we tore
The scant allowance that our tyrants bore.

*   *   *   *   *   *

O may I ne'er review these dire abodes,
These piles for slaughter, floating on the floods,—
And you, that o'er the troubled ocean go,
Strike not your standards to this venom'd foe ;
Better the greedy wave should swallow all,
Better to meet the death-conducting ball,
Better to sleep on ocean's oozy bed,
At once destroy'd and number'd with the dead,
Than thus to perish in the face of day,
Where twice ten thousand deaths one death delay.''

JOHN VAN DYK, (who was on board the Hunter in 1780,) says:

" From the Jersey Prison ship, eighty of us were taken to the pink stern sloop of war Hunter, Capt. Thomas Henderson, commander ; we were taken there in a large ship's long boat, towed by a ten-oar barge, and one other barge with a guard of soldiers in the rear to guard the prisoners. On board the ship Hunter we drew one-third allowance, and every Monday we received a loaf of wet bread, weighing seven pounds for each man—this loaf was from Mr. John Pintard's father, of New York, the American Commissary—and this bread, with the two-thirds allowance of provisions, we found sufficient to live on. After we were on board the Hunter for some time, Mr. David Sproat, the British commissary of prisoners, came on board; all the prisoners were ordered aft—the roll was

called, and as each man passed him, Mr. Sproat would ask,
'Are you a seaman?' The answer was Landsman—Landsman. There were ten landsmen to one answer of half seaman.
When the roll was finished, Mr. Sproat said to our sea officers,
'Gentlemen, how do you make out at sea, for the most of you
are landsmen?' Our officers answered, 'You hear often how
we make out—when we meet our force, or rather more than
our force, we give a good account of them.' Mr. Sproat
asked, 'And are not your vessels better manned than these?'
Our officers replied, 'Mr. Sproat, we are the best manned out
of the port of Philadelphia.' Mr. Sproat shrugged his shoulders, saying, 'I cannot see how you do it.'"

CAPT. THOMAS DRING, whom we have before quoted, says:

"The three Hospital ships, Scorpion, Strombolo, and Hunter,
were used for the reception of the sick from the principal
hulk. The Jersey, at length, became so crowded, and the
mortality on board her increased so rapidly, that sufficient
room could not be found on board the Hospital ships, for their
reception. Under these dreadful circumstances, it was determined to prepare a part of the upper deck of the Jersey, for
the reception of the sick from between decks. Bunks were
therefore erected on the after part of the upper deck, on the
larboard side, where those who felt the symptoms of approaching sickness, could lie down, in order to be found by the
Nurses as soon as possible; and be thereby also prevented
from being trampled upon by the other prisoners; to which

they were continually liable while lying on the deck. I have stated that the number of the Hospital ships was three. One of them, however, was used rather as a store-ship and depot for the medical department; and as a station for the Doctor's Mates and boat's crews attending the whole.—This ship was, I think, the Hunter. I never was on board either of the Hospital ships; and could never learn many particulars in relation to the treatment of the sufferers on board them; for but few ever returned from their recesses, to the Jersey. I knew but three such instances during the whole period of my imprisonment. But I could form some idea of the interior of the Hospital ships, from viewing their outward appearance, which was disgusting in the highest degree. Knowing, as we did, from whence their wretched inmates had been taken, the sight of these vessels was terrible to us, and their appearance more shocking than that of our own miserable hulk. But whatever might be our sensations on viewing the Hospital ships, they were, undoubtedly, in many respects, preferable to the Jersey. They were not so crowded, and of course afforded more room for breathing. They were furnished with awnings, and provided with a wind-sail to each hatchway, for the purpose of conducting the fresh air between decks, where the sick were placed. And, more than all, the hatchways were left open during the night; as our kind keepers were under no apprehensions of danger from the feeble and helpless wretches who were there deposited. When communication between the ships was required, or anything wanted; it was made

known by signals, which were promptly attended to by the
boats from the Hunter. Our condition caused our keepers
much labour; and furnished employment, which to some of
them was far from being agreeable. There were on board the
Jersey, among the prisoners, about half a dozen men, known
by the appellation of 'Nurses.' I never learnt by whom they
were appointed, or whether they had any regular appointment
at all. But one fact I well knew; they were all thieves. They
were, however, sometimes useful in assisting the sick to ascend
from below, to the gangway on the upper deck, to be examined
by the visiting Surgeon, who attended from the Hunter, every
day, (when the *weather* was good.) If a sick man was pro-
nounced by the Surgeon, to be a proper subject for one of the
Hospital ships, he was forthwith put into the boat in waiting
along side; but not without the loss or detention of all his
effects, if he had any; as these were at once taken into possession by the Nurses, as their own property. I will here relate
an incident; not on account of its extreme aggravation; but
because it occurred immediately under my own eye; which
will shew in some degree, the kind of treatment which was
given by these Nurses to the poor, weak and dying men who
were left to their care; and who were about to be transported
to a Hospital ship, and, in all probability, in a few hours, to
the sand bank on the shore. I had found Mr. Robert Carver,
our Gunner while on board the Chance, sick in one of the
bunks where those retired who wished to be removed. He
was without a bed or pillow; and had put on all the wearing

apparel which he possessed, wishing to preserve it, and being sensible of his situation. I found him sitting upright in the bunk, with his great coat on over the rest of his garments, and his hat between his knees. The weather was excessively hot; and in the place where he lay, the heat was overpowering. I at once saw that he was delirious; a sure presage that his end was near. I took off his great coat, and having folded and placed it under his head for a pillow, I laid him down upon it, and went immediately to prepare him some tea. I was absent but a few minutes; and on returning, met one of the thievish Nurses, with Carver's great coat in his hand. On ordering him to return it, his only reply was, that it was a perquisite of the Nurses, and the only one they had: that the man was dying; and the garment could be of no further use to him. I however took possession of the coat; and on my liberation, returned it to the family of the owner. Mr. Carver soon after expired where he lay. We procured a blanket; in which we wrapped his body, which was thus prepared for interment. Others of the crew of the Chance had died previous to that time. Mr. Carver was a man of strong and robust constitution. Such men were subject to the most violent attacks of the fever; and were, also, its most certain victims. I attach no blame to our keepers, in regard to the thievish habits of the Nurses, over whom they had no control. I have merely related this incident for the purpose of more clearly showing to what a state of wretchedness we were reduced."

Dring's Recollections of the Jersey Prison-ship, p. 70-75.

ANDREW SHERBURNE, who was a prisoner on board a hospital-ship, gives the following account of his experience :

"Some time in January, 1783, I was taken sick, and sent on board one of the hospital ships. This circumstance occasioned a distressing scene, both to myself and my uncle. My money was entirely gone; my uncle had yet a few dollars; I think he gave me a dollar or two, and we parted, with little expectation of ever meeting again. The ship on which I entered was called the Frederick, and was very much crowded; so that two men were obliged to lie in one bunk. I was put into a bunk with a young man whose name was Wills; he belonged to Ipswich, in Massachusetts. The bunk sat fore and aft, directly under the ballast port, opposite the main hatchway. Wills was a very pleasant young man, of a serious turn, and was persuaded he should not live. At this time my mind was very fluctuating, and occasionally deranged. My bed-fellow was running down very fast; but I was not, at that time, aware of it. We were obliged, occasionally, to lay athwart each other, for want of room: and I found the poor fellow very obliging and accommodating. He appeared to have his reason until he was speechless, and finally died, stretched across me. The death of a man in that place, and at that time, excited but little notice; for a day did not pass without more or less deaths. I have seen seven dead men drawn out and piled together on the lower hatchway, who had died in one night on board the Frederick. There were perhaps ten or twelve nurses belonging to this ship, and I should say there were about one hundred sick: the nurses lived in the steerage, and whatever property or clothing the deceased left, fell into their hands. If the deceased had only a good head of hair, it was taken off by the nurses and sold. The depravity of the human heart was probably as fully exhibited in those nurses, as in any other class of men. Some, if not all of them, were prisoners; and I believe they had some compensation from the British government for their services. They could indulge in playing cards, and drinking, while their fellows were thirsting for water, and some dying. There were more or less of them among the sick the greater part of the day; but at night the hatches were shut down and locked, and there was not the least attention paid to the sick or dying, except what could be done by the convalescent, who were so frequently called upon, that in many cases they overdid themselves, relapsed and died. After Mr. Wills, my bed-fellow, was dead; I called to the nurses to take him away, as he lay partly across me, and I could not relieve myself: but they gave me very hard words, and let the dead man lay upon me half an hour before they removed him; and it was a great favor to me that they did not take away the blankets that was under us. I had now two blankets left me, a great coat, and a little straw within a sack, under me; but even with these, I suffered extremely with the cold. I have frequently toiled the greatest part of the night, in rubbing my feet and legs to keep them from freezing; and while I was employed with one, it seemed as if the other must absolutely freeze. I must then draw up the coldest and rub upon that; and thus alternately work upon the one and the other, for hours together: I was sometimes inclined to abandon them to their fate, but after a while I would feel excited to bestow a little more labour upon them. In consequence of those chills, I have been obliged to wear a laced stocking upon my left leg for nearly thirty years past. My bunk was directly against the ballast port; and the port not being caulked, when there came a snow storm, the snow would blow through the seams upon my bed. In one instance, in the morning, the snow was three or four inches deep upon my bed; but in those cases there was one advantage to me; when I could not otherwise procure water to quench my thirst. The provision allowed the sick, was a gill of wine, and twelve ounces of flour bread per day. The wine was of an ordinary quality, and the bread made of sour or musty flour, and sometimes poorly baked. There was a small sheet-iron stove between decks, but the fuel was green, and not plenty; and there were some peevish and surly fellows generally about it. I never got an opportunity to set by it; but I could generally get the favor of some one near it to lay a slice of bread upon it, to warm or toast a little, to put into my wine and water. We sometimes failed in getting our wine for several days together: we had the promise of its being made up to us, but this promise was seldom performed. With the money which my uncle gave me, I sent ashore by one of the nurses, and bought a tin pint cup, a spoon, a few oranges, and a pound or two of sugar; but I question whether I got the worth of my money. The cup, however, was of infinite service to me. We were always careful to procure our cups full of water before the hatches were shut down at night; but there was frequently a difficulty attending this: the water was brought on board in casks, by the working party, and when it was very cold, it would freeze in the casks, and it would be difficult to get it out. The nurses had their hands full of employment generally by day, and often depended on the convalescent to serve the sick with water. At the close of the day, a man would sometimes have half a dozen calling upon him at the same time, begging to be supplied. I was frequently under the necessity of pleading hard to get my cup filled. I could not eat my bread, but gave it to those who brought me water. I have given three days' allowance to have one tin cup of water brought to me. I was under the necessity of using the strictest economy with my cup of water; restricting myself to drink such a number of swallows at a time, and make them very small: my thirst was so extreme, that I would sometimes overrun my number. I became so habituated to number my swallows, that for years afterwards I continued the habit, and even to this day I frequently involuntarily number my swallows. There was one circumstance which I must by no means forget. A company of the good citizens of New York, supplied all the sick with a pint of good Bohea Tea, (well sweetened with molasses,) a day, and this was constant. I believe this tea, under God's providence, saved my life, and the lives of hundreds of others.

There was no person of my acquaintance on board this ship; some of our crew had gone on board some other hospital ship before I left the Jersey. In the first of my sickness I was delirious a considerable part of the time. I am not able to say what my sickness might be denominated; at any rate, it was severe. The physicians used to visit the ship once in several days: their stay was short, nor did they administer much medicine. Were I able to give a full description of our wretched and filthy condition, I should almost question whether it would be credited. * * * It was God's good pleasure to raise me up once more, so that I could just make out to walk, and I was again returned to the Jersey prison ship. * * * In a few days, there came orders to remove all the prisoners from the Jersey, on board of transports, in order to cleanse the ship. We were all removed, and directly there came on a heavy storm. The ship on which I went on board, was exceedingly crowded, so that there was not room for each man to lay down under deck, and the passing and repassing by day, had made the lower deck entirely wet. Our condition was absolutely distressing. After a few days we were all put on board the Jersey again. A large number had taken violent colds, myself among the rest. The hospital ships were soon crowded; and even the Jersey herself shortly became about as much of a hospital ship as the others. In a day or two after my return to the Jersey, I was sent off again on board an hospital ship, (her name I have forgotten,) and on descending the main hatchway, the first person I noticed was

my uncle Weymouth. We were in some sense rejoiced in
meeting each other once more. We could indeed sympathize
with each other in some degree, but our situation seemed very
precarious. My uncle was very low spirited, but he was
favored with his reason; and it pleased God to continue my
reason while I remained on board this ship. In the space of a
week, my uncle began slowly to amend; he had a most excellent head of hair, but it had become so tangled, that he
despaired of clearing it, and gave it to a nurse for cutting
it off. While on board this ship, I had some trying scenes to
pass. A man who lay next me had been a nurse, but was
taken sick, and had had his feet, and even his legs, frozen. I
had several times seen them dressed: at length, while they
were dressing his feet, I saw the toes and bottom of his feet
cleave off from the bone, and hang down by the heel. On
board this ship, I found John and Abraham Hall, who were
brothers. John was about twenty-three and had a wife,
Abraham was about sixteen, they were both of our crew,
and were very sick. They lay at some distance from me; I
could not go to see them, nor could they come to see me,
they lay together. One night Abraham made a great outcry
against John, requesting him to get off from him. Some of
the men who were near, swore hard at John, for thus laying
on his brother. John made no reply: when the morning
came, John was found dead, and Abraham but just alive; I
believe he died the same day. Finally, there were but five
out of thirteen of our crew who returned. The remainder

left their bones there. I believe that a much larger proportion
of some other crews died than of ours. * * * While I was
confined with my uncle, on board the second hospital ship, we
had intelligence of peace."

Memoirs of Andrew Sherburne, 1st ed., pp. 110–113.

2d ed., pp. 113–116.

The following extract, with which we conclude this note,
will give a good idea of the character and professional qualifi-
cations of the physicians who attended the sick :

" From Brooklyn heights a Hessian doctor came,
Not great his skill, nor greater much his fame ;
Fair Science never call'd the wretch her son,
And Art disdain'd the stupid man to own.

* * * * * *

He on his charge the healing work begun
With antimonial mixtures, by the ton,
Ten minutes was the time he deign'd to stay,
The time of grace allotted once a day—
He drench'd us well with bitter draughts 'tis true,
Nostrums from hell, and *cortex* from Peru—
Some with his pills he sent to Pluto's reign,
And some he blister'd with his flies of Spain ;
His Tartar doses walk'd their deadly round,
Till the lean patient at the potion frown'd,
And swore that hemlock, death, or what you will,
Were nonsense to the drugs that stuff'd his bill—
On those refusing, he bestow'd a kick,
Or menac'd vengeance with his walking stick :—
Here, uncontroul'd he exercis'd his trade,
And grew experienc'd by the deaths he made."

FRENEAU.

(₄₄) Although it is conceded that the mortality on board
the Jersey was frightful in the extreme, yet it is impossible to

arrive, with any degree of certainty, at or near the correct number of her victims. Some accounts have estimated it at about 11,500; but this, no doubt, is exaggerated, or perhaps intended for the sum total of those who perished on board all the prison-ships and hospital-ships.

THOMAS ANDROS, (a prisoner in the fall of 1781,) in speaking of the sickness and deaths on board the Jersey, says:

" When I first became an inmate of this abode of suffering, despair and death, there were about four hundred prisoners on board, but in a short time they amounted to twelve hundred. And in proportion to our numbers, the mortality increased. All the most deadly diseases were pressed into the service of the king of terrors, but his prime ministers were dysentery, small-pox, and yellow fever. There were two hospital ships near to the Old Jersey, but these were soon so crowded with the sick, that they could receive no more. The consequence was, that the diseased and the healthy were mingled together in the main ship. In a short time we had two hundred or more sick and dying, lodged in the fore part of the lower gun-deck, where all the prisoners were confined at night. Utter derangement was a common symptom of yellow fever, and to increase the horror of the darkness that shrouded us, (for we were allowed no light betwixt decks,) the voice of warning would be heard, 'Take heed to yourselves. There is a mad-man stalking through the ship, with a knife in his hand.' I sometimes found the man a corpse in the morning, by whose side I laid myself down at night. At another time he would become deranged, and attempt, in darkness, to rise and stumble over the bodies that everywhere covered the deck. In this case I had to hold him in his place by main strength. In spite of my efforts, he would sometimes rise, and then I had to close in with him, trip up his heels, and lay him again upon the deck. While so many were sick with raging fever, there was a loud cry for water, but none could be had except on the upper deck, and but one allowed to ascend at a time. The suffering then from the rage of thirst during the night was very great. Nor was it at all times safe to attempt to go up. Provoked by the continual cry for leave to ascend, when there was already one on deck, the sentry would push them back with his bayonet. By one of these thrusts, which was more spiteful and violent than common, I had a narrow escape of my life. In the morning the hatchways were thrown open, and we were allowed to ascend, all at once, and remain on the upper deck during the day. But the first object that met our view in the morning, was a most appalling spectacle. A boat loaded with dead bodies, conveying them to the Long-Island shore, where they were very slightly covered with sand. * * * There were, probably, four hundred on board, who had never had the small-pox—some, perhaps, might have been saved by inoculation. But humanity was wanting, to try even this experiment.—Let our disease be what it would, we were abandoned to our fate. Now and then an American physician was brought in as a captive, but if he could obtain his parole, he left the ship, nor could we much blame him for this. For his own death was next to certain, and his success in saving others by medicine in our situation was small. I remember only two American physicians who tarried on board a few days. No English Physician, or any one from the city, ever, to my knowledge, came near us. There were thirteen of the crew, to which I belonged, but in a short time, all but three or four were dead. The most healthy and vigorous were first seized with the fever, and died in a few hours. For them there seemed to be no mercy. My constitution was less muscular and plethoric, and I escaped the fever longer than any of the thirteen, except one, and the first onset was less violent. There is one palliating circumstance as to the inhumanity of the British, which ought to be mentioned. The prisoners were furnished with buckets and brushes to cleanse the ship, and with vinegar to sprinkle her inside. But their indolence and despair were such, that they would not use them, or but rarely. And, indeed, at this time, encouragement to do so was small. For the whole ship, from her keel to the tafferel, was equally affected, and contained pestilence sufficient to desolate a world; disease and death were wrought into her very timbers. At the time I left, it is presumed a more filthy, contagious, and deadly abode for human beings, never existed among a Christianized people. It fell but little short of the Black Hole at Calcutta. Death was more lingering, but almost equally certain. The lower hold and the orlop deck were such a terror, that no man would venture down into them. ᛣ * * As to religion, I do not remember of beholding any trace of it in the ship. I saw no Bible—heard no prayer,—no religious conversation,—no clergyman visited us, though no set of afflicted and dying men more needed the light and consolations of religion."

Old Jersey Captive, pages 12–19.

SILAS TALBOT, (who was a prisoner in the fall of 1780,) in speaking of the Jersey, and the sickness and deaths therein, says :

" All her ports were close shut and secured, which effectually prevented any current of fresh air between decks, where the prisoners were all shut down from sun-set to sun-rise, and during these melancholy hours, all access to, or intercourse with, the upper deck was prohibited. She had a guard on board, which were forbidden, on pain of severe punishment, to relieve the wants of any distressed prisoner; and was anchored in a solitary nook, called the Wallabout. * * * There were confined, at this time, in this much-dreaded hulk, about eleven hundred prisoners. No berths were constructed for them to lie down in, nor a bench to sit upon. Many were almost without cloaths. The dysentery, fever, phrenzy, and despair, prevailed among them, and filled the place with filth, disgust and horror. The scantiness of the allowance, the bad quality of the provisions, the brutality of the guards, and the sick, pining for comforts they could not obtain, altogether furnished continually one of the greatest scenes of human distress and misery ever beheld. It was now the middle of October, and the weather was cool and clear, with frosty nights, so that the number of deaths per day were reduced, while captain Talbot was on board, to an average of *ten ;* and this number was considered by the survivors but a small one, when compared with the terrible mortality that had prevailed in the ship for three months before. The human bones and skulls, yet bleaching on the shore of Long Island, and daily exposed, by the falling down of the high bank on which the prisoners were buried, is a shocking sight, and manifestly demonstrates that the Jersey prison-ship had been as destructive as a field of battle."

Hist. Sketch of the Life of Silas Talbot, pp. 107–110.

The following extracts have a bearing upon this subject, and will be found interesting :

WHEREAS MARRIOT ARBUTHNOT, Esquire, Vice Admiral of the Blue and Commander in Chief of his Majesty's Ships and Vessels employed and to be employed in North America, &c. &c. &c. has appointed me Commissary General for Naval Prisoners in North America, I do hereby direct all Captains, Commanders, Masters, and prize masters of vessels, who shall bring naval prisoners into this port, that they (immediately on their arrival) send them on board the prison ship appointed for their reception, and report the same at my office.

DAVID SPROAT,
Commissary-General of Naval Prisoners.

N.B. Naval prisoners out on parole in the city or on Long-Island, are desired to send a note to the office, informing me of the place of their residence, in order that I may have it in my power to acquaint them when their exchange shall take place.

New-York, 20 October, 1779.

Rivington, December 4, 1779.

I DO hereby direct all Captains, Commanders, Masters, and Prize Masters of ships and other vessels, who bring naval prisoners into this port, immediately after their arrival to send a list of their names to this office, No. 33, in Maiden Lane, where they will receive an order how to dispose of them.

DAVID SPROAT,

New-York, April 28, 1780.   Commissary-General N. P.

Rivington, Sat. April 29, 1780.

———

WHEREAS it is found by experience, that indulgencies shewn to prisoners have often been abused by them, and favored making their escape.—I do therefore require all Captains, Commanders, Masters and Prize Masters belonging to the Royal Navy, and private vessels of war who shall bring naval prisoners into this port; not to allow any of them to come on shore on any promise or pretence whatsoever, but immediately after their arrival to cause a report of them to be made at the Commissary's Office No. 33 Maiden Lane where they will be directed how to dispose of them—And if notwithstanding some may escape while in charge of the captors or afterwards from on board the prison ships—the person found harboring or concealing them, may depend upon being proceeded against according to the Commandant's proclamation.

DAVID SPROAT,

New-York, 8th Dec. 1781.   Commissary General for

Naval Prisoners.

Rivington, Sat. Dec. 8, 1781.

———

" NEW-HAVEN, *January* 8.

Last Wednesday a Flag of Truce vessel arrived at Milford, after a tedious passage of several days, having upwards of 200 American prisoners, whose rueful countenances too well discovered the ill treatment they received whilst they were prisoners in New York; twenty of these unfortunate people died on the passage, and twenty have died since they landed at Milford."

New Hampshire Gazette, Jan. 21, 1777.

"*Providence, April* 19.

A gentleman from the Westward informs that the enemy at New York continued to treat the American prisoners with great barbarity. Their allowance to each man for 3 days is 1 lb. of beef, 3 worm eaten musty biscuits, and a quart of salt water: the meat they are obliged to eat raw, as they have not the smallest allowance of fuel. Owing to this more than savage cruelty, the prisoners die fast, and in the small space of three weeks (during the winter) no less than 700 brave men have perished. Nothing short of Retaliation will compel these British Barbarians to respect the law of nations."

New Hampshire Gazette, April 26, 1777.

* * * "A cartel vessel lately carried about one hundred and thirty American prisoners from the prison ships in New York to New London, in Connecticut. Such was the condition in which these poor creatures were put on board the cartel, that in that short run, sixteen died on board; upwards of sixty, when they landed, were scarcely able to move, and the remainder greatly emaciated and enfeebled; and many who continue alive, are never likely to recover their former health." * * *

New Hamp. Gazette, Feb. 9, 1779.

Extract from a letter written by a captain of an American privateer while on board a prison ship in New York :

* * * "It is very sickly here—one third of my crew is sick, and all the rest are likely to be so. There is not more than one in five that recovers. * * * There is now 200 out of 6, suffering the pains of this sickness, and it's daily increasing. * * * I am now in the limboes, in the midst of filth and vermin."

Pennsylvania Packet, Aug. 30, 1781.

"New London, *August* 2.

Tuesday, a flag returned here from New York, which brought from the hospital ship 51 American prisoners, 2 of which died on the passage, and the others are in a sickly and emaciated condition."

Pennsylvania Packet, Sept. 4, 1781.

Extract of a letter dated on board the Jersey (vulgarly called Hell) Prison Ship, New York, August 10, 1781 :

"There is nothing but death or entering into the British service before me. Our ship's company is reduced to a small number (by death and entering into the British service) of 19. * * * I am not able to give you even the outlines of my exile ; but thus much I will inform you that we bury 6. 7, 8, 9, 10, and 11 men in a day : we have 200 more sick and falling sick every day ; the sickness is the yellow fever, small pox, and in short, everything else that can be mentioned.

I had almost forgot to tell you that our morning's salutation is, ' Rebels ! turn out your dead !' "

Pennsylvania Packet, Sept. 4, 1781.

———

" NEW LONDON, *May* 3.

Sunday last a flag returned from New York which brought 20 Americans who had been a long time on board a prison ship. About one thousand of our countrymen remain in the prison ships at New York, great part of whom have been under close confinement for more than six months, and in the most deplorable condition ; many of them seeing no prospect of a releasement are entering into the British service to elude the contagion with which the ships are fraught."

Pennsylvania Packet, May 14, 1782.

———

Extract of a letter dated on board the prison-ship Jersey, at New York, April 26, 1782 :

"I am sorry to write you from this miserable place : I can assure you since I have been here we have had only twenty men exchanged, although we are in number upwards of 700, exclusive of the sick in the Hospital ships, who died like sheep ; therefore my intention is, if possible, to enter on board some merchant or transport ship, as it is impossible for so many men to keep alive in one vessel."

Pennsylvania Packet, May 21, 1782.

" PROVIDENCE, *May* 25.

   Sunday last a flag of truce returned here from New York, and brought a few prisoners.

We learn that 1,100 Americans were on board the prison and hospital ship at New York, when the flag sailed from thence ; and that from 6 to 7 were generally buried every day."

         Pennsylvania Packet, June 18, 1782.

SALEM, *December* 5.

A letter from an officer, late of a privateer from this port, dated on board the Jersey prison ship, New-York, November 9th, says :

" The deplorable situation I am in cannot be expressed. The Captains, lieutenants and sailing masters are gone to the provost, but they have only got out of the frying pan into the fire. I am left here with about 700 miserable objects, eaten up with lice, and daily taking fevers, which carry them off fast."

        Pennsylvania Packet, Jan. 2, 1783.

By way of retaliation on the British for the atrocious cruelties inflicted upon American prisoners, the Americans, in 1782, fitted up a prison-ship themselves. It was called the " Retaliation " prison-ship. It was used, however, but for a short time. The following is a notice of her, taken from the papers of the day :

" NEW LONDON, *May* 24.—Last Saturday, the Retaliation prison ship was safely moored in the River Thames, about a mile from the ferry, for the reception of such British prisoners as may fall in our hands ; since which about one hundred prisoners have been put on board."

        Pennsylvania Packet, June 11, 1782.

The following paragraph is the source whence have sprung the reports of the vast numbers who perished in the prison-ships.

Neither Mr. Sproat, the British Commissary, or his deputy, Mr. Robert Lenox, the latter of whom lived in our city for many years after the Revolution, and died here, ever contradicted these reports, although they certainly had it in their power by an official return of those taken, exchanged, and dead, to give the true number.

No such return has ever appeared, and we may therefore safely infer that the reports were true, and that about 11,000 American prisoners perished in the British prison-ships and hospital-ships of the Revolution :

" *Fishkill, May* 18, 1783.
To all Printers of public Newspapers,
Tell it to the world, and let it be published in every Newspaper throughout America, Europe, Asia and Africa, to the everlasting disgrace and infamy of the British King's commanders at New York: That during the late war, it is said, 11,644 American prisoners have suffered death by their inhuman, cruel, savage and barbarous usage on board the filthy and malignant British prison-ship, called the Jersey, lying at N. Y. Britons tremble, lest the vengeance of Heaven fall on your isle, for the blood of these unfortunate victims !

AN AMERICAN.''

" They died—the young—the loved, the brave,
　　The death barge came for them,
And where the seas yon crag rocks lave
　　Their nightly requiem,
They buried them all, and threw the sand
Unhallow'dly o'er that patriot band.

The black ship, like a demon sate,
　　Upon the prowling deep ;
From her, came fearful sounds of hate,
　　Till pain still'd all in sleep—
It was the sleep that victims take,
Tied, tortur'd, dying, at the stake.

Yet some, the deep has now updug,
  Their bones are in the sun ;
And whether by sword, or deadly drug,
  They died—yes—one by one.
Was it not strange to mortal eye,
To see them all so strangely die ?

*　　*　　*　　*

Are they those ancient ones, who died
  For freedom. and for me ?
They are—they point in martyr'd pride,
  To that spot upon the sea,
From whence came once the dying yell,
From out that wreck—that prison'd hell.''

                                    WHITMAN.

The principal causes of the mortality on board the "Jersey"
prison-ship, were :

1st. *Crowding and want of ventilation.*—The prisoners were
so crowded together, that the minimum amount of pure air
necessary for the healthy functions of life, was never enjoyed,
while, on account of the small port-holes and outlets, the circulation was very limited, and as the prisoners were kept
confined, the surrounding atmosphere, saturated with the
exhalations from their bodies and lungs, was too slowly
replaced by that which was fresh and oxygenated.

2d. *The want of food.*—The prisoners did not obtain the
rations required to keep them in health, and what was served
out to them was very poor in quality; the meat being generally tainted, and the flour and bread mouldy and otherwise

deleterious. The water also was generally bad, and the quantity often insufficient. The food was, therefore, debilitating instead of strengthening, and was calculated to produce scurvy, dysentery, and other diseases.

3d. *Cleanliness.*—Although buckets and brooms were allowed the prisoners, the physical and mental prostration caused by the confined air they were compelled to breathe, and the unhealthy and insufficient food they had to eat, rendered them incapable of labor, and no regular measures were taken to enforce sanitary regulations. The reaction of these causes on each other increased the vigor of action of each.

4th. *Miasma.*—The ship was moored at the Wallabout, always and to this day an unhealthy location : in the Revolution it was a low, marshy swamp, well calculated to generate those miasmatic poisons which produce typhus and other low forms of pestilential fevers. In addition to this, the ship itself was very old and very leaky, contaminated with decomposed animal and vegetable matter, and having always a large amount of bilge-water in her hold, which could never be entirely removed by the old-fashioned wooden pump, the only one known on shipboard at that day. Miasmatic exhalations were, therefore, the consequence ; all the elements for the generation of the fevers, to which so many of the prisoners fell victims, being present and greatly abundant. Finally, the physical strength of the prisoners being greatly reduced, they were unable to meet the attack of disease ; when sick, were unattended, until beyond the power of medicine; and when, at last, medical assistance was rendered, the physicians were inattentive, to say the least.

(₄₅) The following extracts will show the manner in which those who died on board the prison-ships and hospital-ships were interred:

CAPT. DRING, (who was present at one of these burials,) gives the following account of the proceedings:

"It has already been mentioned that one of the duties of the Working Party was, on each morning, to place the sick in the bunks, and if any of the prisoners had died during the night, to carry the dead bodies to the upper deck, where they were laid upon the gratings. Any prisoner who could procure and chose to furnish a blanket, was allowed to sew it around the remains of his deceased companions. The signal being made, a boat was soon seen approaching from the Hunter; and if there were any dead on board the other ships, the boat received them, on her way to the Jersey. The corpse was laid upon a board, to which some ropes were attached as straps; as it was often the case, that bodies were sent on shore for interment, before they had become sufficiently cold and stiff to be lowered into the boat by a single strap. Thus prepared, a tackle was attached to the board, and the remains of the sufferer were hoisted over the side of the ship into the boat, without further ceremony. If several bodies were waiting for interment, but one of them was lowered into the boat at a time, for the sake of decency. The prisoners were always very anxious to be engaged in the duty of interment; not so much from a feeling of humanity or from a wish of paying respect to the remains of the dead, (for to these feelings, they had almost become strangers,) as from the desire of once more placing their feet upon the land, if but for a few minutes. A sufficient number of the prisoners having received permission to assist in this duty, they entered the boat, accompanied by a guard of soldiers, and put off from the ship. I obtained leave to assist in the burial of the body of Mr. Carver; whose death was mentioned in the preceding Chapter. As this was done in the ordinary mode, a relation of the circumstances attending it, will afford a correct idea of the general method of interment. After landing at a low wharf which had been built from the shore, we first went to a small hut, which stood near the wharf, and was used as a place of deposit for the hand-barrows and shovels provided for these occasions. Having placed the corpses on the hand-barrows, and received our hoes and shovels, we proceeded to the side of the bank near the Wallabout. Here a vacant space having been selected, we were directed to dig a trench in the sand, of a proper length for the reception of the bodies. We continued our labour until our guards considered that a sufficient space had been excavated. The corpses were then laid into the trench, without ceremony; and we threw the sand over them. The whole appeared to produce no more effect upon our guards, than if we were burying the bodies of dead animals instead of men.

They scarcely allowed us time to look about us; for no sooner
had we heaped the earth above the trench, than the order was
given, to march. But a single glance was sufficient to show
us parts of many bodies which were exposed to view; although
they had probably been placed there, with the same mockery
of interment, but a few days before. Having thus performed,
as well as we were permitted to do it, the last duty to the
dead, and the guards having stationed themselves on each side
of us, we began reluctantly to retrace our steps to the boat.
We had enjoyed the pleasure of breathing, for a few moments,
the air of our native soil; and the thought of returning to the
crowded prison-ship, was terrible in the extreme. As we
passed by the water's side, we implored our guards to allow
us to bathe, or even to wash ourselves for a few minutes;
but this was refused us. I was the only prisoner of our party
who wore a pair of shoes; and well recollect the circumstance,
that I took them from my feet, for the pleasure of feeling the
earth, or rather the sand as I went along. It was a high
gratification to us to bury our feet in the sand, and to shove
them through it, as we passed on our way. We went by a
small patch of turf, some pieces of which we tore up from the
earth; and obtained permission to carry them on board, for
our comrades to smell them. Circumstances like these may
appear trifling to the careless reader; but let him be assured
that they were far from being trifles to men situated as we
had been. The inflictions which we had endured; the duty
which we had just performed; the feeling that we must in a

few minutes re-enter our place of suffering, from which in all
probability, we should never return alive, all tended to render
everything connected with the firm land beneath, and the
sweet air above us, objects of deep and thrilling interest.
Having arrived at the hut, we there deposited our implements,
and walked to the landing place, where we prevailed on our
guards, who were Hessians, to allow us the gratification of
remaining nearly half an hour, before we re-entered the boat.
Near us stood a house, occupied by a Miller; and we had
been told that a tide-mill which he attended, was in its immediate vicinity; as a landing place for which, the wharf where
we stood, had been erected. It would have afforded me a
high degree of pleasure to have been permitted to enter this
dwelling, the probable abode of harmony and peace. It was
designated by the prisoners, by the appellation of the "Old
Dutchman's;" and its very walls were viewed by us, with
feelings of veneration; as we had been told that the amiable
daughter of its owner had kept a regular account of the number of bodies which had been brought on shore for interment
from the Jersey and the hospital ships. This could easily be
done in the house, as its windows commanded a fair view of
the landing place. We were not, however, gratified on this
occasion, either by the sight of herself, or of any other inmate
of the house. Sadly did we approach.and re-enter our foul
and disgusting place of confinement. The pieces of turf which
we carried on board, were sought for by our fellow-prisoners,
with the greatest avidity; every fragment being passed by

them from hand to hand, and its smell inhaled, as if it had been a fragrant rose."

Dring's Recollections of the Jersey prison-ship, pp. 76–82.

EBENEZER FOX says:

" When any of the prisoners died in the night, their bodies were brought to the upper deck in the morning, and placed upon the gratings. If the deceased had owned a blanket, any prisoner might sew it around the corpse, and then it was lowered with a rope, tied round the middle, down the side of the ship into a boat. Some of the prisoners were allowed to go on shore, under a guard, to perform the labor of interment. Having arrived on shore, they found in a small hut some tools for digging, and a hand-barrow on which the body was conveyed to the place for burial. Here in a bank near the Wallabout, a hole was excavated in the sand, in which the body was put, and then slightly covered ; the guard not giving time sufficient to perform the melancholy service in a faithful manner. Many bodies would, in a few days after this mockery of a burial, be exposed nearly bare by the action of the elements." *Rev. Adventures of Ebenezer Fox, 1st ed., p. 108.*
2d ed., pp. 111–112.

" Each day, at least six carcases we bore
And scratch'd them graves along the sandy shore,
By feeble hands the shallow graves were made,
No stone, memorial, o'er the corpses laid ;
In barren sands, and far from home they lie,
No friend to shed a tear, when passing by ;
O'er the mean tombs insulting Britons tread,
Spurn at the sand, and curse the rebel dead."

FRENEAU.

ALEXANDER COFFIN, JR., gives an instance of the premature manner in which these interments were sometimes made. He says:

"A man of the name of Gavot, a native of Rhode Island, died, as was supposed, and was sewed up in his hammock, and in the evening carried upon deck to be taken with others who were dead, and those who might die during the night, on shore to be interred, (*in their mode of interring.*) During the night it rained pretty hard: in the morning, when they were loading the boat with the dead, one hammock was observed by one of the English seamen to move; he spoke to the officer and told him that he believed the man in that hammock (pointing to it) was not dead. *In with him,* said the officer, *if he is not dead he soon will be:* but the honest tar, more humane than his officer, swore he never would bury a man alive, and with his knife ripped open the hammock, when behold—the man was really alive. What was the cause of this man's reanimation, is a question for doctors to decide: it was at the time supposed, that the rain during the night had caused the reaction of the animal functions, which were suspended, but not totally annihilated. This same man, Gavot, went afterwards in the same flag with me to Rhode-Island. Capt. Shubael Worth of Hudson was master of the flag, and will bear testimony to the same fact."

Interment of the Martyrs, p. 35.

Another authority says:

"The haste and indignity with which they were committed to the earth were such, that many skeletons have been discovered in positions which clearly indicate and prove, that the graves, or holes, which were dug were too confined to receive them at full length, and that, either from want of time or inclination to enlarge them, the bodies were crowded and pressed down into the earth without decency or humanity."

Interment of the Martyrs, p. 5.

JEREMIAH JOHNSON, (who was born near the Wallabout, and died there on the 20th Oct., 1852, in the 87th year of his age,) in his Recollections of Brooklyn and New York, says:

"I saw the sand-beach, between a ravine in the hill and Mr. Remsen's dock, become filled with graves in the course of two months; and before the first of May, 1777, the ravine, alluded to, was itself occupied in the same way. * * * It was no uncommon thing to see five or six dead bodies brought on shore in a single morning; when a small excavation would be dug at the foot of the hill, the bodies be cast in, and a man with a shovel would cover them, by shoveling sand down the hill upon them. Many were buried in a ravine of the hill; some on the farm. The whole shore, from Rennie's Point to Mr. Remsen's door-yard, was a place of graves; as were also the slope of the hill,* near the house; the shore, from Mr. Remsen's barn along the mill-pond to Rappelye's farm; and the sandy island, between the flood gates and the mill-dam; while a few were buried on the shore on the east side of the Wallabout. Thus did *Death* reign *here*, from 1776, until the peace. The whole Wallabout was a sickly place

* This part of the hill was dug away by Mr. Jackson, where he obtained the bones for the "*dry bone procession.*"

during the war. The atmosphere seemed to be charged with
foul air, from the prison ships, and with the effluvia of the
dead bodies, washed out of their graves by the tides. We
believe that more than half of the dead, buried on the outer
side of the mill-pond, were washed out by the waves at high
tide, during north-easterly winds. The bones of the dead lay
exposed along the beach, drying and bleaching in the sun, and
whitening the shore; till reached by the power of a succeeding storm, as the agitated waters receded, the bones receded
with them into the deep—where they remain, unseen by man,
awaiting the resurrection *morn !* when, again joined to the
spirits to which they belong, they will meet their persecuting
murderers at the bar of the supreme Judge of 'the quick and
the dead.' We have, ourselves, examined many of the *skulls*
laying on the shore. From the teeth, they appeared to be
the remains of men in the prime of life."

Naval Magazine, Vol. I., pp. 467–469.

By the action of the tide the bones were washed from their
shallow graves, and during the progress of excavations for the
U. S. Navy Yard, were still further disturbed. For years
they lay whitening the Long Island shore, crying loudly for
the respect which was their due. Attempts were made at
different times to give them a proper sepulture and a fitting
monument, but though Congress was petitioned, and the subject brought before other bodies, yet nothing effectual was
accomplished until the year 1808, when the Tammany Society,
composed then of many revolutionary patriots, took the lead

in the good work. Previous to this, however, Mr. Benjamin
Aycrigg, having often noticed, with painful regret, the negligence shown to those relics of departed worth, made at length
an agreement in 1805 with a Mr. Amos Cheney, residing near
the locality, who engaged to gather them together, at the rate
of one cent per pound. Nearly twenty hogsheads were
thereby collected, and in 1808, a vault for their reception was
commenced in Jackson street, now Hudson Avenue, upon land
which had been set aside for the purpose by the late John
Jackson, Esq., and on the 13th day of April of that year, the
corner-stone of a monument was laid with considerable ceremony. The stone bore the following inscription :

" In the name of
THE SPIRITS OF THE DEPARTED FREE.
Sacred to the Memory of that portion of
AMERICAN SEAMEN, SOLDIERS, AND CITIZENS,
Who perished on board the
Prison-ships of the British,
At the Wallabout, during the
REVOLUTION.
This Corner-stone of the Vault was erected by the
TAMMANY SOCIETY ;
Or Columbian Order,
Nassau Island, Season of Blossoms, Year of Discovery
the 316th, of the Institution the 19th, and of
American Independence, the 32d."

On the 26th day of May following, the burial took place. The
procession moved from the Park in New York, and was one
of the most solemn and imposing ever seen in the city. In
the procession was a black horse, on which was mounted a

trumpeter, dressed in character, (black relieved with red) and
wearing a helmet, ornamented with flowing red and black
feathers. In his right hand he bore a trumpet, to which was
suspended a black silk flag, edged with red and black, upon
which appeared the following memorable words, in letters
of gold :

"MORTALS AVAUNT!

11,500

SPIRITS OF THE MARTYRED BRAVE.

Approach the Tomb of Honor, of Glory, of

VIRTUOUS PATRIOTISM !"

A noted feature in the procession was the " Grand National
Pedestal," so called, consisting of a square stage, erected on a
large truck carriage, the margin of which represented an iron
railing ; below this dropped a deep festoon which covered the
wheels ; on the stage was a pedestal eight feet long, six feet
high, and four wide, and made to imitate black marble. On
the four pannels of the pedestal were the following inscriptions :

(FRONT)

" AMERICANS ! REMEMBER THE BRITISH."

(RIGHT SIDE)

" YOUTH OF MY COUNTRY ! MARTYRDOM
PREFER TO SLAVERY."

(LEFT SIDE)

" SIRES OF COLUMBIA ! TRANSMIT TO
POSTERITY THE CRUELTIES PRAC-
TISED ON BOARD THE BRITISH PRISON SHIPS."

(REAR)

" TYRANTS DREAD THE GATHERING STORM,—
WHILE FREEMEN, FREEMEN'S OBSEQUIES PERFORM."

An elegant blue silk American flag, eighteen feet by twelve, floated from a staff at the top of the pedestal, and the staff was surmounted by a globe, upon which stood the American eagle, enveloped in a cloud of crape. Upon the pedestal was the "Genius of America," represented by Josiah Falconer, a member of the Tammany Society, and the son of a Revolutionary patriot. He wore a loose under-dress of light blue silk reaching to his knees; over it was a long flowing white robe, relieved by a crimson scarf and crape. He had sandals on his feet, and on his head a magnificent cap, adorned with elegant feathers. On the stage and around the pedestal stood nine young men, each holding by a tassel the end of a cord connected with the flag. These young men represented, respectively, Patriotism, Honor, Virtue, Patience, Fortitude, Merit, Courage, Perseverance, and Science, and were called "The Attributes of the Genius of America." They were all dressed in character, with plumes of feathers in their hats, and they all wore white silk scarfs, relieved with black crape. Each "Attribute" also wore a scarlet badge, with a blue silk fringe, on which the name of his character was embroidered in gold, and each one bore in his hand a blue silk banner, emblematic of the institution to which he belonged. The whole structure was drawn by four horses, in charge of two grooms, who were appropriately dressed with ribbons and crape.

The bones, which had been placed in thirteen coffins, made, it is said, by one John Mead, a cabinet maker, were under the charge of the tribes of St. Tammany, each tribe having one of the coffins in its custody. One hundred and four Revolutionary patriots acted as pall-bearers, all wearing white scarfs, relieved with crape. Numerous banners, bearing appropriate devices, appeared in the procession. Though under the direction of the Tammany Society, yet the procession was participated in by the State and city authorities, the military, and civic associations, with a full representation of all trades and professions, beside a vast number of citizens, among whom were many persons of distinction.

After passing through various streets, it crossed over to Brooklyn, where, being again formed, it proceeded to the tomb. At the vault, an oration was delivered by Benjamin De Witt, a prayer by the Rev. Ralph Williston, and a fitting benediction closed the services of the day. The whole ceremony was an exciting and heart-rending scene, and met the approving voice of the many thousands there assembled.

Notwithstanding this splendid, imposing pageant, and the feelings of deep sympathy which it seemed to create, no monument was erected; and in 1832, the very lot in which the relics of the Martyrs were interred, was assessed as private property, and actually put under the hammer, and—*sold for taxes!* A patriot of the Revolution, and a fellow-sufferer at the hands of the British, came forward, and rescued that lot from sacrilege. That patriot—that sufferer—was Benjamin Romaine. He took the sacred relics under his watchful care, and with jealous eye and untiring vigilance, guarded and protected them to the last moment of his life. Over the tomb he caused to be erected a wooden structure in the shape of a mausoleum, which he called " *The Ante-Chamber to the Tomb.*" He surmounted it by an eagle, embellished it with appropriate ornaments, and covered it with inscriptions commemorative and patriotic. Nor did he stop here. With the view to protect from desecration those sacred relics, he bequeathed the plot as a family vault to his heirs and their descendants forever, and directed that he, himself, should be buried there. Upon the death of that truly estimable man in the month of February, 1844, his remains were placed by the side of those whom he, while living, had cherished with such fond, faithful devotion. There they now lie. United in life, let them not be separated in death. Honor, all honor to Benjamin Romaine—the pure, noble-hearted, ever-to-be remembered and lamented, Benjamin Romaine—the man who had not only the heart to feel, but the will to execute. His name should be written in letters of gold. Had he lived in the days of Rome, and done an act like this, he *himself* would have had a splendid monument, and a statue too, erected to his memory. Americans—you who have become wealthy by the pursuits of commerce, or by the profits of trade—you who, by your lucrative callings or professions, have been raised to affluence—you who dwell in splendid palaces--who are arrayed in purple and fine linen—who live sumptuously, and have your tables and coffers full, and to overflowing— remember, in your abundance and prosperity, to whom you

THE TOMB OF THE MARTYRS,

As it originally appeared.

owe these blessings. Think of the poor Martyrs of the Revolution, who, in the flower of their youth, in the prime of their lives, in the midst of their usefulness, became victims to British cruelty, and in the prison-ships and hospital-ships of the Wallabout, miserably, horribly died, that you—you might be free, and rich, and happy! Go to the spot where lie those noble men who were immolated on the altar of Freedom. Behold their place of interment—in a locality, used as a receptacle for filth and refuse, and where even the coarse, disgusting noise of swine is heard. Go there, and after viewing that repulsive spot, tell me, as I look you in the eye, will you give those bones a fitting sepulture—will you raise over them a proper monument? Arise, then, my wealthy countrymen—arise from your velvet seats, your chairs of ease—arise in the power of your wealth, and in the majesty of your power, and proclaim that those bones shall be no longer "*unwept, unhonored* and *unsung*." Erect over them a worthy, a glorious, an enduring monument—one that shall tower to the clouds above—one that shall first catch the modest peep of the rising sun—one that parting day shall love, and be wont to linger, and dwell upon. Show to the world that our republic is not an ungrateful republic—that we are not like the Athenians of old, merely knowing what is right; but that we, like the Lacedemonians, also *practise* it. Show to the world that we, too, can respect, and not only respect, but honor,—aye, *adore*, Virtue—Patriotism—Martyrdom. It is a shame upon us as an enlightened people—it is a damning stigma on us as Americans, that this tribute to Revolutionary devotion has been so long, so unjustly, so disgracefully withheld. God grant that I may see the day when this blot upon our national character, and our own honor, shall be washed out forever. "*Si sum creatus cælestis stirps, cedo nota tantus genus.*"

(₄₆) Burgoo. This was what is here called "*mush,*" or in New England, "*hasty-pudding,*" and was made of oat-meal and water. It was served out to the prisoners once a week. The oat-meal, of which it was composed, was scarcely ever sweet; on the contrary, it was generally so musty and bitter, that none but persons in their condition, and suffering as they did, could eat it.

(₄₇) Thomas Andros, in his narrative, gives a different account of this occurrence. Having been a prisoner on the Jersey at the very time it took place, and perhaps an eye witness to the whole proceedings, his version is, therefore, probably the most correct. He says:

"A secret, prejudicial to a prisoner, revealed to the guard, was death. Captain Young of Boston, concealed himself in a large chest belonging to a sailor going to be exchanged, and was carried on board the cartel, and we considered his escape as certain; but the secret leaked out and he was brought back, and one Spicer of Providence being suspected as the traitor, the enraged prisoners were about to take his life. His head was drawn back, and the knife raised to cut his throat, but having obtained a hint of what was going on below, the guard at this instant, rushed down and rescued the man. Of his guilt at the time, there was to me, at least, no convincing evidence. It is a pleasure now to reflect that I had no hand in the outrage." *Old Jersey Captive, p.* 17.

(₄₈) The regular crew of the Jersey consisted of a Commander, two mates, a steward, a cook, and about twelve sailors. The crew of the ship had no communication whatever with the prisoners. In addition to the regular officers and seamen, there were also on board about a dozen old invalid marines, but the actual guard was composed of soldiers detached from the different regiments quartered on Long Island.

CAPT. DRING speaks of them as follows:

"The number usually on board, was about thirty. Each week, they were relieved by a fresh party. They were English, Hessians, and Refugees. We always preferred the Hessians, from whom we received better treatment than from the others. As to the English, we did not complain; being aware that they merely obeyed their orders in regard to us; but the Refugees or Royalists, as they termed themselves, were viewed by us with scorn and hatred. I do not recollect however, that a guard of these miscreants was placed over us more than three times; during which, their presence occasioned much tumult and confusion; for the prisoners could not endure the sight of these men, and occasionally assailed them with abusive language; while they, in return, treated us with all the severity in their power. We dared not approach near them, for fear of their bayonets; and of course, could not pass along the gangways where they were stationed; but were obliged to crawl along upon the booms, in order to get fore and aft, or to go up or down the hatchways. They never answered any of our remarks respecting them; but would merely point to their uniforms; as if saying,—We are clothed by our Sovereign, while you are naked. They were as much gratified at the idea of leaving us, as we were at seeing them depart. Many provoking gestures were made by the prisoners, as they left the ship, and our curses followed them, as far as we could make ourselves heard. * * * The only duty, to my knowledge, ever performed by the old Marines was to guard the water butt; near which, one of them was stationed with a drawn cutlass. They were ordered to allow no prisoner to carry away more than one pint of water at once; but we were allowed to drink at the butt, as much as we pleased; for which purpose two or three copper ladles were chained to the cask. Having been long on board, and regular in the performance of this duty, they had become familiar with the faces of the prisoners; and could thereby, in many instances, detect the frauds which we practiced upon them in order to obtain more fresh water for our cooking than was allowed us by the regulations of the ship. Over the water, the soldiers had no control. The daily consumption of water on board, was at least, equal to seven hundred gallons. I know not whence it was brought, but presume it was from Brooklyn. One large gondola or boat, was kept in constant employment, to furnish the necessary supply."

Dring's Recollections of the Jersey Prison-ship, pp. 88–91.

The conduct of some of the guard towards the prisoners was not only harsh and unfeeling, but, sometimes, even brutal in the extreme. A few instances of this we will give.

THOMAS PHILBROOK, (who was for several months a prisoner on board the Jersey,) says:

" As the morning dawned, there would be heard the loud, unfeeling and horrid cry, '*Rebels, bring up your dead.*' Staggering under the weight of some stark stiff form, I would at length gain the upper deck, when I would be met by the salutation, 'What! *you* alive *yet?* Well, you are a *tough* one."

WILLIAM BURKE, (a native of Newport, in the State of Delaware,) was a prisoner on the Jersey for about fourteen months. He says:

" Among other cruelties which were committed, I have known many of the American prisoners put to death by the bayonet: in particular I well recollect, that it was the custom on board the ship for but one prisoner at a time to be admitted on deck at night, besides the guards or centinels. One night, while the prisoners were many of them assembled at the grate at the hatchway, for the purpose of obtaining fresh air, and waiting their turn to go on deck, one of the centinels thrust his bayonet down among them, and in the morning twenty-five of them were found wounded, and stuck in the head, and

dead of the wounds they had thus received. I further recollect that this was the case several mornings, when sometimes
five, sometimes six, and sometimes eight or ten were found
dead by the same means."

Interment of the Martyrs, p. 90.

"Two young men, brothers, belonging to a rifle corps, were
unfortunately made prisoners, and sent together on board the
Jersey. The elder took the fever, and in a few days became
delirious. One night, (his end was fast approaching,) he
became calm and sensible, and lamenting his hard fate, and
the absence of his beloved mother, begged for a little water.
His brother, with tears, entreated the guard to give him some,
but in vain. The sick youth was soon in his last struggles.
The other in this distress offered the guard a guinea, for an
inch of candle, only that he might see him die ; and even this
was refused.—The language of the survivor expresses the irre-
sistible sentiments of nature and humanity.—' *Now,*' says he,
drying up his tears, ' *if it please God I ever regain my liberty,
I'll be a most bitter enemy !*'—This awful appeal was not in
vain. He regained his liberty—he rejoined the army—and
when the war ended he returned home in safety and triumph,
with eight large and one hundred and twenty-seven small
notches on the stock of his rifle ! ! !—*A tremendous, but just
revenge !*"

Historical Sketch of the Life of Silas Talbot, p. 108.

(49) BENJAMIN WHIPPLE was born in the year 1755, and was
a tailor by trade. After the revolution, he moved from Rhode

Island to the city of Albany, and held for many years the
situation of door-keeper to the House of Assembly of the State
of New York. He was elected to this office in 1802, and held
it by successive elections for the period of eighteen years, and
to the time of his death. His predecessor in office was Peter
Hanson, and his successor was Henry Bates. Mr. Whipple's
house was on the corner of Lodge-street and Maiden Lane, now
the site of St. Peter's Church Rectory. The upper rooms were
used for a Masonic Lodge, of which he was the keeper. He
was in great favor with the craft. He died in Albany, on the
30th day of April, 1819, at the age of sixty-four years.

(50) BENJAMIN DEXTER was the son of Andrew Dexter, of
Smithfield, R. I., who was a cooper by trade. His mother's
maiden name was Lydia Jencks. Her father was a resident
of Smithfield, and was, by occupation, a farmer. The subject
of this notice was of the fifth generation of Rev. Gregory
Dexter, a native of Northampton county, Eng., who was born
in 1610, and came to Rhode Island in 1644, in company with
Roger Williams, who was then on his return home from a
visit to England. Benjamin Dexter was born in Smithfield,
in the year 1754, and was brought up to the trade of a blacksmith. His wife's maiden name was Phebe Marsh, by whom
he had one son and three daughters. Mr. Dexter was a man
of industrious habits, and was much esteemed for his integrity
of character. He died in the town of Foster, R. I., on the
26th day of March, 1837, at the age of about 83 years.

(51) JABEZ HAWKINS was probably the one whom we find alluded to as a private in Colonel Robert Elliot's regiment, that regiment being one of three raised by Rhode Island for defence of the State, in December, 1776, at the time of the invasion of Newport by the British troops. These regiments were raised first for 15 months, ending March 16, 1778. They were then by an act of the General Assembly ordered to be re-enlisted for 12 months longer, ending March 16, 1779, and then for the third time re-enlisted, pursuant to the same authority, for 12 months more, ending March 16, 1780, making altogether three years and three months before they were disbanded. We find the name of Jabez Hawkins also among those recruits who enlisted for the campaign of 1782 from the town of North Providence, R. I.

(52) "NEW-YORK, October 15.

We find the following account of this storm published in the papers of the day:

About 12 o'Clock last Saturday, we had an exceeding hard Gust of Wind, attended with Thunder, and a heavy Shower of Rain mixed with large Hail. The Lightning struck a House on the New Dock, but it did little or no Damage. Two small Boats overset in the River, but no Lives were lost."

Gaine, Monday, Oct. 15, 1781.

(53) WILLIAM WATERMAN was born in the year 1758. He took an active part in the revolutionary war, and showed

himself to be a brave soldier. He fought in the battle of White Plains, where he was wounded through the thigh. In the course of the war he was taken prisoner, and put on board the Jersey prison-ship off New York, from which he made his escape by swimming to Long Island. He subsequently rejoined the army, and continued in active service to the end of the war, discharging his duties faithfully. He died in Royalton, Vermont, on the 10th day of March, 1845, at the age of 87 years.

(54) HELL GATE or HURL GATE, a celebrated strait in the East River, near the west end of Long Island Sound, opposite Harlem, and about eight miles N. E. of New-York city, formerly remarkable for its whirlpools, which made a tremendous roaring at certain times of the tide. These whirlpools were occasioned by the narrowness and crookedness of the passage, and a bed of rocks which extended quite across it. In the year 1780, the British frigate Huzzar, of 28 guns, Capt. Charles Morice Pole, in attempting to pass through, struck the rocks, and was so much injured, that after sailing a short distance, she sunk in deep water, where her hull still remains. Attempts have been made to raise her, but without success, though by means of diving-bells and other sub-marine contrivances, many articles have been brought up, but no specie has yet been discovered, though she was reported to have had an amount on board. In former times, this passage was very dangerous to navigation; but of late years, the obstructions

have been removed by blasting, so that there is now 21 feet of water at low tide, and the largest vessels can therefore pass through without any fear of injury. There is a tradition among the Indians that at an early period, their ancestors could step from rock to rock, and cross this arm of the sea on foot.

(55) NEWTOWN lies in Queen's County, L. I., about eight miles east of New-York. The number of inhabitants of the town, in 1810, was 2,312, of which 512 were slaves. In 1852 the population was 7,208. There are many private graves in this town, and a great number of tomb-stones. Many of the latter were wantonly destroyed during the revolutionary war by the British troops who were then stationed here.

(56) The Hessians were soldiers hired by Great Britain of the petty princes of Germany. The first employment of these mercenary troops by the English Government, was in the year 1726. At the commencement of the American revolution, England stood in great need of troops, and at first contemplated the hiring of 20,000 men from Russia, but it was finally decided to abandon this plan, and a treaty was subsequently entered into with the Duke of Brunswick, the Landgrave of Hessen-Cassel, and the Count Hanau, who conjointly agreed to furnish the men required. Of these the Landgrave of Hessen-Cassel furnished the greater part, and, from this circumstance, all the German soldiers received the common appellation of Hessians. The compensation received by the

NOTES. 289

rulers of the several states, was generally at the rate of thirty
crowns or about thirty-five dollars for each man contributed,
and an additional sum of the same amount for each one killed,
or for three wounded, beside the cost of outfit and two
months' extra pay. A still further sum was given in gross to
the several vendors, and the Landgrave of Hessen-Cassel found
a favorable occasion in the urgent necessity for troops by the
British government to obtain the liquidation of a previously
discovered debt of £80,000 incurred by that government
during the seven years' war. The Hessian troops were first
opposed to the Americans in the battle of Long Island
in 1776. They were afterwards in service at Trenton, Saratoga, and other engagements during the war. A lady de-
scendant of one of the Hessian officers who came to America,
informs us that a part of the Hessian forces mutinied, and
were unwilling to leave their country, knowing that they had
been sold. The mutiny was at length quelled, but only by the
arrest of the leaders, who were six of them shot to death in
the market of Hessen-Cassel. A Mr. DeWitt, who was confined
a prisoner in New York, and made his escape in 1777, says he
" saw six hundred Hessians confined on board the men of war,
for laying down their arms, and that the foreigners only
waited for a favorable opportunity to go off in a body." The
Hessian troops were peculiarly desirous to desert the service,
so as to remain in our country, and hid themselves in every
family where they could possibly secure a friend to aid their
escape. Those who were successful, generally became thriving

tradesmen and farmers, and many of them acquired wealth. "At the Bank of England," says a paragraph in the Lady's Magazine for December, 1786, "the sum of £471,000 was transferred by Mr. Van Otten, on account of the Landgrave of Hessen-Cassel, being so much due for Hessian soldiers lost in the American war at thirty pounds a man. According to this calculation, the number of Hessians lost in the said war was 15,700."

(₅₇) JAMAICA, a beautiful and flourishing town in Queen's County, L. I., about 13 miles from the city of New York. In the year 1810, the whole township contained 1,661 inhabitants. In 1852 the population was 4,247.

(₅₈) JAMAICA PLAINS is the name given to the western portion of the extensive plains known as *Hempstead Plains*,— a vast tract of level land lying between Jamaica and Hempstead, commencing about 16 miles from the west end of Long Island, and extending 12 miles east, with a breadth of five to six miles. Hempstead Plains have been considered from the earliest settlement of the country, a great natural curiosity. The attention of strangers was always called to them, and scarcely any traveler of note in former times, but mentioned them, and deemed them worthy of minute description. In its original state, this whole tract appeared to the eye as smooth and unbroken as the sea in a calm. A few scattered clumps upon the borders, being just visible above the surface, in the distance, had the appearance of small islands. In the summer, the rarefaction of the air over so large a surface, exposed to the sun's hot rays, occasioned the phenomena of "looming," as seen in the harbors near the sea, which elevating these tree-tops as a mass, and causing the surrounding soil, shrouded in a thin, and almost transparent vapor, to look like water, made the deception complete. These plains were used for horse races as early as 1670 ; in the Revolution were called "Ascot Heath," and the "New Market Course" after the celebrated one in England, and they were greatly noted not only in the North American colonies, but even in Europe. The races were held twice a year, for a silver cup, and were attended by the gentry of New York and New England. In former times, Hempstead Plains were considered almost barren, but the hand of cultivation has of late years caused them to blossom and bloom, so that they are now occupied by fields of grain, have been enclosed by one and another, whereby they have lost their original appearance, and in a few years more, no vestige whatever of their former condition will remain.

(₆₉) The phenomenon alluded to, was, doubtless, that known as the "*ignis fatuus*," or more popularly, the "Jack O'Lanthorn," or "Will o' the Wisp;" a changeable, flickering and momentary light engendered in hot weather, in moist localities, from the exhalation of gases, highly combined with phosphorus. It is frequently noticed in meadows and bogs, and is also observed in the vicinity of grave-yards, where the decaying animal matter furnishes an ample reservoir of the elements which give rise to the phenomenon. This association of place and circumstance recalls naturally to the superstitious and ignorant, unacquainted with the cause of the appearance, the idea of ghosts and "goblins dire," and has, perhaps, contributed considerably to continuance in the belief of spiritual visitations. In localities favoring its development, it presents to the detained traveler at night, the appearance of a light from a lanthorn blown about by the wind, and frequently acts as a lure to a bootless chase, often causing him to wander from his way—

> " An *ignis fatuus*, that bewitches
> And leads men into pools and ditches."
>
> *Hudibras, Part I., Canto* 1.

(60) The whole of Long Island being under British control from 1776 to 1783, the farmers there were subjected to many severe regulations and exactions by the enemy. They were required to furnish from year to year, for the use of the army, not only the greater part of their hay, straw, grain, vegetables and other farm produce, but also the teams and draught animals necessary to convey them to the place of deposit, under the penalty of imprisonment and having their whole crops confiscated. The owners of woodlands had not only to supply the fuel required, but were also compelled to cut and deliver it, and the pay being fixed by the king's commissioners, if the farmer objected and demanded more, he often lost the whole. The use of horses and oxen was also fre-

quently required, sometimes under pay, but often with no compensation whatever. Owing to the great and constant drain made by the army, the necessaries of life often became excessively scarce and proportionably high, but the rise was of little benefit to the farmer, whose supply had perhaps already been so reduced by pilfering and foraging parties of the enemy, as to be inadequate for the wants even of his own family. To these hardships were added the annoyance of constant surveillance; passes and permits being required for everything they did, and wherever they went; while the utmost condescension was exacted by the British officers, even to the uncovering of the head in their presence. If a farmer neglected to do this, he rendered himself liable to summary chastisement, although the haughty Britain would scarcely deign to notice him, much less return the civility. It is no wonder, then, that the expulsion of the British was beheld by the farmers with great exultation, and that they viewed with infinite satisfaction the abject mortification with which their red-coated oppressors finally left the country they had attempted so very unsuccessfully to subdue.

The following extracts will be read with interest in this connection :

Forage-Office, New-York, Sept. 10, 1778.

THE Farmers on New-York-Island, Long, and Staten-Island, are hereby required immediately to thrash out their grain, as the STRAW is wanted for the use of his Majesty's troops, for which they will be paid at the usual rate, on producing certificates of the delivery from the deputy Commissaries at the different posts of Brooklyn and Flushing, on Long-Island; at Coles-Ferry on Staten-Island; and at

Kings-bridge, Marston's Wharf, and Bear-Market, on New York Island; with the same allowance for transportation as they received last year.

GEORGE BRINLEY,
Commissary of Forage.

Rivington's Gazette, Wed., Jan. 13, 1779.

New-York, February 24.

Mr. Benjamin James, Commissary in the forage department, has drawn a prize in the British state lottery of Five Thousand Pounds.

Rivington, Wed., Feb. 24, 1779.

By the Commandant of New-York—

PERMISSION will be granted to the Farmers and Gardeners, of these islands (that have not wood on their lands proper for fencing) to cut railing for fences, on the lands of persons not under the protection of Government, on Long Island, or Staten Island.

Complaints have been made, that the wood cutters have broke down the fences, and done other damage on cultivated lands, such offenders will upon proof be severely punished, and forfeit their claims to any future Permits.

The Permits granted to cut firewood for the use of the city are to expire the first day of March next.

New Permits will be granted.

Applications are to be made to the Police of New-York.

New-York, February 5, 1779.   D. JONES,
                                                Maj. Gen.

Rivington, Wed., March 3, 1779.

THE FARMERS in general are requested to THRASH out their GRAIN immediately, and the STRAW to be delivered at the following places, where proper persons will attend, and give receipt at Marston's Wharf, and the Bear Market, or York Island.

Brooklyn, Flushing, and to Mr. John Cutler, Collector of Forage, on Long-Island.

And at the Forage-Yard, on Staten-Island.

GEORGE BRINLEY,
Forage-Office, October 1, 1779.　　　　Commissary of Forage.

Rivington, Dec. 18, 1779.

———

"Saturday last departed this Life at Newtown on Long-Island, in the 45th year of his Age, Mr. John Sweeten, Deputy-Commissary of Forrage."

Gaine, Mon., Aug. 21, 1780.

———

By Major GENERAL JONES, Commandant of
NEW-YORK.

PROCLAMATION,

BY a Proclamation of his Excellency Sir Henry Clinton, dated New-York, December 20, 1778, the farmers of Long-Island and Staten-Island, were ordered to thrash and bring to market, by stated periods, such proportions of wheat, rye. and Indian corn, in their possession, as they did not stand in need of for the support of their families, and the sowing their lands : They were required also, to give an account to the Colonels of militia of their respective districts, what quantity of grain they possessed, and what it might be necessary to reserve for the above uses. The Commander in Chief has been pleased to order that Proclamation to remain in force, and be strictly observed, the rates excepted, which, as an encouragement for an ample supply of the markets are to be as follows :

Shillings.

Wheat,.............. 26 curency per bushel.
Wheat Flour,........ 80 .... per cwt.
Rye,................ 10 .... per bushel.
Rye Meal,........... 30 .... per cwt.
Indian Corn, ... 10 .... per bushel.
Indian meal,......... 28 .... per cwt.
Buckwheat,... ..... 7 .... per bushel.
Buckwheat meal,.... 26 .... per cwt.

It is therefore ordered, that from and after the first day of February next, no greater price for any of the above articles, shall be demanded, offered or received, on the penalty of the person offending, forfeiting (on being convicted on oath, before the Police of New York, or the Colonel of the militia of the district on Long-Island or Staten-Island, where the offence is committed) the grain, flour, corn, or meal, so offered, to be sold or purchased, or the value thereof, and to suffer imprisonment till the said forfeiture is paid; the one half of the forfeiture to be paid to the informer, and the other half for the use of the poor of this city, or the township where the offence is committed.

The Police of New-York, and the Colonels of militia on Long-Island, and Staten-Island, are hereby required, to take an account of what quantities of wheat, rye, Indian corn, grain, flour, or meal are in their respective districts, and in whose possession ; and report the same as soon as possible to the Commandant of New-York.

New-York, January 22, 1779.

D. JONES,
Major-General.

☞ The above Proclamation is reprinted by order of Brigadier General BIRCH, Commandant of this City, that no person may plead ignorance of the Regulations therein contained.

Rivington, September 30, 1780.

By Lieutenant General
JAMES ROBERTSON,
Governor of New-York, &c.

WHEREAS it appears necessary that two Thirds of the Fresh Hay produced on the islands of New-York, Staten-Island, and Long Island, be set apart for carrying on the King's service, all persons whatsoever possessed of Hay are required to bring the above proportions into the King's magazines most contiguous to them.

The Hay produced on New York island to be delivered at the magazine near Fort Knyphausen, at Marston's Wharf, and the city of New-York, the Hay of Staten-Island at the magazines there, and the produce of the Western part of Long Island at the magazines of Brooklyn Ferry, Flushing and Jamaica. As this quantity must be furnished without any deduction, all persons proprietors of the same will be considered accountable for the number of tons that grow on their grounds, and are ordered to cut it without delay, so that the requisition be fully complied with before the 15th of August ensuing. The usual price will be paid for the Hay and Carting, and the magazines, as well as mode of transportation, for the Eastern part of Long Island, will be pointed out at a future day.

Rivington, Wed., July 25, 1781.

Proclamation.

By his Excellency

Lieut. *General Robertson,*

Governor of New-York, &c.

AS the reduction of *Horses* and *Waggons* belonging to the Quarter Master General, will occasion a call on the country to supply the Magazines, and to assist in other extraordinary duty, a return has been made of those belonging to the inhabitants of Long-Island, that each district may perform its proportion of this service, and be regularly paid.

On application for the requisite number from the Commissary General or his Deputy, to the several Captains of Militia, they are to furnish them in rotation, weekly from their companies. Certificates will then be given for the service and pay allowed at the rate of Fourteen Shillings per day for each Waggon, with two Horses and a Driver.

And as this is the proper season to lay up Forage for the Army, the Farmers of King's and Queen's Counties, and of Huntington in Suffolk, are required to bring in half their fresh Hay to the nearest Magazine before the end of the ensuing month of August, for which they will receive Six Pounds per ton, and the usual cartage. Those who comply with this requisition to be protected in keeping the remaining half, and considered by their officers as having employed their teams for the time on public duty.

Rivington, Sat., Aug. 3, 1782.

(₆₁) JERICHO, (which is located at the place described) is a pleasant village near the centre of the town of Oyster Bay, upon the Jericho turnpike road, in Queen's County, L. I., about

27 miles from the city of New York. The ground on which the village was erected, was a part of the purchase made by Robert Williams in 1650, and was early settled upon by a number of substantial Quaker families, whose posterity still remains. This place was the residence of the celebrated Elias Hicks, who officiated for many years in the Friends' meeting-house located here. The Indian name of Jericho was Lusum.

(62) OYSTER BAY, a town in Queen's County, Long Island. It derives its name from that of the beautiful bay on its northern limits, which has long been, and still is distinguished for its fine oysters and other marine productions. The first plantation of the town was commenced on the site of the present village of Oyster Bay in 1653, although it is probable that individuals had located in other parts of the town some years before, but without any permanent organization as a community. In the year 1810 it contained 4,548 inhabitants, of whom 134 were slaves. The population in 1852 was 6,900.

(63) The surrender of Cornwallis and his army at Yorktown, Va., on the 19th October, 1781, to the allied American and French forces, was an event which created the wildest excitement among the American people. On no occasion during the war did they manifest so great a degree of joy and exultation. To the Giver of all good, they united in rendering, with grateful hearts, thanksgiving and praise for the decisive victory which, through His gracious mercy, they had been

enabled to gain. Nor was this all. The glorious news spread through the land with rapid pace, and was everywhere received with huzzas, bonfires and illumination. In Philadelphia the glad tidings came by express at midnight, and the faithful watchman, as he patrolled his weary round, crying the hours as they passed, roused the inhabitants from their slumbers by the startling, but welcome and cheering intelligence that "*Cornwallis was taken.*" So rapturous and intense were the emotions of joy which this brilliant success occasioned, that several citizens were deprived of their senses, and one aged patriot, then door-keeper of Congress, actually expired under the excitement. When the news reached Britain, she was struck with dismay. The loss of a second entire army had extinguished all hope of conquest. Those of her ministers who had before been averse to the war, were now greatly emboldened in their opposition. The heavy burdens which her people had hitherto borne with patience, now pressed with intolerable weight, and Britain was at length compelled to acknowledge with bitter disappointment and galling mortification, the *Independence of America.*

(₆₄) SNOW'S TAVERN was situated in the lower part of Main street, Sag Harbor, L. I., and was afterwards kept, and perhaps owned by Mr. William Duvall. After him, the premises were owned by Asa Partridge; have since been repeatedly burnt over; and now belong to the heirs of Thomas

Brown, deceased, and are at this time occupied by a coal-yard, hay-press, etc.

(⁶⁵) REV. JOSEPH SNOW, Jr., was the son of Joseph Snow, and was born in Providence, R. I., about the year 1713. He was by occupation a house carpenter, and without education took to preaching. He was for many years, and up to the time of his death, pastor of the Beneficent Congregational Church and Society in Providence. He died in that city on the 10th day of April, 1803, in the 89th year of his age, and the 58th of his ministry. The Rev. Stephen Gano, at that time pastor of the First Baptist Church in Providence, preached his funeral sermon.

(⁶⁶) SAG HARBOR—a post town and port of entry in Suffolk County, N. Y. It is situated on a bay of the same name, at the eastern extremity of Long Island; is about 110 miles east of the city of New York, and was incorporated in 1803. It has an excellent harbor, and is finely situated for trade and navigation. Before the Revolution, the town was thinly settled, but since the peace of 1783, the population and business have greatly increased, and a valuable whale fishery is now carried on from this place. The population in 1852 was 3,000. Sag Harbor is noted for the brilliant exploit performed here by Major Meigs in the month of May, 1777.

(⁶⁷) During the time that Long Island was under the control of the British, an active contraband trade existed between the

island and the opposite Connecticut shore, and marauding and
kidnapping was constantly carried on between them. On the
Connecticut side, the smuggling was done with great secrecy,
and if the goods thus obtained, were discovered by honest persons, they were advertised and the owners requested to come
and take them. The Tories, being so closely watched, were
not usually engaged in this trade, and it was reserved for pro-
fessed friends of the patriot cause to thus gain gold by their
country's misfortunes. Persons who were otherwise considered fair and honorable, were engaged in it; but if they
were discovered, they were at once subjected to opprobrium
and insult. No occupation could be mentioned that was
more odious, nor could anything more excite the public indig-
nation against a man than to call him a Long Island trader.
Though rigorously watched, though houses were searched and
men imprisoned, yet the trade flourished still; the enormous
profits inducing many persons to encounter the perils and
risks necessary to bring the goods across the Sound. Vessels,
laden with contraband goods, were occasionally intercepted
by the State cruisers, and the more serious history of these
sad times was often enlivened by ludicrous anecdotes of the
adventures and mishaps of these midnight traders. Thus a
story is told of two men from the Great Neck shore of New
London, who put off one night in a whaleboat with a large, fat
ox on board. The animal got loose from its fastenings, and
became so unmanageable, that the men, in danger of sinking,
were glad to make for a country sloop near by, and meekly

surrender their ox to confiscation and themselves to imprisonment. On the Long Island side, the harbors were infested with bands of the lowest and vilest refugees, whence many a plundering descent was made on the Connecticut coast, and robbery and extortion of every kind committed. The small sloops and boats in which these piratical excursions were made, had the familiar name of "*Shaving-Mills.*" They were the terror of the coast, often committing the most atrocious robberies.

(₆₈) Through the whole year 1777, New London was blockaded by the British almost with the strictness of a siege. The Amazon frigate kept a continual watch at the mouth of the river Thames, capturing and destroying coasters and fishing vessels without mercy. Several British ships also wintered in Gardiner's Bay, and the Sound was the common haunt of the enemy. A host of privateers fitted out at New York and Long Island, moreover, infested the whole of the New England coast, so that the inhabitants were therefore at length driven in self-defence to build privateers and arm as cruisers whatever craft they had left or could seize in their turn from the enemy, and send them afloat to defend their property. Several rich prizes having been taken by them, the British became exasperated, and in the latter part of the year 1781, sent an expedition against the town, under the traitor Arnold, who, after assaulting Fort Griswold and massacring its brave defenders in cold blood, entered New London, and fired the town, destroying public and private property of immense value.

(69) MONTAUK POINT constitutes the extreme eastern end of Long Island, and is distant 140 miles east of New York. It is called in the Indian deed of conveyance to East Hampton, "Womponenit." The word "Mon" in the Mohegan vocabulary, is said to mean island, while the terminal "auke" means land. The term was applied to a powerful tribe of Indians who once inhabited this point, and who were called, by the English, Montauks or Islanders, with the broad sound of *a*, equivalent to Matonwacs of the Dutch. The locality is covered with rolling hills, intermixed with boulders of rock, terminating in an abrupt bluff sixty feet high, on which stands a stone light-house, erected in 1795 by the U. S. Government, at an expense of $22,300, which shows a fixed light, elevated 160 feet above the ocean level; and is visible 18½ nautical miles. There is, adjacent, a public house, which is much resorted to in the summer season. It is supposed that the point for about five miles from its terminal bluff, was once surrounded by water. Of this there are decisive indications from the sea to the Sound, in a tract of sand, in the middle of which are found the imbedded bones of a whale. Montauk is the most celebrated Indian locality on Long Island. Though within the knowledge of the whites, the Montauks have never been beyond 300 or 400 in number, yet tradition reports them to have been once " as numerous as the blades of grass." This

tribe was constantly at war with the Narragansetts of Block Island and the mainland, who inflicted great havoc among them, and compelled them to seek the protection of East Hampton. The chief Sachem of the Montauks was Wyandanch, whose name appears in most of the Indian conveyances of land in Suffolk County. He died of an infectious disease about the year 1658. After his death, his widow or Sungsqua, together with her son Weoncombone, under advice of his guardians Lion Gardiner and his son David Gardiner, governed the tribe. There are near Fort Pond, remains of several Indian forts; and the burial places of generations of Indians who lived on this point, are still to be seen. Remnants of the Montauk tribe, consisting of four or five families, still live there; and of these, some have intermarried with negroes. They are unable to resist the temptation of fire-water, and are, therefore, rapidly disappearing. The point was conveyed to the town of East Hampton by Wyandanch and his successors, in consideration of the kindness of that town in protecting him from Ninigret or Janemo of Rhode Island, his merciless enemy, who had not only slaughtered his chiefs, but carried his daughter into captivity, from which she was recovered by Lion Gardiner. A few Indian traditions still lirger around the point.

(70) STONINGTON—a seaport town, with an incorporated borough of the same name, in New London County, Conn. The borough, or principal village, is on a rocky point of land

which projects half a mile into the east end of Long Island Sound, and is generally called Stonington Point. It is noted for a spirited and successful defense made here in the month of August, 1814, against a British squadron, which, under Sir Thomas Hardy, commenced a bombardment, but were compelled to retire with considerable loss. The town has a good harbor, which is protected by a breakwater constructed by the Government, at an expense of $50,000. The inhabitants are chiefly employed in the whaling and maritime trade. The town was settled in 1658, and the population in 1852 was 5,431.

(71) SAYBROOK—a town in Middlesex County, Conn., at the mouth of the Connecticut river, and 41 miles south of Hartford. This place is one of the oldest in the State, and derives its name from Lords Say and Brook, who purchased the land and caused the first settlement in 1635. Col. Fenwick, whose wife, the daughter of a British nobleman, was buried here, was one of its founders. This was the place for which Cromwell and his compatriots were embarked, when they were forbidden by King Charles 1st to leave England. The building lots assigned to them by the colonists are still pointed out. Yale College was in operation here from 1707 to 1717. Saybrook is a flourishing town, and has extensive manufactories of ivory combs, augers, etc. The inhabitants are many of them employed in the shad fisheries. The population of Saybrook in 1853 was 2,904.

(72) POP ROBIN. This was a common dish at that time in some parts of New England. It was also a favorite meal in New York, and is still used here to this day among some of the old Knickerbocker families. The name given to it here is " *thickened milk.*" By the Dutch it is called " *dikke melk.*"

(73) The house where John Waterman lived, and where Mr. Hawkins lodged and was so hospitably entertained, is still standing. It is occupied by John Waterman, the grandson of the first named. It retains its original appearance, with the exception of the door near the corner, which has since been added, and the two lower windows on the front end of the house, which have been enlarged to accommodate a shop now kept there. The barn spoken of by our author, has long since been removed. Its site is now occupied by a meeting house.

(74) JOHN WATERMAN was born about the year 1710, and was, we believe, a native of Rhode Island. He was bred a seaman, and became master of a vessel, but having a preference for the mechanic arts, he soon left the pursuits of commerce, and built a paper-mill about two miles from Providence, which was probably the first one erected in the colony of Rhode Island. In the year 1769, he purchased the press and types, which had been for many years owned and perhaps used by Samuel Kneeland, of Boston. With these he opened a printing house near his paper-mill, but he seems to have

done but little in the typographic line. The building used by
him for printing purposes, was near his residence, and stood
adjoining the barn spoken of by our author. Mr. Waterman's
residence was situated in what is now known as Olneyville,
about two miles from the centre of Providence, but now
within the limits of the city. He was a kind-hearted, charitable and benevolent person, no better evidence of which need
be given than the manner in which he sympathized with and
entertained the hero of our narrative, then a poor wanderer,
returning with wearied steps, from a wretched captivity with
the enemy. We have strong reasons to infer, likewise, from
the narrative, that he was a courteous gentleman, a warm
friend to his country, and a true Christian. Mr. Waterman
died in the year 1787, at the age of 77.

(75) "THE GREAT BRIDGE," so called, is erected over the
stream of water which separates the eastern part of the city
of Providence from the western. The bridge is built of wood,
with heavy timber, and is covered with earth and paved with
cobble stones. It is kept in order by appropriations made for
the purpose. In former times, the funds for repairing it were
raised by lotteries granted by the General Assembly of the
State of Rhode Island.

(76) OLNEY WINSOR was born in Johnston, R. I., on the 24th
day of August, 1763. His father, Samuel Winsor, was for
many years pastor of the First Baptist Church in Providence,

and died in January, 1803, at the age of 80. His mother, Lydia Olney, was a daughter of John Olney, of North Providence, a farmer by occupation, and a grandson of the first Thomas Olney, of Providence, who succeeded Roger Williams as Pastor of the church established there.

Olney Winsor, the subject of this notice, was a graduate of Brown University, and was for many years a member of the college corporation. He commenced business in Providence, thence moved to Alexandria, Va., but soon returned to Providence, where he resumed and continued business as a merchant until the year 1792, when he was elected Cashier of the Providence Bank, the first institution of the kind in Rhode Island. He continued to occupy this position until the year 1811, about which time he moved to his small country place in North Providence, where he remained till his death.

His first wife was Freelove Waterman, daughter of Charles Waterman, of Johnston, by whom he had five children, four of which died in infancy. A daughter survived her father until November 7, 1850. His second wife was Hope Thurber, daughter of Samuel Thurber, of Providence, a paper manufacturer. This lady died, July 24, 1826, aged nearly 72 years. By her Olney Winsor had one daughter, named Sarah J., who is still living.

Mr. Winsor was a man of great integrity of character, of large general information, and of very genial feelings, and was much respected and esteemed. He had the air and manner of a gentleman of a school which has passed away. He died in North Providence, March 15, 1837, at the age of nearly 84 years, and was buried in his family lot in the "North Burial Ground," in Providence, R. I.

(₇₇) We have before stated that our author, when about twenty years of age, was married to Miss Dorcas Whipple. This lady was born in Smithfield, R. I., in the year 1767. She was a member of the Baptist church, and was much beloved for her many estimable traits of character. She died at Newport, N. Y., on the 7th day of January, 1821, in the 54th year of her age.

The names of their children were as follows:

1. Susannah, born   1785 at Smithfield, R. I.   died Dec., 1856, at Piseco, Hamilton Co. N.Y.
2. Amy   "   1786.   "   "   "   June 11, 1822.
3. Catharine   "   1788.   Fairfield, N. Y.   "
4. Christopher " Mch. 8. 1791.   "   "   still living.
5. Nancy   "   1793.   "   "   died, 1845, at Newport, N.Y.
6. Experience "   1796.   "   "   "   1842, in Ohio.
7. Abigail   "   1798.   "   "   "   1843, at Newport, N.Y.

The name of "Hawkins" is evidently of English origin, and is of great antiquity, running back as far as the year 1358. Several of the name have risen to distinction, and among these is Sir John Hawkins, the celebrated naval commander of the time of Queen Elizabeth, who, as rear-admiral, signalized himself against the invincible armada of Spain. Another Sir John Hawkins, an eminent lawyer, editor of an edition of Walton's Angler, and author of a valuable history of Music, lived in the time of George the third, and was an intimate friend and companion of the celebrated Dr. Johnson. We find also at this period the name of Christopher Hawkins, an author, and a member of Parliament, who was knighted by the King, June 21, 1791. In the Encyclopædias of Heraldry are described several coats of arms which were granted to persons bearing the name of "*Hawkins*."

ADDENDA.

The following items having been accidentally omitted in their proper places, they are accordingly inserted here, and the indulgent reader will please take them in where they belong:

At page 51, third line from the bottom, after the word " *discovery*," take in the following note :

(A) Among the many traits which have ever distinguished the sailor from the landsman, none is more striking than his superstition. There is hardly anything occurs on shipboard out of the ordinary way that he is not at once ready to ascribe to some supernatural agency. Deprived as he generally is of the advantages of early education, and denied subsequently the benefits of intelligent intercourse, it is not at all singular that he should do so, and that it is so difficult to wean him from his erratic notions after they have been once formed. His objections to going to sea on a Friday, and to sailing in a vessel on which a clergyman is a passenger, are well known instances of his superstitious feelings.

The following instances of this superstition in the British

Navy, occurring as early as the close of the 17th century, are
taken from " Capt. Cowley's Voyage Round the Globe," made
in the years 1683, 4, 5 and 6 :

> " We had moreover this Day great Feasting on Board us, and the
> Commanders of the other two Ships returning on Board their Vessels,
> we gave them some Guns, which they returned again.   But it is
> strangely observable, that whilst they were loading their Guns they
> heard a voice in the Sea, crying out, *Come help, come help, a Man over
> Board*, which made them forthwith bring their Ship to, thinking to take
> him up, but heard no more of him.   Then they came on Board of us,
> to see if we had not lost a Man ; but we nor the other Ship had not a
> Man wanting, for upon strict examination we found that in all the three
> Ships we had our Complement of Men, which made them all to conjec-
> ture that it was the Spirit of some Man that had been drowned in that
> Latitude by accident."
>
> *Hacke's Collection of Original Voyages, Lon : 1699, pp. 40–41.*

> " Then haling away S. W. we came abreast with Cape *Horn* the 14th
> Day of *February*, where we chusing of Valentines, and discoursing of
> the Intrigues of Women, there arose a prodigious Storm, which did
> continue till the last Day of the Month, driving us into the lat. of 60 deg.
> and 30 min. South, which is further than ever any Ship hath sailed
> before South ; so that we concluded the discoursing of Women at Sea
> was very unlucky, and occasioned the Storm."
>
> *Hacke's Collection of Original Voyages, ut supra citat, pp. 6–7.*

At page 157, 13th line from the top, after the word " *killed*," take in the
following :

Among the houses that suffered injury from the broadside
of the Asia upon this occasion, was the celebrated one known
as " Fraunces' Tavern," kept by Samuel Fraunces, who on
account of his swarthy complexion, was frequently called by
the familiar sobriquet of " *Black Sam*."   Philip Freneau, the

well known poet of that day, gives the following account of the affair :

> " At this time arose a certain king SEARS
> Who made it his study to banish our fears :
> He was, without doubt, a person of merit,
> Great knowledge, some wit, and abundance of spirit ;
> Could talk like a lawyer, and that without fee,
> And threaten'd perdition to all that drank TEA.
> Ah ! don't you remember what a vigorous hand he put
> To drag off the great guns, and plague captain *Vandeput*.*
> That *night*† when the HERO (his patience worn out)
> Put fire to his cannons and folks to the rout,
> And drew up his ship with *a spring on her cable*,
> And gave us a second confusion of *Babel*,
> And (what was more *solid* than scurrilous language)
> Pour'd on us a tempest of *round shot* and *langrage* ;
> Scarce a broadside was ended 'till another began again—
> By Jove ! it was nothing but *Fire away Flannagan !* ‡
> At first we suppos'd it was only a sham,
> 'Till he drove a *round ball* thro' the roof of *black Sam* ; §
> The town by their flashes was fairly enlighten'd,
> The women miscarry'd, the beaus were all frighten'd ;
> For my part, I hid in a cellar (as sages
> And Christians were wont in the *primitive ages :*)
>   *   *   *
> Yet I hardly could boast of a moment of *rest*,
> The dogs were a-howling, the town was distrest !—
> But our terrors soon vanish'd, for suddenly SEARS
> Renew'd our lost courage and dry'd up our tears."

At page 195, after the 15th line from the top, take in as follows :

The following extract gives some further particulars :

" NEW-YORK, August 18.

   Thursday was brought in here by some of his Majesty's ships, the rebel brig MARIAMNE, —— *Whipple*, master, of 16 six pound-

---

* Captain of the Asia man of war.   ‡ A cant phrase among privateers men.
† August, 1775.   § A noted tavern keeper in New York.

ers, and 47 men; four days out from Providence, Rhode Island, on a
cruize, but had taken nothing: She was captured last Monday morning.

When the Mariamne left Rhode Island, all the French fleet were in
Newport harbour.—The rebels at Providence were equipping a number
of small privateers, but had none out, except a small ship of 20 guns,
commanded by a person named Olney."

Rivington, Saturday, Aug. 18, 1781.

At the end of page 195, add the following:

The last chapter of her tale of sorrow is told in the following notice:

" *New-York*, 1*st December*, 1781.

NOTICE is hereby given to the officers and company of his Majesty's
Ship Amphitrite, Robert Biggs Esq. Commander, who were
actually on board the 30th day of July, 1781, at the capture of the
Schooner Neptune, in company with his Majesty's ships Medea and
General Monk, and privateer Triumph and Hibernia; and 6th of
August, at the capture of the privateer ship Bellisarius in company
with the Medea and Savage; and 13th day of said month August, at the
capture of the privateer brigantine Mariamne, in company with the
Medea, that they will be paid their respective shares of said captures on
Wednesday the 5th inst. at the office of the Subscriber, and the shares
not then demanded will be recalled every day (Sundays excepted) for
three years to come, when the unclaimed shares will be paid into
Greenwich Hospital, agreeable to Act of Parliament.

SAMUEL KEMBLE,

Rivington, Sat. Dec. 1, 1781.   Agent."

EXPLANATION

BOATSWAIN—An officer on board ship who has charge of the boats, sails, rigging, colors, anchors, cables and cordage. His duty is to summon the crew to their duty, to relieve the watch, assist in the necessary business of the ship, seize and punish offenders, etc. He has a mate who has charge of the long boat for setting forth and weighing anchors, warping, towing and mooring.

BULKHEAD—A partition built up in a ship to form separate apartments.

CABLE-TIER—A place on the orlop deck where cables are coiled away.

CAT-HEAD—A piece of timber projecting over a ship's bow, to which the anchor may be raised and secured.

COMPANION-WAY—The staircase to the cabin.

FLUKE—The broad part or arm of an anchor, which takes hold of the ground.

FORECASTLE—A short deck at the fore part of the ship, before the mast.

HATCHWAY—A square or oblong opening in the deck of a ship, affording a passage from one deck to another, or into the hold or lower apartments.

HOLD—The whole interior cavity of a ship, between the floor and the lower deck.

KEDGE-ANCHOR—The smallest anchor used on board ship.

LARBOARD—The left hand side of the ship. The right hand side is the *starboard*.

LEE—That side of a vessel which is opposite to the side against which the wind strikes.

LUFF—Bringing the head of a ship near the wind.

MAIN-SAIL—The sail of the main-mast, or principal sail of a ship.

MOOR—To confine a ship by anchors, and cables or chains.

QUARTER-DECK—The portion of the uppermost deck of a ship between the main and mizzen masts. This is the *parade* in men of war.

SHOT-LOCKER—A strong frame of plank near the pump-well in the hold, where shot are deposited.

SQUARE-RIGGED—Noting a vessel, as a ship, the principal sails of which are extended by yards which are suspended horizontally and by the middle, and not by stays, booms, and gaffs, or lateen or lug-sail yards.

STANCHION—A piece of wood or iron used to support the deck, the quarter-rails, the netting, awnings, and the like.

TAFFRAIL—The rail or upper part round a vessel's stern.

TARPAULIN—A piece of canvas well daubed with tar, to render it water-proof, and used to cover the powder magazines, guns, etc., and also the hatchways of a ship to prevent rain or water from entering the hold.

YAWL—A small ship's boat, rather narrow, and usually rowed by four or six oars.